Christ
and
Community

Praise for *Christ and Community*

"Probing the correlations of *Christ* and *community* in the New Testament Gospels, this new book by Suzanne Watts Henderson shows how the Gospel narratives consistently link the presentation of Jesus—his mission, message, and identity—to the identity and activity of the Christian communities being formed by these narratives. Henderson highlights distinctive features of each Gospel's profile of Jesus and his followers, within their various settings, but also has a keen eye for themes and affirmations that cut across the whole Gospel tradition. Another hallmark of the work is the author's vigorous insistence on rooting the Gospel presentations of Jesus's messianic career in judiciously chosen Jewish texts and traditions rather than exploiting distorted notions of early Judaism as (negative) foil for emerging Christian beliefs. Henderson's *Christ and Community* offers a fresh, illuminating, and accessible introduction to the New Testament Gospels."

—John T. Carroll, Harriet Robertson Fitts Memorial Professor of New
Testament, Union Presbyterian Seminary, Richmond, VA

"Suzanne Watts Henderson's new book, *Christ and Community*, illumines how each Gospel, in its own way, presents Christ's work as something he intended his followers to share with him and each other. The book is warm and accessible and will be welcomed in academic and church settings."

—Richard Vinson, Associate Dean for Undergraduate Studies and
Professor, Salem College, Winston-Salem, NC

Christ
and
Community

The
Gospel Witness
to Jesus

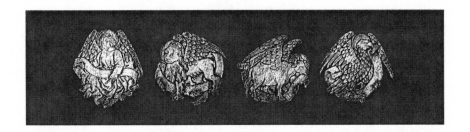

Suzanne Watts Henderson

Abingdon Press
Nashville

CHRIST AND COMMUNITY:

THE GOSPEL WITNESS TO JESUS

Library of Congress Cataloging-in-Publication Data has been requested.

ISBN 978-1-4267-9308-0

15 16 17 18 19 20 21 22 23 24—10 9 8 7 6 5 4 3 2 1
MANUFACTURED IN THE UNITED STATES OF AMERICA

For Bob, Abbie, Will, and Hannah:
my inspiration and my delight

Contents

Preface

Over two decades ago, my work in the Gospel of Mark led to an interpretive hunch: What if long-standing doctrinal interest in Jesus's messianic mission and identity has led readers to miss the wider landscape of the gospel message? What if we read the Gospels not mainly as dogmatic statements but as community literature—that is, as stories that interpret Jesus's mission and identity for those whose lives bear witness to his messiahship? In many ways, this book offers a synthetic response to these questions, exploring the Gospels' persistent connection between Christ and community in light of Jesus's mission and identity.

In a sense, the perspective offered here reflects my interest in recovering the Gospel witness to Jesus through the lens of literary and historical inquiry. I hope those curious about how these texts might have functioned in their first-century settings, then, will find this reading refreshingly free of christological assumptions that often underlie Gospel studies. That is not to say, however, that the findings here lack implications for theological reflection; quite to the contrary. Perhaps paradoxically, to reclaim the Gospel witness to Christ and community is to expose in these ancient texts important dimensions of the church's calling today.

I am indebted to many who have shared this journey and supported me along the way. My editors at Abingdon Press, Kathy Armistead and David Teel, have ably shepherded this project from start to finish. Thanks go, too, to Kelsey Spinnato, who has steered the book toward production. My home institution, Queens University of Charlotte, has provided a highly collaborative undergraduate setting that has challenged me to make biblical studies accessible to nonspecialists and to those from a range of faith traditions (or none at all). In particular, my Queens colleagues Lynn Morton, Norris Frederick, and Diane Mowrey have actively supported my efforts along the way. Meanwhile, librarians at both Queens and Union Presbyterian Seminary in Charlotte, North Carolina, have provided both assistance and hospitality. Finally, my students consistently push me to keep my research fresh, to communicate clearly, and to consider connections between ancient texts and real life.

I would be remiss not to mention my debt to a web of colleagues and friends who have read parts of this book as it has taken shape. My Duke PhD advisor and cherished friend Joel Marcus remains one of my most ardent and supportive critics. Since supervising my dissertation, he has progressed from red pen to inline comments, but his incisive questions have saved me from countless gaffes (the ones that remain are my responsibility alone). Others who have interacted helpfully with my work—by way of conversation or written response—include Elizabeth Bridges, Mollie James, Greg Jarrell, Van and Jean King, Diane Lipsett, Davina Lopez, Emily Reeve, Rick Vinson, and Chrissy Williamson.

Mostly, I am grateful to my family—my husband Bob and our three young-adult "children," Abbie, Will, and Hannah, one of whom aptly called this a "great empty nest project." Their constant love anchors all that I am and all that I do. The sheer joy they bring to my life is beyond measure. With deepest love, I dedicate this book to them.

Introduction

"Are you the Christ?" (Mark 14:61; see also Matt 26:63; Luke 22:67).[1] With this pointed question, the high priest gets to the heart of the Gospel witness to Jesus. For, despite their differences, all four New Testament accounts of Jesus's life, death, and resurrection answer the question in the affirmative: Jesus is, they maintain, God's Christ, God's messiah, God's "anointed one."[2] What is more, each Gospel writer shares John's[3] concern that those who hear the gospel story will come to "believe that Jesus is the Christ, God's Son" (John 20:31). The Gospel witness to Jesus, then, is christological at its core. As a result, this book examines the Gospel witness to Jesus the Christ through the lens of his messianic mission and identity. What does each evangelist say about who Jesus was, what he stood for, why he died, and what happened after his death? And how do these stories about his mission and identity fit the foundational gospel claim that Jesus is, indeed, the Christ? Along the way, we will detect both the common claims and the distinctive features of the four New Testament (NT) Gospels.

But if the Gospels are about Jesus the Christ, they are not *just* about Jesus. Careful attention to their witness suggests that Jesus cannot be

---

1. Most of the biblical quotations throughout this book come either from the Common English Bible or my own translation (marked AT).

2. Both the word *Christ* (Greek: *christos*) and its Hebrew-based cognate *messiah* (Hebrew: *mashiach*) derive from the verb "to anoint."

3. While the actual authors of the four NT Gospels remain unknown to us, we will identify both Gospels and their authors by the traditional titles.

understood apart from the community formed by those who "come after" him—both in his lifetime and beyond. Indeed, each Gospel is "more the biography of a movement, or at least that movement's beginnings (*archē*), than . . . the biography of an individual."[4] This book, then, draws the wider horizon of that movement into view. As we shall see, all four Gospels forge clear lines of connection between Christ and community. In these narrative portraits of God's "anointed one," Jesus's own messianic mission and identity shape in turn the mission and identity of the communities established in his name.

The discussion that follows, then, explores a familiar topic in a new light. Like many studies that have come before, this book traces the contours of Jesus's messiahship as depicted in the four NT Gospels. Yet rather than taking each Gospel in turn, we work thematically, treating different aspects of Jesus's mission and identity found across the four accounts. What is more, rather than emphasizing Jesus's exclusive status as the Christ, we expose Gospel evidence that sketches out clear communal implications of his messiahship. It turns out that the Gospels do more than simply affirm that Jesus is the Christ; they cast a vision of messianic community for those who would call him Lord, in the first century and beyond.

The Gospel Witness to Jesus: The Case for Christ and Community

Since the approach taken here differs from other studies of the Gospels, we begin with the evidence we will consider, as well as the book's relationship to trends in NT scholarship. Traditionally, books that explore the Gospel portraits of Jesus both assume and maintain his unique identity as the Christ. This study takes a more nuanced tack. Without denying the central significance of Jesus's own story in the Gospels, we also follow the Gospel witness itself to its logical and paradoxical end: To understand Jesus as the Christ is to recognize the inclusive impulse of his messiahship. Indeed, the Gospel witness to Jesus suggests that his messianic status gains

---

4. Joel Marcus, *Mark 1–8: A New Translation with Introduction and Commentary*, Anchor Bible 27 (New York: Doubleday, 1999), 66. Marcus's claim for Mark applies to all four NT Gospels.

validity in part through the witness of those who take up his messianic mission.

In a sense, this book detects in the Gospel witness to Jesus more *correlation* than *distinction* between Jesus and his followers. But though this emphasis is far from commonplace in either academic study or popular religious discussion, it is also not entirely new. Building on Gospel evidence as well as important findings in recent scholarship, this study makes a case for Christ and community that sheds new light on several questions that have long plagued Gospel study.

Christ and Community: Gospel Evidence

It is important to note from the outset that all four Gospels forge connection between Christ and community. A few examples help to illustrate this claim. First, just as Mark portrays Jesus's messianic career in terms of teaching, miracle working, and suffering, so too does Mark's Jesus impart a similar calling to his followers. Like Jesus, they proclaim the message and wield God's power (Mark 3:15; 6:7); like him, they face a sacrificial destiny (Mark 8:34; 9:35; 10:39). Matthew calls both Jesus himself (e.g., Matt 2:15) and those who make peace (e.g., Matt 5:9 AT) "sons of God." And while Matthew's Jesus appears as the "Son of the Human" or the "Human One,"[5] who will judge the nations from "his majestic throne" (Matt 25:31), the disciples likewise will "sit on twelve thrones," judging "the twelve tribes of Israel" (Matt 19:28). In Luke, an expansive group of seventy (or seventy-two) apostles mount so effective a campaign against evil forces that Jesus watches "Satan fall like lightning from heaven" because of their deeds (Luke 10:18 AT). And Luke devotes an entire sequel—the book of Acts—to reporting the apostles' display of authority and sacrifice after the resurrection. Even the Fourth Gospel, so noted for its high Christology, connects Christ and community in significant ways. After several impressive "signs" bear witness to his messiahship, Jesus says believers will do even "greater works than these" (John 14:12). What is more, besides affirming his own mystical union with the Father, John's Jesus imparts his

---

5. The Common English Bible uses this language.

God-given glory to believers, so that "they can be one...I'm in them and you are in me" (John 17:22-23). Perhaps in light of these and other examples, the second-century church leader Irenaeus wrote, "our Lord Jesus Christ [did] become what we are, that he might bring us to be even what He is Himself."[6]

Christ and Community: Correlation or Distinction?

If such connection between Christ and community appears across the Gospel landscape, why has it been so widely neglected? Several related developments in early Christianity led to an increasing interpretive interest in Jesus's inimitable, exclusive status as the messiah. First, his followers throughout the Mediterranean world soon heralded Jesus not just as Christ but also as Lord, a term used in Judaism for God alone. This raised the contentious question of his divine nature. As a result, many looked to the Gospels to support their views about his unique relationship to God.

In a related trend, when God's kingdom did not appear in the way that many Jews and early Christians expected, many of Jesus's followers began to rethink, and spiritualize, the concept. Already in Luke, and especially in John, we can detect this increasingly "realized" view of God's kingdom. That is, rather than looking toward a future cataclysmic renewal of the earth, Jesus's followers increasingly thought of God's kingdom as either a present spiritual reality or a personal destiny in the afterlife. Such a shift, in turn, partly reflects the influence of Western interpreters, who approached the subject as a matter of individual salvation. As a result, the Jewish messianic worldview that shaped both Jesus and the Gospels largely faded from view—and along with it, the hope that God's kingdom would prevail on earth, among the faithful community.

Finally, the early church's developing hierarchy shored up its authority in part by appealing to Jesus's distinction from, rather than solidarity with, faithful humanity. Already in Ephesians, the writer bases the husband's "headship" within the family on the notion that "Christ is the head of the

---

6. Irenaeus, *Against Heresies* 5, in *Ante-Nicene Fathers*, vol. 1, *The Apostolic Fathers, Justin Martyr, Irenaeus*, ed. Alexander Roberts and James Donaldson (Peabody, MA: Hendrickson, 1994).

church" (Eph 5:23). By the fourth century CE, when Constantine Christianized the Roman Empire—or Romanized Christianity—ecumenical councils rallied around the doctrine of Jesus's divine identity at least in part to legitimize religious and political power. As a result of all these trends, the inclusive portrait of Jesus's messianic mission and identity—preserved within the Gospels themselves—has been mostly neglected ever since.

Modern interpreters have both reinforced this sense of distinction between Christ and community and paved the way for rethinking it. Notably, those concerned with Christology tend to assume the distinction, since they read the Gospels for evidence of early Christian beliefs about—and religious devotion to—the risen Lord. Over the last decade, a number of studies have weighed in on the question, "How on earth did Jesus become God?"[7] For his part, Larry Hurtado traced the origins of Jesus's divine status to his earliest—and thoroughly Jewish—followers. Thus he challenged Wilhelm Bousset's view that Jesus's "divinization" came about through Greco-Roman religious influence and so was not native to Jesus's own religious landscape.[8] And while other scholars have proposed competing views of both the timing and influences behind belief in Jesus's divinity, they consistently assume that NT Christology promotes distinction between Jesus, with his Godlike status, and his earliest followers, who come to worship him as God.

On the other hand, several developments in NT scholarship have paved the way for examining the Gospel witness to Jesus through a wider angle lens. One trend that informs our study is the increasing tendency to read Jewish texts on their own terms, without recourse to Christian assumptions. The scrolls found in caves by the Dead Sea, for instance, have shed important light on Jewish hopes for God's coming kingdom. These scrolls, of course, are inherently communal in scope, since they look toward the social and religious renewal that manifests God's dominion. The

---

7. This is the title of a book by Larry Hurtado (Grand Rapids: Eerdmans, 2005). His more thoroughgoing study is found in *Lord Jesus Christ: Devotion to Jesus in Earliest Christianity* (Grand Rapids: Eerdmans, 2003).

8. See Wilhelm Bousset, *Kyrios Christos: A History of the Belief in Christ from the Beginnings of Christianity to Irenaeus*, trans. John E. Steely (1913; Nashville: Abingdon, 1970).

group's defining document, the Community Rule (1QS), calls its initiates "sons of light" who live together as advance scouts for God's coming kingdom. In this scroll, the faithful people of God even serve in "messianic" roles such as instruments of end-time judgment and peace. In other Jewish texts, too, scholars increasingly note that "messianic" figures often mediate God's power and presence within the gathered community. It is among the faithful that God's kingdom takes root on earth.

In another trend, those who study the "historical Jesus" also have noted the communal dimension of Jesus's own mission. For instance, historians such as E. P. Sanders and others take the tradition about "the Twelve" disciples—a central feature of Jesus's career—to symbolize Israel's restoration within God's coming reign. Gerd Theissen goes so far as to call Jesus's followers a "messianic collective," in part because of Gospel traditions that cast the Twelve as end-time judges (Matt 19:28; Luke 22:30).[9] In light of these examples, most would concede on a historical level that Jesus took the formation of messianic community to lie at the heart of his own mission.

As these examples suggest, messianic community plays an indispensable role in Gospel backgrounds, both in Jewish traditions and in Jesus's own career. But to what extent do the Gospels preserve conceptual ties with both traditions? Put differently, if the Gospels bear witness to Jesus as Lord and Christ, do they necessarily portray his messianic mission and identity in exclusive terms, as many maintain? As we shall see, the evidence suggests this is not the case. Perhaps surprisingly, even what Hurtado calls the early and "explosive" tendency to worship Jesus did not forge as great a divide between Christ and community as many have assumed. Throughout the Gospels, Jesus's messianic mission and identity supply a pattern for the faithful communities that coalesced around his memory.

Interpretive Payoff

This study of Christ and community thus builds on findings that have come before. In turn, our more expansive approach to the Gospel witness

---

9. See, e.g., Gerd Theissen and Annette Merz, *The Historical Jesus: A Comprehensive Guide*, trans. John Bowden (Minneapolis: Augsburg Fortress, 1998), 216.

to Jesus offers a "way through" several important issues that continue to divide scholars. Indeed, our broader inquiry into Christ and community helps make coherent sense of many Gospel features that have stumped interpreters.

One persistent puzzle that has plagued NT scholarship concerns Jesus's messianic "self-consciousness." Especially in the Synoptic Gospels, Jesus seems reticent about—and sometimes implicitly denies—his identity as the Christ. Yet historians agree that he was crucified under a messianic banner ("King of the Jews"), and his earliest followers both named and apparently worshiped him as "the Christ." How might we understand such an important paradox? Typically, scholars either deny that Jesus thought of himself as the Christ (and attribute the statements to post-resurrection traditions) or fail to explain adequately the Gospel accounts of his demurral. But once we explore Jesus's messianic self-consciousness in light of Jewish thought, the "problem" fades from view. It turns out that Jewish texts portray messianic figures not as those who seek their own repute but as those who point to, and often preside over, God's renewal of the world. In this light, both Jesus's reticence about his own status and his followers' affirmation of it fit the communal concerns of Jewish messianic thought.

Along related lines, this study makes the case for understanding continuity rather than discontinuity from Jesus's earthly ministry to the post-resurrection age. That is not to say that his death and resurrection did not generate the significant development, even "explosion," of devotion to Jesus as Lord and Christ. But as we trace those lines of development across the Synoptic Gospels and into the latest—and most emphatically christological—Fourth Gospel, we find that claims about Jesus's messianic mission and identity continue to carry weighty implications for Gospel communities as well. What begins within his earthly career lives on, and grows exponentially, after his death: Through *their* deeds of power, radical self-sacrifice, and ultimate vindication, Jesus's followers appear as active participants in his messianic mission. They even reflect vital aspects of his messianic identity.

Another fault line in NT scholarship often separates interest in Jesus's Galilean career on the one hand from a focus on his death and resurrection in Jerusalem on the other. Perhaps swayed by Paul's letters, which make scant mention of Jesus's teaching or miracles, many take the essence of Jesus's messiahship to lie in his passion. Others balk at the saving significance of his death and fashion their view of his mission around a "wisdom Jesus," whose teachings seem better suited to modern sensibilities. Yet such a chasm is artificial rather than organic. As the Christ, Jesus appears in the Gospels as the one anointed to institute God's dominion on the earth. And it turns out that all dimensions of the gospel story—his teaching, his miracles, his sacrificial death, and his resurrection—contribute to this role. Indeed, the Gospels themselves treat Jesus's passion as the culmination of his messianic mission, rather than a departure from it. Both his earthly ministry and his death and resurrection bear witness to God's sovereign power unleashed within the human realm. In both facets of his story, God works through Jesus to defeat those forces that would compromise human dignity and wholeness, as the same divine power evident in his teaching and miracles can be seen, in an ultimate sense, in his passion as well.

Our study of Christ and community also confirms both the sociopolitical and the religious nature of the Gospel witness to Jesus. Generally, scholars take sides, insisting either that Jesus challenged the values and structures of Roman occupation or that he heralded God's coming kingdom on religious terms. Yet, as we shall see, Jesus's mission and identity in the Gospels grows out of his faith that God's coming reign will triumph over all forces that resist it. In the Gospel accounts, Jesus is no ascetic living in the caves by the Dead Sea, waiting for God's armies to make their way to earth. Nor is he a Cynic philosopher-activist stoking sociopolitical resistance, at least in the conventional sense. Rather, Jesus takes up the mantle of biblical prophets to stake a claim for God's kingdom, a kingdom that recalibrates the scales of earthly justice. In this way, the Gospel witness to Jesus traces the deep religious roots of his mission and identity while casting a sociopolitical vision for human community that testifies to God's kingly power.

Finally, the innate Gospel connection between Christ and community challenges the persistent—and dogmatically driven—separation of Christology from "ecclesiology" (the view of the church) in NT studies. On the one hand, those who assume Jesus's exclusive status or identity often emphasize his distinction from the faithful community, which stands in need of salvation. Once we trace the Gospels' organic link between Christ and community, though, even devotion to an increasingly Godlike Jesus, seated at God's right hand, does not preclude his followers' role as deputized agents of God's kingdom; indeed, such participation is assumed and broadly affirmed. What is more, alongside their hints at the worship of Jesus as Lord (see John 20:28), the Gospels consistently confer all aspects of his "lordship"—his power, his sacrifice, and his exaltation—upon the faithful community (see Mark 10:42-44).

On the other hand, those who read the Gospels mostly as teachings for the church sometimes isolate and elevate human agency and downplay the significance of Jesus's abiding presence. Together, the Gospels cast a vision of messianic community that operates not through human ingenuity or resources *alone* but through perpetual reliance on a living Lord. Just as Mark's Jesus promises to "[go] ahead of" his disciples in post-resurrection age (Mark 16:7), Matthew's risen Christ says he will be "with you . . . until the end of this present age" (Matt 28:20). In both Luke and John, Jesus assures his companions that the divine spirit will come upon them, giving life to the community as they reflect God's life-giving power to the world.

More than just *belief in* or even religious devotion to Jesus the Christ, then, the Gospels promote active *embodiment of* his messianic mission and identity. Together, they sketch the contours of a messianic community that manifests God's power and presence on the earth. As we shall see, the Gospel witness to Jesus the Christ portrays his mission and identity as a pivotal part of God's unfolding redemption of the world, both in Christ and, through him, in the post-resurrection community.

The Gospel Witness to Jesus: Messianic Mission and Identity

The chapters that follow explore two broad features of the shared Gospel witness to Jesus: his messianic mission and his messianic identity. Within each section, we explore both the unity and diversity of that

Gospel witness. Against the backdrop of Jewish messianic thought, the Gospels tell the story of Jesus the Christ by affirming in similar terms the central elements of Jesus's career, as well as key facets of his identity. In each case, though, the Gospels highlight aspects of Jesus's messiahship that relate directly to their earliest settings. And it is at this intersection of text and context that the Gospel witness to Christ and community comes into view.

Chapter 1, "Foundational Questions," explains the assumptions and interpretive methods used in the rest of the study. In addition, basic information about the nature of the Gospels, their own sociohistorical settings, and the meaning of the term *Christ* will guide those new to the academic study of the Gospels.

Part One: Messianic Mission

In the book's first main section, we trace the contours of Jesus's messianic career. Taken together, his message, his divine power, his self-sacrifice, and his defeat of death all signal the dawn of God's reign upon the earth. Along the way, the Gospels forge connection between Christ and community for each dimension of this mission.

Chapter 2, "Messianic Message: 'Announcing God's Good News' (Mark 1:14)," begins with Jesus's own starting point in the Synoptic Gospels: his proclamation of God's coming reign (Mark 1:15; Matt 4:17; Luke 4:43). Just as this message plays a central role in both Jewish messianic thought and in Jesus's historical career, so too do the Gospels underscore its significance for their story of Jesus the Christ. Even the Fourth Gospel, which makes little mention of God's coming reign per se, opens with the poetic claim that in Jesus, God's word (or "message"; Greek: *logos*) has become flesh (John 1:1-18). What is more, all four Gospels maintain that Jesus's followers emerge as heirs to that message and bear it in turn to the wider world.

Chapter 3, "Messianic Power: 'Authority over All the Power of the Enemy' (Luke 10:19)," explores the common and distinctive elements of the Gospel portrait of Jesus as one who wields divine authority over the forces of evil that would oppose God's reign. This treatment of the miraculous elements of the Gospels explores Jesus's power over the created order as early evidence of God's coming reign, within which human dignity and wholeness flourish. Along the way, Jesus engages the faithful community as active partners in his decisive triumph over evil.

Chapter 4, "Messianic Sacrifice: 'To Give Up One's Life' (John 15:13)," considers the motif of Jesus's sacrificial suffering, which is unprecedented in Jewish messianic thought. But traditions that hail God's coming reign do anticipate oppression, and even death, for those devoted to its just ways. This chapter frames Jesus's suffering and death as part of that apocalyptic showdown, which extends in turn to the messianic community. Indeed, the pattern of Jesus's self-sacrifice proves foundational for Gospel communities that find themselves in the midst of the "birth pangs" (Mark 13:8 NRSV) of the messianic age. Perhaps surprisingly, even the Fourth Gospel takes Jesus's death to reflect the kind of sacrificial servanthood he promotes among his own (John 15:12-13).

Chapter 5, "Messianic Resurrection and Reign: 'Inherit the Kingdom' (Matt 25:34)," explores the Gospel accounts of Jesus's victory over death itself, as well as his ascension to the heavenly throne room, where he reigns with God. Consistently, the evangelists anchor Jesus's own resurrection within broader hopes for the "resurrection" of believers, either in the end-time or in the afterlife. What is more, the Gospels also suggest a corresponding reign for the faithful community (Matt 19:28). In both Christ and community, then, God's decisive triumph over the powers of death will culminate in an age of justice over which they will preside.

Part Two: Messianic Identity

Our second section considers the Gospel witness to Jesus's messianic identity. In these two chapters, we examine the titles and the traits that play a prominent role in each Gospel. Again, we note that Jesus's messianic identity serves as pattern for the identity of the messianic community he enlists and empowers.

Chapter 6, "Messianic Titles: Son of the Human, Son of God, Lord, and Christ," explores names for Jesus found in all four Gospels. In this chapter, though, we focus attention on the title that is especially prominent in each evangelist's account. Once again, we frame our study of the Gospel claims about Jesus the Christ in relation to Jewish messianic thought on the one hand and the community's own setting on the other. In each case, the titles in use carry important implications for the audience's identity and purpose within the messianic age.

Chapter 7, "Messianic Traits: Servanthood, Righteousness, Prophetic Power, and Mystical Union," explores the dominant qualities and attributes ascribed to Jesus in each Gospel. While all of these traits appear in all four Gospels, each evangelist casts particular facets of Jesus's identity in a messianic light. And just as these traits characterize Jesus as the messiah, they also extend to members of the faithful community, who manifest God's power and presence for the world to see.

Conclusion: Christ and Community: The Gospel Witness to Jesus

Our concluding chapter synthesizes findings to capture each evangelist's vision for messianic community. Written for those living in the post-resurrection age, these stories portray Jesus's messiahship as the decisive turning point in the disclosure of God's kingdom upon the earth. As they look toward the salvation of the world, the evangelists cast a vision for faithful community that bears witness to that messiahship. In each case, the Gospels insist that the risen Lord remains with them. His abiding presence, then, provides the bridge between his own messianic career and the messianic community established in his wake.

Study Questions

1. Give one example of the connection between Christ and community in each of the NT Gospels.

2. Explain one development in early Christianity that led readers to overlook the connection between Christ and community in the Gospels.

3. Explain one trend in NT scholarship that has paved the way for reconsidering the connection between Christ and community in the Gospels.

4. Explain an example of one "interpretive payoff" promised in this study of Christ and community.

For Further Reading

Bousset, Wilhelm. *Kyrios Christos: A History of the Belief in Christ from the Beginnings of Christianity to Irenaeus*. Translated by John E. Steely. Nashville: Abingdon, 1970.

Catchpole, David. *Jesus People: The Historical Jesus and the Beginnings of Community*. Grand Rapids: Baker Academic, 2006.

Ehrman, Bart D. *How Jesus Became God: From Good Teacher to Divine Savior*. New York: HarperOne, 2014.

Horrell, David G., and Christopher M. Tuckett, eds. *Christology, Controversy, and Community*. Supplements to Novum Testamentum 99. Leiden: Brill, 2000.

Hurtado, Larry W. *Lord Jesus Christ: Devotion to Jesus in Earliest Christianity*. Grand Rapids: Eerdmans, 2003.

Robinson, H. Wheeler. *Corporate Personality in Ancient Israel*. Edited by John Reumann. Facet Books: Biblical Series 11. Philadelphia: Fortress, 1964.

Theissen, Gerd, and Annette Merz. *The Historical Jesus: A Comprehensive Guide*. Minneapolis: Fortress, 1998.

Chapter One
Foundational Questions

Few books are as deeply admired as the Bible. Yet most readers have little sense of how, when, and for whom it was written. This is especially true for the Gospels. Together, these four accounts preserve stories and sayings that take us back to the time of Jesus, capturing his mission and identity in ways that continue to inspire billions of followers today. But most readers of the Gospels have little idea where the Gospels came from, what Jesus's world was like, or even what basic phrases like the "kingdom of God" meant to him. Few realize that the Gospels were written decades after Jesus's death and recast his story in settings that differ from both Jesus's world and our own. As a result, it is important to explain several basic concepts that will undergird this study of the Gospel witness to Jesus. In this chapter, those well-acquainted with NT scholarship will find themselves in familiar terrain. But our discussion of Gospel backgrounds and methods lays a foundation that will prove indispensable to the study of Christ and community that follows.

What Are the Gospels?

The word *gospel* (Greek: *euangelion*) means "good news" and was often used in ancient Greek to express a favorable outcome in battle: "we won!" This connotation lies behind the Gospels, since all four authors think that, in Jesus's life, death, and resurrection, God's life-giving power has defeated the armies of evil, including death itself (see 1 Cor 15:55). Among Gospel

1

writers, only Mark introduces the story by calling it a "gospel" ("good news"; Mark 1:1). But the term was soon used in a generic sense to designate stories about Jesus, and by late in the second century, scribes added titles identifying their traditional authors.

In their written accounts, the Gospel writers (evangelists) combine earlier oral and written traditions to narrate what Luke calls "the events that have been fulfilled among us" (Luke 1:1), events related to a man named Jesus of Nazareth. On one level, Jesus himself was historically insignificant in his own time: non-Christian writers barely mention him. On another level, his historical significance is immeasurable, since the movement he left behind now includes about one-third of the world's population. Together, the NT Gospels provide our earliest glimpse of both the man and his movement.

The four accounts of this "good news" about Jesus the Christ have much in common. To begin with, all four Gospels say that Jesus's story fulfills Jewish messianic hopes. Thus, he is, for all four writers, a decidedly *Jewish* Christ. As a result, the Gospels consistently appeal to Jewish scripture to confirm Jesus's role as messiah. It is this common portrait that will serve as starting point for our study.

As they tell the story of his messiahship, the Gospels share many specific details. For one thing, they all include Jesus's spirited interaction with figures such as John the Baptist, his twelve disciples, his mother, Mary, and other women, and even both Jewish and Roman opponents. They agree, too, that he spent most of his time in the northern region of Palestine called the Galilee, where he taught about the "kingdom of God" and performed miracles as a way of channeling divine power. In each Gospel, Jesus travels to Jerusalem, which stood at the center of religious and political power, where he suffers betrayal, hostile interrogation, and death on a Roman cross during the Jewish Passover celebration. Finally, all four evangelists maintain that devoted women who returned to his tomb "on the third day" found it empty.

Yet the Gospels also differ in both trivial and meaningful ways. The names of places and even Jesus's disciples change, as does his itinerary. More significant are the shifting relationships among characters in the stories. Jesus's relationship to God, for instance, varies across the Gospels, as does the tone and spirit of his interaction with his disciples.

To understand those differences among Gospel accounts, it is important to note several details about their composition. The first has to do with the time gap between Jesus's own career and the written accounts themselves. While Jesus died sometime around the year 30 CE, the first Gospel (Mark) was probably written around 70 CE, and the latest (John) took shape sometime after 90 CE. The significance of this span is hard to overestimate. For one thing, it means that the stories and sayings they report were preserved orally for decades before they were written down. As a result, many details related to Jesus's story changed over time; competing accounts of the same stories circulated alongside one another; and even different impressions of Jesus himself emerged. All of these differences show that the modern question of "factual accuracy" is out of place in the first-century world of oral tradition.

But if the stories changed over time *before* they were written down, that trend continues *within* the Gospels themselves. Notably, a second-century bishop named Papias shows little regard for historicity in the modern sense as he explains the Gospel-writing process. In something of a defense of Mark's reliability, Papias notes that the author "neither heard the Lord nor followed him, but afterward...he followed Peter, who adapted his teaching to the needs of his hearers, but with no intention of giving a connected account of the Lord's discourses, so that Mark committed no error while he thus wrote some things as he remembered them."[1] As Papias notes, not only is Mark's task a selective one, but it is an interpretive one as well, since the evangelist recounts Peter's instruction, which in turn was tailored to the "needs of his hearers."[2] In light of this, the temporal and conceptual distance between Jesus and the Gospel accounts of his earthy career is greater, and perhaps more significant, than many modern readers assume.

---

1. Eusebius, *Ecclesiastical History*, 3.39, in vol. 1 of *The Nicene and Post-Nicene Fathers*, series 2, ed. Philip Schaff and Henry Wace (Peabody, MA: Hendrickson, 1999).

2. In addition, of course, the Gospels were written in Greek, while Jesus spoke Aramaic, a difference that forges even greater distance between the Gospels and the stories and sayings they relate.

It is this gap that helps explain the many differences among the Gospels—differences that range from Jesus's origins to his post-resurrection appearances. Sometimes, the variances are insignificant and easy to explain: for instance, an editorial change that better fits Palestinian geography (Mark 5:1; cf. Matt 8:28). In other places, the differences reflect the authors' distinctive "spin." Consider the story of Jesus's arrest, which takes place in all four Gospels in a garden (called Gethsemane in Matthew, Mark, and Luke). While Mark shows Jesus in anguish as he faces his destiny, Matthew and Luke tone down his agony, and John omits it altogether (compare Mark 14:32-44 with Matt 26:36-46; Luke 22:40-46; John 18:1-12). This is but one example of a tendency, found among the four Gospels, to highlight certain features of Jesus's messianic story and downplay others.

What then can we say about the Gospels? Dating to the last third of the first century CE, they tell the story of a man named Jesus of Nazareth. They are called "gospels" because they tell the "good news" that, in him, God's life-affirming power has secured a foothold on earth. As God's anointed one, Jesus heralds and initiates God's coming reign; as the Christ, he wields, in a decisive way, the authority over evil associated with that reign; as the messiah, he inaugurates a "new creation" marked by human dignity and wholeness.

But Jesus's story is not a solitary one. Others play a vital part in this unfolding drama of God's sovereign power at work in his messianic mission and identity. What is more, each writer forges deliberate ties between Jesus's own story as the *Christ* and the calling of the *communities* left in his wake. Each Gospel detects in Jesus's messianic role a pattern for messianic community. But this is no mere succession plan, as if Jesus's followers simply take up where he left off. Rather, each evangelist assures those who call Jesus "lord" that he remains with them; it is his empowering post-resurrection presence that equips and sustains their life together. The Gospel witness to Jesus, then, is both decidedly christological—in that the stories depict him as the Christ—and intrinsically communal—since his messianic mission and identity lives on among those who follow and trust in him.

4

How Will We Read the Gospels?

The answer to this question is both deceptively simple and suggestively complex. Simply put, we read the Gospels mainly on their own terms. This approach begins by establishing interpretive distance between today's reader and the Gospels' first-century setting. That means setting aside prior beliefs about Jesus and his saving significance and turning to the Gospels with fresh eyes to read their claims anew. To read the Gospels "on their own terms," then, means reading the text in context—that is, using interpretive tools associated with literary and historical criticism.

Reading the Text: Narrative, Source, and Redaction Criticism

In terms of method, our study of Gospel witness to Jesus begins with a strategy known as "narrative criticism." This approach explores the story's artistry—its language, plot, characterization, and other literary devices—as a "way in" to its meaning. To read the text closely and carefully exposes details long overlooked for theological reasons. This is especially the case with Gospel passages that attribute Christlike power and authority to his followers. For instance, many interpreters either overlook or downplay the Fourth Gospel's claim that believers will do "greater works than these" (John 14:12), since it seems incompatible with the Gospel's high Christology.

Already, though, our approach grows more complex. For to read each Gospel portrait "on its own terms" leads beyond the *text itself* to questions about its relationship to the other accounts included in the NT. Since the canon includes four Gospels, not one, careful attention to one invites comparison with the others. In modern times, that comparison has led to an interpretive strategy called "source criticism." This approach examines such questions as these: Which Gospel came first? What traditions does each writer incorporate? What can we say about the composition of the Gospels?

Since Matthew, Mark, and Luke share so many stories and narrative details, they are called the "Synoptic" (literally, "seeing together") Gospels. Most scholars today think the Four-Source Hypothesis offers the best explanation of their similarities and differences. In this view, *Mark* was the first written Gospel and served as a source for both Matthew and Luke. Because these two Gospels make vastly different use of Mark, experts think they worked independently. Yet Matthew and Luke both include about 220 verses—mostly sayings—that are not found in Mark. To explain this material, scholars widely assume the existence of a hypothetical "sayings source" called *Q* (short for the German noun *Quelle*, or "source"). Finally, stories and sayings unique to Matthew and Luke are designated *M* and *L*, respectively. While debate about this hypothesis persists, it remains the best account of the Synoptic Gospels' compositional history.

The question of John's sources is murkier, partly because the Fourth Gospel[3] seems to have been written in stages. For instance, many take the post-resurrection stories found in John 21 as a later addition, since John 20:30-31 sounds like a Gospel ending.[4] And while most scholars think the Fourth Gospel was compiled independently from the synoptic accounts, similarities in some places indicate that John may have shared some underlying sources with the synoptic writers. In any case, source criticism allows us to view both the Synoptic Gospels and John as collections of stories woven together to produce distinctive accounts of Jesus's messianic career.

Source criticism also supports our efforts to read the text on its own terms because it brings to light, through comparison, the distinctive features of each Gospel. This leads to another important reading strategy used here. "Redaction criticism" builds on source-critical findings to highlight the evangelists' editorial ("redactional") and thematic concerns. For example, since Matthew incorporates about 90 percent of Mark's Gospel, we can trace the ways in which Matthew changes, reorganizes, and occasionally omits material from the Markan source. These editorial choices, combined with the special "M" traditions found in the Gospel, shed important interpretive light on the evangelist's editorial concerns. The re-

---

3. Since John is likely the work of more than one author, many scholars prefer to refer to the Gospel by this phrase.

4. "Then Jesus did many other miraculous signs in his disciples' presence, signs that aren't recorded in this scroll. But these things are written so that you will believe that Jesus is the Christ, God's Son, and that believing, you will have life in his name" (John 20:30-31).

dactional handiwork of Mark and John is harder to detect, since we lack direct access to the literary sources they used. In the case of these two Gospels, then, we employ simple comparative strategies to note the themes and details that contribute to their distinctive accounts.

Reading in Historical Context: Jewish and Early Christian Settings

This study of the Gospels in relation to one another leads to another set of interpretive questions that guide our study. For as the evangelists both adopted and adapted earlier sources, their work was shaped by both Jesus's own Palestinian Jewish context and the experience of the post-resurrection communities for whom they wrote. We can think of the Gospels' Jewish roots and early Christian audiences as the "bookends" that help us understand the Gospel messages on their own terms.

On the one hand, since all four Gospels preserve traditions about Jesus's innately Jewish mission, it is important to anchor these stories within the sociohistorical landscape of first-century Jewish thought. In other words, when the evangelists call Jesus the "Christ," what do they think that term signifies? How does Jesus's interest in the "kingdom of God" fit within patterns of Jewish response to the Roman occupation of Palestine? And how would Jesus's companions have understood his miracles? Such details from Jesus's historical ministry, preserved within the Gospel accounts, anchor Jesus's career within the soil of Jewish thought. It turns out that each dimension of Jesus's messianic mission and identity grows out of Jewish hopes for God's reign taking root upon the earth. Rather than looking to Jewish traditions to confirm Christian beliefs about Jesus's messianic status, we will work in the other direction, noting ways in which Jewish messianic thought informs the Gospel witness to Jesus. To take the Gospels on their own terms thus requires that we grapple with questions of Jesus's historical setting in Judaism, especially its various strains of messianic thought.

Finally, though no direct, external evidence of the Gospel settings remains, scholars generally agree that they originally addressed small groups of Jews and Gentiles who thought that, in Jesus of Nazareth, the messianic age of God's reign had begun.[5] To outsiders, their minority view—that Jesus was indeed the Christ—was problematic; after all, his humiliating death on a Roman cross seemed, as the Apostle Paul put it, "a scandal to Jews and foolishness to Gentiles" (1 Cor 1:23). On some level, the Gospel stories provide a foundational narrative to support their first audiences' devotion to Jesus's messiahship. But they also make sense of each community's own experience that grows out of that devotion. For instance, most scholars think that Mark comforts and inspires a persecuted community by linking their own "way of the cross" to Jesus's suffering. And the fact that some Christians were probably excluded from late first-century synagogues explains, to many scholars, John's virulent indictment of "the Jews." Both the Gospels' background in Jewish thought and their foreground in the evangelists' settings shed important light on our study of the text itself. Taken together, they reflect the approach called "historical criticism," which examines the worlds that shaped the texts.

Reading in Postmodern Perspective?

Our discussion of reading strategy would be incomplete without naming the significance of our own sociohistorical setting. After all, postmodern critics would rightly call it naïve to suggest that one can take the Gospels on their "own terms." Even the act of reading is interpretive, since we understand the text through the lens of our preexisting worldview—a worldview shaped in turn by our social location. As a result, we note here two contemporary trends that contribute to our approach to the Gospels.

The first arises in the wake of the Holocaust, which has rightly prompted interpreters to revisit the long-standing tendency to read Jewish traditions through a christological lens—that is, as "prequel" to the story of Jesus the Christ. This approach relegated Jewish scripture to a supporting role for Christian doctrine, sowing seeds of dangerous anti-Semitic ideologies along the way. Increasingly, NT scholars take care to explore Jewish messianic thought as backdrop for, rather than confirmation of,

---

5. On the minority view, see Richard Bauckham, ed., *The Gospel for All Christians: Rethinking the Gospel Audiences* (Grand Rapids: Eerdmans, 1997). This collection of essays, which challenges the mainstream view, emphasizes the mobility of early Christian communities.

Jesus's career and its depiction in the Gospels. To set aside assumptions about Jesus's unique or exclusive status opens the way for studies that expose the communal nature of both Jewish and early Christian texts.

In a parallel trend, the evolving relationship between church and culture has loosened the grip of authoritative doctrine on biblical studies in general, and the NT Gospels in particular. For one thing, after almost two millennia of "Christendom" in the West, the church's influence in the northern hemisphere has waned dramatically, first in Europe and now even in the United States. Gone are the days when social and religious hierarchy could be taken for granted. Indeed, the prevailing postmodern, postcolonial, and postinstitutional worldview means that entrenched authoritarian claims about belief and church power no longer hold sway. But the demise of hierarchy and belief does not signal the end of Christianity: far from it. Indeed, the far-flung popularity of Pope Francis—with his rejection of status and solidarity with the poor—testifies to what one scholar calls the "age of the spirit."[6] This shift carries weighty implications for our own reading of the Gospels, since it frees us from the need to find in them confirmation of prior doctrinal beliefs.

How then will we read the Gospels? This section has shed light on a wide range of interpretive strategies in play in this book. In short, we explore the Gospels' witness to Jesus less for doctrinal claims about Jesus's messianic *status* than for their narrative depiction of his messianic *role*, which extends in turn to the communities they address. In all four Gospels, Jesus's messianic mission encompasses his message, his deeds of power, his suffering, and his resurrection and reign—dimensions that apply to the messianic community established in his wake. What is more, the Gospels use messianic titles and traits to identify both Jesus and his followers. Together, the Gospels bear witness both to the *Christ*, who manifests God's power and presence on earth above all in his own life, death, and resurrection, and to the *community* that resides as an outpost of the messianic age he establishes. Though this study neither presumes nor requires religious conviction, its findings offer a compelling vision of

---

6. Harvey Cox, *The Future of Faith: The Rise and Fall of Belief and the Coming Age of the Spirit* (New York: HarperCollins, 2009).

Christian community for those who read the Gospels through the lens of faith today.

For Whom Were the Gospels Written?

As intimated above, the question of "original audience" is a particularly thorny one. Since the Gospels were written anonymously, their authors remain unknown to us; titles added about a century later preserve traditions about authorship but are not historically verifiable. Besides not naming their authors, the Gospels also remain mostly silent about their intended hearers. On both counts, the Gospels differ from most other NT writings and cast the question of original audience in a speculative light.

In spite of this reticence about authorship and audience, though, the Gospels do provide important clues about the socioreligious settings they address. Scholars use these clues to infer, however tentatively, details about the evangelists' communities that help make sense of the Gospel accounts. Notably, consensus views about each Gospel's setting have emerged that will prove useful for our study.

Mark

Already we have seen that Mark was probably the first written among NT Gospels. According to the tradition discussed above and preserved in a fourth-century church history by Eusebius, the second-century church leader Papias seems to attribute this Gospel to a man named Mark, who served as the Apostle Peter's interpreter. Yet even this attribution comes from generations after the Gospel took shape. Though the author's precise identity remains impossible to confirm, scholars widely agree that Mark was written in the 60s or early 70s CE for a community outside Palestine that included both Jewish and Gentile Christians. While some accept the Gospel's traditional ties to Rome, many scholars today find in the Gospel itself evidence that it was written for a community closer to Palestine—either in Syria to the north, or in Alexandria to the south and west.

Despite differing views of Mark's location, scholars generally concur that Mark's community faced dire persecution. The evidence comes mostly from the Gospel itself. In the first place, Jesus's warning about trials before religious "councils...governors and kings" (Mark 13:9) sounds to many like "*ex eventu* prophecy," a term that refers to "predictions" made after the fact. One verse in particular addresses Mark's audience rather overtly: "When you see the disgusting and destructive thing standing where it shouldn't be (the reader should understand this), then those in Judea must escape to the mountains" (Mark 13:14). This reference to the "disgusting and destructive thing" in the Jerusalem temple alludes to the Old Testament (OT) book of Daniel (Dan 9:27; see also 11:31). There it probably refers to the "desolating monstrosities" the Syrian overlord Antiochus IV Epiphanes placed in the temple. Thus Mark's story likens the oppressive second-century BCE occupation to that of Rome, whose presence in Jerusalem was formidable in Jesus's time, and likely even more so in Mark's. Indeed, the editorial aside, "the reader[7] should understand this," suggests that Mark's audience, too, would hear this verse as Jesus's prediction for *their* own place and time. Thus many scholars infer that Mark wrote in the midst or aftermath of the Jewish War (66–70 CE), an unsuccessful insurgency suppressed ultimately when Rome left the temple in rubble that tourists can still see today.

In writing for a community in turmoil, Mark recounts the "good news" that Jesus's messianic career has inaugurated the coming reign of God, despite all evidence to the contrary. Early in the story, Jesus himself delivers the "good news" that "God's kingdom has drawn near" (Mark 1:15 AT); later, he suggests that it will soon arrive "in power" (Mark 9:1). On one level, then, Mark thinks his audience's plight, like Jesus's, can be understood as the "beginning of the sufferings" (Mark 13:8; see Isa 13:13, 14:30; 19:2) that accompany the onset of the messianic age. In this way, Mark imbues their experience with cosmic significance. But Mark also portrays Jesus's messianic career in ways that engage the community in the unfolding defeat of evil. Like Jesus, they not only proclaim the "good news" of God's coming kingdom but also wield its authority over evil; like Jesus, such words and deeds mean that they will "take up [a] cross" (Mark

---

7. The term can be misleading, since the low literacy rate in the ancient world (around 10 to 15 percent at best) suggests that most of Mark's audience would have heard, rather than read, the Gospel.

8:34) as they are drawn into conflict with the powers that be; like Jesus, they will take their place in the eternal kingdom of God, gathered together as "his chosen people" (Mark 13:27).

The writer of Mark's Gospel, then, recounts Jesus's story for what one scholar has called a "community of the new age,"[8] a group of Jesus's followers who think that, in his life, death, and resurrection, God's kingdom has dawned. As they await its full disclosure, they carry forward his messianic mission. Their own suffering makes sense in light of his. But rather than promoting passive endurance while God's redemption takes root, Mark's story suggests that this messianic community plays an active role as advance agents of God's kingdom on the earth (see e.g., Mark 13:10), a role that leads in turn to their redemption.

Matthew

Early church tradition associates this Gospel with Matthew, the tax collector named as one of Jesus's disciples (Matt 9:9; 10:3),[9] but questions about its authorship, too, remain hypothetical. While Augustine and others thought Matthew was written first among NT Gospels, source critical findings discussed above suggest that Matthew used Mark as a written source. As a result, Matthew's editorial imprint—and thus the social and religious setting of its audience—comes into focus when we compare this account with both Mark (which it uses) and Luke (with which it shares the Q source); the material found only in Matthew (the M source) offers especially revealing clues about this evangelist's first hearers.

Redaction critics highlight several distinctive features found in this Gospel. In the first place, Matthew takes care to portray Jesus's messiahship as the explicit fulfillment of Jewish scripture. Examples include an opening genealogy that traces Jesus's lineage to Abraham (Matt 1:1-2) through King David (Matt 1:6) and the repeated use of "fulfillment citations" to explain Jesus's life and death in light of Jewish scripture (e.g., Matt 1:22-23; 2:5b-6; 2:15b; and so on). Moreover, Matthew depicts Je-

---

8. See Howard Clark Kee's book by this title: *Community of the New Age: Studies in Mark's Gospel* (Philadelphia: Westminster, 1977).

9. Eusebius, *Ecclesiastical History*, 3.39.

sus as a "new Moses" who goes up a mountain to deliver not the Jewish law itself (Torah) but his authoritative interpretation of it (Matt 5–7). The Gospel even includes five major sets of Jesus's teachings, a literary structure that may deliberately recall for hearers the five books of Moses. This insistence on Jesus's Jewish identity—and his Moses-like authority—signals to many that Matthew writes for a mostly Jewish audience closely aligned with Torah.

At the same time, this Gospel treats Jewish religious leaders harshly. Matthew repeatedly maintains Jesus's superiority to the religious leaders of his day, calling their righteousness inadequate because it is self-serving and nominal. Indeed, Matthew elaborates on Mark's account of Jesus's conflict with Jewish leaders in important ways. For example, Matthew's Jesus tell hearers that their righteousness must surpass that of legal experts and the Pharisees (Matt 5:20), and Matthew devotes an entire chapter to Jesus's tirade against this group's misuse of religious authority (Matt 23).

What do these features tell us? Most find important interpretive clues about Matthew's setting in this narrative tension between *Jesus's Jewishness* on the one hand and the *failure of the Jewish leadership* on the other. If Matthew was written around 80 CE for a mostly Jewish community, it addresses those who stood at a crossroads in their relationship to Judaism, which was reinventing itself after the destruction of the temple in 70 CE. Matthew thus retells this story about Jesus the Christ in ways that respond to that socioreligious setting. For one thing, since the rabbis (the Pharisees) played a decisive role in reshaping Judaism to emphasize the ongoing interpretation of Torah, Matthew presents Jesus as "rabbi among rabbis." For another thing, Matthew retains and draws out hopes for God's coming reign in a religious setting that had begun to tamp down messianic expectation. Though messianic figures still appeared on the Jewish landscape for decades to come, a subtle shift was occurring: the disastrous outcome of the Jewish War, which had been stoked by messianic hopes, led at least some to question the wisdom of such a radical worldview.

Finally, Matthew's explicit interest in the gathered community seems to address a group forging its own socioreligious identity. Among NT Gospels, only Matthew uses the word *church* (literally, "called out gathering";

Greek: *ekklēsia*), a rather generic expression for political or religious bodies. Thus Matthew appropriates a common cultural term to designate the "called out" community the Gospel addresses. Matthew also accentuates Peter's authority; only in this Gospel does this disciple walk on water or receive the "keys of the kingdom" (Matt 16:19). What is more, Matthew ends with a Great Commission charging Jesus's followers to "make disciples of all nations" (or "Gentiles"; Greek: *ethnē*; Matt 28:16-20). Thus Matthew portrays Jesus as a quintessentially Jewish messiah whose own mission and identity live on in the messianic community anchored in Jewish tradition and extending, through them, to "all nations."

Luke

The oldest existing manuscript of this Gospel attributes it to Luke, but it comes from the late second century CE, about a century after Luke was written, making the claim possible but historically unreliable. Early church tradition locates Luke's community in Antioch, though the Gospel itself only suggests a location outside Palestine, within the wider Mediterranean world.

Like Matthew, Luke incorporates material from both Mark and Q as sources. Indeed, Luke even acknowledges previous Gospel accounts, implying at least partial dependence on them. Among evangelists, Luke is the most explicit about the Gospel-writing task and introduces the account this way: "Many people have already applied themselves to the task of compiling an account of the events that have been fulfilled among us. They used what the original eyewitnesses and servants of the word handed down to us. Now, after having investigated everything carefully from the beginning, I have also decided to write a carefully ordered account for you, most honorable Theophilus. I want you to have confidence in the soundness of the instruction you have received" (Luke 1:1-4). In distilling sources into a "carefully ordered account," Luke exercises no small degree of editorial license, using only about half of Mark and rearranging material along the way. And the special "L" material found throughout the Gospel—especially within the Travel Narrative (Luke 9:51–19:27)—provides a window into issues that were pressing for Luke's community.

What can we say about Luke's earliest audience? Among the Gospels, only Luke names an addressee: Theophilus (Luke 1:3). But the name, which means "God-lover," does not tell us much. If it refers to a specific person, we know nothing else about him. It is more likely that the name serves a generic purpose, including anyone who "loves God"—Jew or Gentile—within its audience. Indeed, the term echoes language sometimes used to describe Gentiles devoted to Israel's God but not full-fledged converts: they were called "God fearers." Already, then, we find incidental support for the view that Luke's Gospel addresses a mostly Gentile audience.

In some ways, the socioreligious setting of Luke's Gospel stands in contrast with Matthew's. For if Matthew makes the case for Jesus's messiahship within Judaism, Luke makes the same case for those outside of it. On the one hand, Luke casts Jesus's story as a decidedly Jewish one and devotes special attention to Jerusalem: Luke's Jesus is circumcised at the Jerusalem temple (Luke 2:21-38), comes of age there (Luke 2:41-51), and returns to Jerusalem after the resurrection (Luke 24:36-49). Only in Luke does Jesus begin his public ministry in the synagogue at Nazareth (Luke 4:14-30). At the same time, Luke highlights the expansive and inclusive nature of Jesus's messianic mission; even in his (Jewish) hometown, he declares his own prophetic calling to serve those outside Israel's borders. Stories found in the Travel Narrative consistently illustrate this calling, as women, Samaritans, tax collectors, and sinners all experience the kind of salvation unleashed through this messiah.

Luke goes beyond both Mark and Matthew to highlight the faithful community's role in that redemptive story. Though it is not a focus of this book, Luke's sequel, the Acts of the Apostles, makes just this point: at Pentecost (Acts 2:1-11), God's spirit equips believers to bear witness to Jesus to the "ends of the earth" (Acts 1:8). But even in the Gospel itself, Luke casts the community as partners in Jesus's messianic mission. For instance, only Luke includes a report of seventy(-two) apostles,[10] whose success "in [Jesus's] name" constitutes Satan's defeat (Luke 10:17). Here and elsewhere,

---

10. The discrepancy can be found among ancient manuscripts, some of which designate seventy-two apostles (which may carry symbolic significance as a multiple of twelve). Others—perhaps based on the earlier traditions—indicate that there were seventy.

God's spirit acts through both Jesus and his followers to manifest divine power at work to restore God's just reign throughout the cosmos.

This motif leads to a final observation about Luke's "spin" and setting. Luke's message about God's coming kingdom is less disruptive than Mark's and less divisive than Matthew's. Instead, Luke works with greater subtlety to tell a story about Christ and community that is subversive at its core. Rather than a frontal assault on the social or political powers of the Greco-Roman world, Luke casts a narrative vision that places a premium on living as if God, not Caesar, is sovereign. Without eliminating hopes for God's decisive victory on earth, Luke shifts attention to the audience's "meantime" role as its vanguard. For Luke, both Christ and those who receive his spirit bear active witness to the "upside down" value system of God's reign, a reign that will bring universal forgiveness and salvation.

John

In its present form, John is probably the latest of the NT Gospels, dating to the end of the first century or the beginning of the second. Early church tradition identified the author with John of Zebedee, and in turn with the "disciple whom [Jesus] loved" (John 19:26; 21:20-24), though the Gospel itself makes no such connection. As noted above, John is likely the work of more than one author. Numerous rough literary transitions suggest that a variety of sources were combined to form this Gospel. What is more, John seems to weave together material that reflects developing and sometimes competing ideas about Jesus's divine nature as well as the community's relationship to Judaism. These features lead many to think the Gospel as we have it today reflects several stages of composition. Long associated with Ephesus, the precise location of John's community is also difficult to confirm. Still, several literary motifs help expose important facets of the setting that this Gospel first addressed.

One prominent feature found in the Fourth Gospel is its scathing indictment not just of Jewish leaders (as in Matthew) but of "the Jews" in a broader sense. The term appears some seventy times in this Gospel, almost always designating those who oppose Jesus, even though Jesus and his followers were Jewish. John's language can also be extreme, going so far as to have Jesus call his opponents children of "your father . . . the devil" (John 8:44). Elsewhere, the narrator speaks of Jesus's followers being "expelled from the synagogue" (*aposynagogēs*; John 9:22; see also John 12:42; 16:2), a practice that occurred only sometime after 80 CE. Together, these anachronistic tendencies suggest that John's audience felt deeply at odds with—probably even alienated by—their own Jewish communities. The Fourth Gospel, then, moves beyond the synoptic accounts to cast the claim that Jesus is "the Christ" as a dividing line between insiders and outsiders in the community.

This sense of distinction appears, too, in the sharply dualistic language used throughout the Gospel. In John, there is little neutral ground. Binary opposites such as light and darkness, flesh and spirit, and truth and falsehood, and even love and hate work consistently to distinguish "believers" from those set against Jesus and his messiahship. These lines of demarcation suggest to many that John's community is sectarian in nature—that is, one that sees itself as separate or "cut off" from the wider world. In addition, John's concern for deep unity among believers (John 17:21-23) fits the literary tendencies of other sectarian groups.

Not only does belief in Jesus's messiahship function as a "boundary marker" for John's audience, but it also leads to what John calls "life in his name" (John 20:31). This promise reflects John's radical reworking of Jesus's teaching for a new setting. While the Synoptic Gospels all retain Jesus's keen interest in a future ideal age established under God's reign, the Fourth Gospel accommodates the delay of its arrival mostly by transposing it: rather than a future, earthly renewal, John presents God's kingdom as a spiritual condition available in the present, and in the afterlife, to those who believe in Jesus the Christ. In this way, John personalizes Jesus's message of salvation in ways that have had a lasting impact on Christian theology.

Yet John's sharpened focus on personal belief in Jesus does not diminish the role of the faithful community. As in the other Gospels, John's witness to Jesus carries weighty implications for their life together. Indeed, John devotes the entire Farewell Discourse (John 13–17) to extending Jesus's mission to his disciples in the post-resurrection age. Beginning with his pattern of sacrificial servanthood, Jesus teaches them to "love one another as I have loved you" (John 13:34 AT). By "remaining" in him, he says, they will bear fruit that grows organically out of his sustaining presence. Ultimately, Jesus even incorporates his own companions, and those who will believe because of them, into his mystical union with God (John 17:21). In all these ways, John's decidedly christological story, then, engages the messianic community in the redemption of the wider world as well (John 17:18). Even for John's sectarian, excluded community, the Gospel witness to Jesus goes beyond belief—pivotal though it may be—toward the reflection of Jesus's messianic mission and identity in their life together.

Christ and Community

Despite their differing emphases and varied settings, the Gospel writers share at least two aims. First, they portray Jesus as the Jewish messiah whose life, death, and resurrection signal the dawn of God's presence and power unleashed in the world. All four Gospels frame Jesus's story against the backdrop of Jewish tradition and see his messianic mission as part of the wider landscape of God's restoration of the world.

Second, in each case, the Gospel witness to Jesus includes but moves far beyond beliefs about Jesus's messiahship, or even devotion to him as Lord and Christ. Together, the Gospels promote connection rather than distinction between Christ and the community each evangelist addresses. Thus each writer translates Jesus's messianic mission and identity for an audience devoted to Jesus the Christ in a setting at some remove, in time and space, from his own career. As community literature, the Gospels tell the foundational story of Jesus and his disciples to engage their readers in God's redemption that continues to unfold in their midst. Thus the evangelists craft their Gospel accounts in light of their social, historical, and religious settings. In so doing, they underscore the contemporary relevance of Jesus's messianic mission for their own place and time.

What Do the Evangelists Mean When They Call Jesus "the Christ"?

Already, we have seen that the Gospel witness to Jesus is inherently christological, since the Gospels together present Jesus as the Christ, the messiah, the "anointed one." But what meaning does that term signify? To answer that question, we begin with the Jewish tradition that shaped both Jesus's own worldview and the Gospel stories. As we shall see, when the evangelists call Jesus "the Christ," they refer neither to his divine identity nor to his privileged status per se, but rather to his authoritative role at the dawn of God's reign upon the earth. In this section, we explore the term *messiah*, as well as the wider conceptual landscape to which it belongs.

Throughout Jewish scripture, prophets, priests, and kings are "anointed" in a symbolic act that designates them as earthly representatives of God's heavenly rule (see, e.g., 1 Kings 19:16; Lev 6:20-22; 1 Sam 16:3). But in 587 BCE, the Babylonians destroyed Jerusalem's temple and deported much of its population, wreaking havoc on Israel's political and religious institutions. Even after their return from exile about fifty years later, the people lived mostly under a series of foreign overlords, whose sometimes brutal tactics made many look forward to the day when God's just reign would prevail on earth. Over time, Jewish writers increasingly used the term *messiah* to designate a figure who would play a pivotal role in establishing that reign.

The Gospel witness to Jesus as the "Christ" grows out of Jewish hopes that God's kingdom might soon prevail upon the earth. But though the Gospels often say that Jesus fulfills a precise messianic script (e.g., Luke 24:45-47), the Jewish texts that look forward to God's coming reign are quite diverse, reflecting the writers' own context and worldview. What is more, figures we might identify as "messianic" are not always called the "messiah." Thus the conceptual landscape to which Jesus's messiahship belongs is fluid and variegated. In light of this complexity, it is important to clarify the terms we will use to describe it.

Throughout this study, we use the word *apocalyptic* to describe the Jewish worldview that longs for God's reign. In some texts, God's sovereign power makes itself known in the human realm by way of an "apocalypse" or "revelation" (Greek: *apocalypsis*). Scholars use the term *apocalypse* as a literary designation for those writings that relate just such a vision. In Jewish scriptures, both Ezekiel and Daniel feature "revelations" of the heavenly realm. The NT includes the book of Revelation, which is the "apocalypse" of John's heavenly vision. But the word also characterizes, more broadly, the view that the coming reign of God "reveals" heavenly power on earth. In this vein, a post-exilic prophet implores Yahweh, "If only you would tear open the heavens and come down" (Isa 64:1), expressing hopes that God's kingly power in heaven will soon triumph throughout creation. In what follows, we will use the term *apocalyptic* in its broadest sense—to designate the worldview that longs to see God's power disclosed "on earth as it's done in heaven" (Matt 6:10). Though not all the Jewish texts considered here fit the narrower literary genre of "apocalypse," they all look forward to a new world order that reflects God's reign.

But if these hopes are "apocalyptic," they are often called "eschatological" as well. This term comes from the Greek word *eschaton* ("end") and refers, broadly speaking, to the end of the world as it now exists. But this end is not really an end in the ultimate sense. It rather designates the point at which God defeats the forces of evil so that the "renewal of all things" (Matt 19:28 NRSV) might begin. Thus the "end" carries a connotation of completion, of the fulfillment of time (Mark 1:15 AT), more than the final destruction of the created order itself. Typically, that "end" brings a final judgment that eradicates unrighteousness in order to establish God's just reign. This end-time judgment, in turn, leads to eschatological salvation for those who qualify to live as citizens of that kingdom. As Mark puts it, "whoever stands firm until the end will be saved" (Mark 13:13).

But in what sense are these hopes "messianic"? Several points about messianic figures that appear in Jewish traditions have direct bearings on our study of the Gospel witness to Jesus as "the Christ." For one thing, Jewish hopes for a restored world order do not generally revolve around the messianic figures themselves, or even require their involvement. For instance, the decidedly apocalyptic Dead Sea Scrolls rarely refer to the figure by name. Where the term does appear, the Scrolls sometimes mention two "messiahs," with the priestly messiah taking precedence over the political one (1QS 9:10-11). Other texts from roughly the same time period also use "messianic" language with great flexibility. In the Similitudes of *1 Enoch*, for example, the "messiah" is also called the "righteous one," the "chosen one," and the "son of the human."

Besides such diverse terminology, the messianic figures themselves encompass a wide range of roles. For instance, Daniel's "Son of a Human"[11] will establish God's dominion on earth only *after* the violent "fourth kingdom" meets its demise (see Dan 7:1-14 AT). By contrast, the *Psalms of Solomon* implore God to raise up a Davidic ruler who will play a more active role in the regime change: he will "shatter unrighteous rulers... [and] purge Jerusalem from nations that trample (her) down to destruction" (*Psalms of Solomon* 17:22).[12]

This diversity among messianic figures, including those not called "messiah," leads to another important point. When they do appear, messianic figures work in relation both to *God*, whose reign they establish, and to the *faithful community* that often participates in that reign and consistently benefits from the deliverance it brings. Thus a wide range of figures are messianic in this more generic sense: they serve as divinely authorized agents of God's dominion through their words and deeds. Together, these figures disclose God's righteous and holy ways in all they do, so that the faithful will see, and reflect, those ways. Indeed, these messianic figures generally show little interest in their own status or authority; rather, they impart God's power to the faithful, who emerge as an outpost of God's coming kingdom. As those who inaugurate God's sovereign reign on the earth, they play a pivotal role in eclipsing the divide between heaven and earth. In so doing, they establish God's just ways on earth in and through those living under God's sovereign sway. When we speak of Jewish messianic hopes, then, the term refers broadly to the hopes for that coming rule.

What can we say about that worldview and the framework it provides for understanding Jesus's messiahship? We can now offer a synthetic summary of the apocalyptic worldview to which it belongs. As many have

---

11. This rather jarring translation of the more familiar "Son of Man" serves two related aims. First, as a more literal translation of the phrase, it preserves the more generic and thus inclusive Aramaic phrase *kebar enash*, which means "like a human being." Second, as we shall explore more deliberately in chapter 6, it captures more faithfully the representative function of this figure in both the Gospels and the Jewish background texts on which they rely, including Daniel.

12. The translation of this and all references to the Old Testament Pseudepigrapha come from James H. Charlesworth, ed., *The Old Testament Pseudepigrapha*, vols. 1–2 (New Haven, CT: Yale University Press, 1983–85).

noted, hopes for God's coming kingdom arise out of a deep sense of tension between the way things are and the way things might yet be. In this view, measured reform of the status quo will not bring deliverance from evil's destructive and oppressive regime; such "salvation" comes only at God's initiative, and through divine—not human—power. Yet, if the Jewish apocalyptic worldview stresses God's sovereignty, it is also decidedly communal in nature, since it anticipates a coming social and religious order recalibrated to reflect God's just ways among the faithful. Thus while Jewish apocalyptic writings follow no set scheme, they generally feature a combination of these elements:

- Things are bad and getting worse: The spiritual force of evil works in the world to stymie human dignity and wholeness in ways that are both unjust and beyond human repair.

- But God is still in charge: In the heavenly realm, God's sovereign reign is marked by justice and righteousness remains in force.

- Hang on; hope is coming: Soon and very soon, God's kingdom will come to earth, perhaps along with a "messiah" or other chosen figure who will preside over the regime change at hand.

- God will sort things out: As the forces of evil lose their grip, creation will face a "day of judgment" that will establish justice, promising eternal salvation to the righteous and condemnation to the unrighteous.

- Creation will reflect God's glory: In the "renewal of all things," all the nations of the earth will be drawn into the sway of God's righteous ways and the eternal peace they bring.

Broadly understood, then, Jewish messianic thought is part of a larger plan for God's sweeping redemption of the whole world. In the "new creation," social and political and religious systems will bear witness to God's just and righteous ways. When "messianic" figures play a part in this unfolding drama, they do so as specially authorized agents, working on God's behalf, to herald and establish God's reign among the renewed human community that lives under its sway.

By calling Jesus the "Christ," the evangelists imply that Jesus stands at the cusp of the new world order calibrated according to God's just, holy, and righteous ways. On the one hand, Jesus appears as the "anointed one," specially designated by God to inaugurate this new age; both his messianic mission and his messianic identity bear witness to God's power conferred on him as its authorized agent. On the other hand, Jesus's "anointed" role means that he makes that power available among the faithful, who join in God's unfolding salvation of the world. Like the messianic figures found throughout Jewish writings, this "Christ" establishes a community that perpetuates his messianic mission and identity.

As we turn to the Gospel witness to Jesus, we will explore his messianic mission and identity in light of Jewish messianic hopes as well as the first-century settings of the earliest audiences. For though most scholars think the evangelists crafted their Gospel stories for the wider Greco-Roman world, they all portray Jesus as the Christ, the one anointed to disclose God's reign on the earth. Just as these earliest followers found in his messianic career palpable evidence of God's presence and power, so too did they find assurance that God's redemptive ways continued to work, through the power of the spirit, in their life together.

Study Questions

1. What does the word *gospel* mean? How does that meaning affect your understanding of the NT Gospels?

2. Explain three critical approaches used in this study.

3. Identify a key thematic concern found in each of the four Gospels.

4. What are the five main elements of Jewish apocalyptic thought?

For Further Reading

Anderson, Paul N. *From Crisis to Christ: A Contextual Introduction to the New Testament*. Nashville: Abingdon, 2014.

Blomberg, Craig L. *Jesus and the Gospels: An Introduction and Survey.* 2nd ed. Nashville: Baker, 2009.

Collins, John J. *The Scepter and the Star: The Messiahs of the Dead Sea Scrolls and Other Ancient Literature.* New York: Doubleday, 1995.

De Jonge, M. "The Use of the Word 'Anointed' in the Time of Jesus." *Novum Testamentum* 8 (April–October 1966): 132–48.

Dunn, James D. G. *Unity and Diversity in the New Testament: An Inquiry into the Character of Earliest Christianity.* 2nd ed. London: SCM Press, 1990.

Horbury, William. *Jewish Messianism and the Cult of Christ.* London: SCM, 2012.

Reddish, Mitchell G. *An Introduction to the Gospels.* Nashville: Abingdon, 1997.

Part One
Messianic Mission

In the chapters that follow, we trace the contours of Jesus's messianic mission as they appear in all four Gospels. For, despite their diversity, all four accounts share a narrative interest in Jesus's messianic message, his messianic power, his messianic sacrifice, and his messianic resurrection and reign. In each aspect of Jesus's career, then, the evangelists portray him as the Christ—that is, the one who discloses God's coming kingdom. In this sense, his career is pivotal in the unfolding "good news" of God's redemption of the earth.

As we consider each Gospel's witness to Jesus's christological mission, we begin by noting the connections between Jesus's career and the Jewish hopes it fulfills and elaborates. Rather than imposing Christian beliefs on Jewish traditions, we ask what light Jewish thought might shed on the Gospel witness to his mission. In addition, we consider the ways in which each writer crafts the Gospel story to address the first-century community for which it is written. The background of Jewish hopes and the foreground of early Christian experience work together to bring the Gospel witness to Jesus more fully to light.

Chapter Two
Messianic Message

"Announcing God's Good News" (Mark 1:14)

Scholars widely agree that Jesus proclaimed the "good news" that God's kingdom was coming soon. Indeed, many think it was this message that led some to hail him as "messiah" while others conspired to bring about his death. In this chapter, we begin our study of Jesus's messianic career by exploring the message he delivers in all four Gospels. What is it about this message that is "messianic"? In what ways is it rooted in Jewish thought? What aspects of Jesus's message does each Gospel highlight for its audience? And how does his message forge a connection between Christ and community? Despite their distinctive accounts, all four evangelists anchor Jesus's messianic message in a Jewish worldview that looks forward to God's life-affirming new world order. What is more, all four evangelists think Jesus's messianic message lives on in the post-resurrection communities devoted to him.

Clearly, Jesus's "good news" about God's coming kingdom proves central to his career in the Synoptic Gospels. In Mark, Jesus opens his public ministry with this pithy announcement: "The time has been fulfilled, and the kingdom of God has come near; repent, and trust in the good news" (Mark 1:15 AT). Both Matthew and Luke adapt this message in important ways, but they too see it as foundational for Jesus's mission (Matt 4:12-17; Luke 4:43). In John, the content of Jesus's message shifts rather dramatically. Rather than spreading word about God's coming kingdom, John's Jesus imparts a messianic message that points the way to "life in his name" (John 20:31). By casting Jesus as the "word-become-flesh" (see John 1:14), John says the messianic message has taken on bodily form. For the Fourth Gospel, Jesus's earthly mission discloses the "messianic" promise of God's powerful, life-giving presence in the world. Thus both the Synoptic Gospels and John affirm that Jesus's messianic message is central to his role as the Christ.

To understand Jesus's messianic message in the Gospels, we begin by exploring Jewish texts that lie behind these stories. As many have noted, Jesus's message about God's coming kingdom takes its conceptual cues at least partly from Isaiah, especially the oracles composed in exile and beyond.[1] Thus we consider key passages from this prophetic book that provide a gospel framework for the synoptic accounts of Jesus's message. In addition, examples from the Dead Sea Scrolls carry forward Isaiah's hopes for God's reign centuries later. In John, Jesus's messianic message reflects the impact of Hellenistic Jewish ideas about God's wisdom and presence in the world. Thus we include a brief study of Jewish wisdom traditions that were current in the first century as backdrop for Jesus's messianic message in the Fourth Gospel.

In a sense, to consider this wider Jewish landscape allows us to set aside the assumption that Jesus's messianic message mainly concerns himself and his own status. Instead, as we turn to each Gospel, we find distinctive aspects of Jesus's message that consistently point toward both the coming reign of God and its implications for the community he establishes. Mark's Jesus promises the palpable nearness of God's kingdom and calls urgently for a faithful response. Matthew preserves this apocalyptic message and underscores its eschatological significance, promoting a "way of righteousness" that will qualify the faithful for eternal life. Luke downplays the role of future judgment, shifting attention to a renewed social order that bears witness to God's kingdom "among you" (Luke 17:21). Finally, though Jesus's message in John makes little mention of God's kingdom, it is "messianic" because it shows the way to "life abundant"

---

1. Scholars use the terms "Second" and "Third" Isaiah to designate Isaiah 40–55 and 56–66, respectively, since they seem to come from two separate settings. In this chapter, we include oracles from both sections of the book, which had already been combined in the first century CE.

that comes from God and becomes available, through Jesus, to those who believe in him. All four Gospels, then, convey Jesus's messianic message of God's power and presence taking root on the earth.

Thus the Gospels affirm not just the messianic nature of Jesus's message but also its vision for messianic community. On one level, the message is communal in nature because it points to a renewed world in which God's power works to affirm human dignity and wholeness for all people. On another level, Jesus consistently involves others in the message's proclamation. As they carry forward this "word" about God's power at work in Jesus the Christ, faithful communities in the first century and beyond share in Jesus's messianic message. As a central part of Jesus's mission as the Christ, the messianic message also proves foundational for the community that lives on in his name.

Messianic Message in Jewish Tradition

To understand Jesus's messianic message in the Gospels, we begin our study with selected Jewish writings that influenced both Jesus and the evangelists. By exploring these background texts on their own terms, we gain important insights for our Gospel study. Both the Synoptic Gospels and John deliberately link Jesus's message to Jewish hopes for God's salvation of the world.

The Good News according to Isaiah and Its Interpreters

The good news that defines Jesus's messianic message, especially in the Synoptic Gospels, takes its cues at least partly from the book of Isaiah, especially the oracles written in the time of exile and its aftermath (Isa 40–66). Here, both Jesus and the evangelists found rich promises first offered to those taken captive in 587 BCE by their Babylonian conquerors. To the oppressed people of Israel, the prophet brings the good news that, by God's power, their suffering would not be in vain. Indeed, their "salvation" from their captors was imminent, and their restored life together would soon show the whole world the saving and life-giving ways of a sovereign God.

29

Sometimes, the Gospels show direct evidence that these oracles provide a framework for Jesus's story. For example, Mark cites Isaiah as part of the Gospel's prologue (Mark 1:2-3).[2] In Luke, Jesus reads from the Isaiah scroll in his first hometown appearance (Luke 4:16-30). On a more subtle level, all four Gospels draw on literary themes such as the "new exodus" and Israel's role as suffering servant. We turn, then, to three passages from Isaiah that shed important light on Jesus's message in the Gospels.

We begin with the opening oracle of Second Isaiah—chapters likely written during the exile itself (Isa 40–55). Scholars widely agree that Isaiah 40:1-11 helps to define the good news found in the Gospels. After a word of comfort, the prophet heralds the news that God will soon defeat the forces that hold Israel captive:

> Get you up on a high mountain,
> O one announcing good news [*euangelizomenos*] to Zion;
> Lift up in strength your voice,
> O one announcing good news [*euangelizomenos*] to Jerusalem....
> Say to the cities of Judah: Behold your God.
> See, the Lord comes with strength and his arm with lordship. (Isa
>   40:9-10 AT)

Though Jerusalem lies in ruins, the prophet assures the exiled people that God, not Nebuchadnezzar, is lord. As a result, this Lord will soon appear in "strength" to reestablish the captives in their homeland, Zion. Here, the good news heralds Israel's victory wrought not through her own military might but through God's decisive power. Isaiah's good news promises human freedom secured through divine restoration of the earth.

Later, the prophet praises the messenger who utters this "good news," this time elaborating in greater detail on its content. God's sovereign power will bring, Isaiah writes, wholeness and deliverance:

> How beautiful upon the mountains are the feet of the one
> who announces good news [*euangelizomenou*] [of] peace,

---

2. Though Mark attributes this opening citation to "Isaiah the prophet," the verses conflate excerpts from Exod 23:20 and Mal 3:1 with Isa 40:3.

who announces good news [*euangelizomenos*]
who announces salvation,
who says to Zion, "Your God reigns!" (Isa 52:7 AT)

When God's heavenly reign makes its way to earth, it will not only bring the defeat of oppressive powers but also usher in an era of peace (Greek: *eirēnē*; Hebrew: *shalom*). What is more, it promises salvation, or deliverance from captivity.

Yet if Isaiah signals that God's coming reign will secure wholeness and deliverance, this good news also describes the impending renewal of the sociopolitical order—a renewal that is especially prominent in the post-exilic oracles of Third Isaiah. More than spiritual concepts, the peace and salvation that accompany God's reign find real-life expression in a just human community. The anointed prophet thus makes clear the value system of God's reign:

The LORD God's spirit is upon me,
    because the LORD has anointed [*echrisen*] me.
He has sent me
    to bring good news [*euangelisasthai*] to the poor,
    to bind up the brokenhearted,
    to proclaim release for captives,
        and liberation for prisoners,
    to proclaim the year of the LORD's favor
        and a day of vindication for our God,
    to comfort all who mourn,

. . . .
They will be called Oaks of Righteousness,
    planted by the LORD to glorify himself. (Isa 61:1-4)

Those who have suffered the most under Babylon's power stand the most to gain from this good news. The oppressed, the brokenhearted, the captives, and the grieving will find their fortunes reversed in the "year of the LORD's favor," even as their overlords face God's judgment.

31

What is more, this restored community will so reflect God's righteousness that they become a billboard for divine glory. Elsewhere, the prophet marvels at the expansive reach of that aura, as "Nations will come to your light / and kings to your dawning radiance" (Isa 60:3). In turn, even Gentiles will "bring good news of the Lord's salvation" (Isa 60:7 LXX). More than just God's rescue of the oppressed people of Israel, Isaiah's "good news" expands to entail God's sweeping renewal of the whole world, evident among the liberated who radiate of God's righteous ways to all the nations.

Isaiah's gospel, then, announces God's coming reign and its reflection among the restored faithful community. Though the prophet sometimes focuses on the "one bearing good news" (Isa 52:7 AT; see also 61:1), ultimately even outsiders will share in its proclamation. Thus Isaiah looks forward both to God's decisive victory and to the community established in its wake. God's universal sovereignty, in Isaiah's view, takes root wherever its subjects reflect God's glory by promoting God's righteous ways.

Over time, Jewish communities facing new oppressors continued to find hope in Isaiah's good news about God's coming kingdom. Often, they applied that good news to their own setting. The scrolls found near Qumran by the Dead Sea reflect this interpretive impulse. And while these texts bore no direct influence on either Jesus or the evangelists, they provide a helpful example of another messianic group that claimed Isaiah's strong promises that God was establishing a foothold, through their righteous community, on the earth.

Like the captives Isaiah reassures, the community at Qumran understood themselves to live in exile. Their dislocation to the Judean wilderness was probably voluntary, not coerced, but the Qumran covenanters found in Isaiah's gospel message a scriptural blueprint for their impending salvation. Such a conceptual framework is evident, for instance, in the Community Rule (1QS), the group's charter document. Echoing Isaiah 40, the Rule urges its members to "prepare in the wilderness the way of the Lord" and identifies the "holy ones" as those who will "walk in the desert to open there [God's] path" (1QS 8:11, 13; see Isa 40:3).

Elsewhere, the War Scroll (1QM) anticipates a cosmic battle in which God will defeat the Roman occupiers (the "Kittim"). After God's decisive victory, this Scroll promises, there will be a "time of salvation for the people of God and a period of dominion for all the men of his lot" (1QM 1:5). Finally, a small but significant fragment quotes Isaiah 52:7, announcing to the community the "good news" that God does indeed rule (11QMelch 2:15-25). For this messianic community, God's reign in heaven was making its way toward earth; through their righteous ways, they bore witness to the "good news" of that reign.

These examples from the Dead Sea Scrolls carry forward Isaiah's vision of God's kingdom that would soon prevail against oppressive forces, both spiritual and political, and that the faithful community would serve as its vanguard. Both Isaiah and the Scrolls declare the good news that God reigns—not just in heaven, but soon, throughout the created realm as well. And in turn, God's coming kingdom will feature a social order that reflects God's just ways. Moreover, those who live as subjects of God's kingdom share in its proclamation. Indeed, only where the faithful community incorporates God's affirmation of human dignity and wholeness does the message about God's sovereignty grow credible.

The Word in Hellenistic Judaism

In John, the nature of Jesus's messianic message shifts rather dramatically from a keen interest in God's coming kingdom to the more enigmatic concept identified in Greek as "*logos*" ("word" or "message"). From the Gospel's outset, Jesus both embodies and proclaims God's word. Scholars generally find in this language evidence of both Jewish and Greco-Roman influence. To understand the background of Jesus's messianic message in John, then, we turn to the *logos* in Hellenistic Judaism. How might this concept provide a bridge between the synoptic message about God's coming kingdom and John's view of Jesus as the word-become-flesh?

Although the *logos* designates a cosmic principle that reflects the order of the created world according to Greek Stoicism, Jewish writers often used the term to refer to the mediating presence of God's wisdom in the world. The intimate connection between God and the word appears already in the first Genesis creation story, where divine speech is the mode of creation: "God said, 'Let there be light'" (Gen 1:3). Perhaps in response to Stoic and Platonic philosophers, later Jewish writers often personified the concept of "word" and assigned it a special role in God's creative work. In the first century, for instance, the Alexandrian Jew Philo characterizes the *logos* this way: "To his word, his chief messenger…the Father of all has given the special prerogative to stand on the border and separate the creature from the creator. And this same word is continually a petitioner to the immortal God on behalf of the mortal race, which is exposed to affliction and misery; and is also the emissary, sent by the Ruler of all, to the subject race."[3] As the passage continues, Philo calls the *logos* neither created nor uncreated but "in the middle of both extremes"[4]—a mediator that spans the divide between God and mortals.

In this account of God's *logos*, Philo also merges the term with notions about God's wisdom found elsewhere in Jewish thought. Often, wisdom is personified as a female who works closely within the created order. For instance, the hymn found in Proverbs 8:22-31 says that she was created at the "beginning of [God's] way" to work "beside [God] as a master of crafts" in creation itself. Later, the Wisdom of Solomon says that wisdom works on God's behalf to instill God's righteous ways on earth (Wisdom 9:2-3). And in Sirach 24, Wisdom speaks these words:

> Then the creator of all things
> gave me a command;
>> the one who created me pitched my tent.
>> and said, "Make your dwelling in Jacob,
>> and let Israel receive your inheritance."
>
> . . . .
>
> I ministered before him in the holy tent,
>> and so I was established in Zion. (Sir 24:8, 10)

---

3. Philo, *Who Is the Heir of Divine Things*, 42:205, in *The Works of Philo: Complete and Unabridged*, trans. C. D. Yonge (Peabody, MA: Hendrickson, 1993).

4. Ibid., 42:206.

As these examples suggest, Hellenistic Judaism saw God's word and God's wisdom almost interchangeably. Together, they manifest God's presence and cultivate God's righteousness on earth.

Against this backdrop, the Fourth Gospel anchors Jesus's messiahship in the notion that, in him, God's word has taken on human form. Just as that word was "with God in the beginning" (John 1:2)—that is, at *creation*—so too the word-become-flesh (John 1:14) works with God in the *new creation* that bears witness to the messianic age. What is more, Jesus's messianic message points the way to the life that age promises. Yet, as with both word and wisdom in Jewish thought, this message points less to his own messianic status than to the life-giving power his messiahship unleashes.

Messianic Message in the Gospels

We turn now to Jesus's messianic message in the Gospels. Growing out of Jewish traditions discussed above, that message confirms that Jesus is indeed the Christ, but it also points beyond his status toward God's renewal of the world and its impact on human community. Like Isaiah and the Dead Sea Scrolls, the Gospels affirm that God is at work to restore a disoriented, dislocated, and disempowered people. Like the wisdom traditions, the Gospels affirm a message of restoration that entails God's life-giving presence unleashed upon the earth. Above all, Jesus's message is messianic because it heralds a radical reorientation of creation toward the creator, a shift evident wherever God's righteous ways shine forth. Thus, all four Gospels cast Jesus's messianic message in terms that bear directly upon their own audience, bringing both meaning and hope as they chart a course in the messianic age. Christ and community together proclaim the good news that God's life-giving power and presence have been set loose in the world.

Messianic Message in Mark: "The Kingdom of God Has Drawn Near" (Mark 1:15 AT)

We begin with the earliest NT account of Jesus's life, death, and resurrection: the Gospel of Mark. To some readers, Mark appears more interested in forging distinction than correlation between Jesus as messiah and his followers, who often seem misguided and obtuse. Moreover, many take the "good news about Jesus Christ" (Mark 1:1) to signal the personal salvation available through faith in Jesus. In this view, Mark uses the term *gospel* (or *good news*) as a cryptic reference to Jesus's exclusive status as God's anointed one.

Yet careful attention to Mark's story suggests that Jesus's gospel message heralds not his own identity but God's coming kingdom, as well as its implications for those who trust in its power. Take, for instance, what Mark says about Jesus's first public appearance:

> After John was handed over, Jesus came to Galilee proclaiming the gospel
> of God and saying:
> The time has been fulfilled, and the reign of God has drawn near.
> Repent and trust in the gospel. (Mark 1:14-15 AT)

What is the gospel that Jesus proclaims? Rather than his own messianic identity, he heralds the dawning rule of God. For Mark's Jesus, the good news concerns God's power breaking onto the earthly scene. And that good news beckons a response. To "repent [literally, "turn around"] and trust in the gospel" means to take the winning side; since God's victory is in view, those who trust God's power will find life in it. Already, Jesus's messianic message both points to God's sovereignty and cultivates human loyalty to it. The passage that follows only underscores this point. Here, Jesus tells four fishers to "come after me, and I will make you fish for people" (Mark 1:17 AT). From the outset of his ministry, Mark's Jesus makes it clear that his messianic mission is no solitary endeavor; his followers, too, will play an active role in recruiting citizens for God's kingdom (see Jer 16:16-21).

In the Gospel's early chapters, Jesus's mission unfolds with the disciples mostly on the sidelines fulfilling their calling to "come after" him. These opening scenes shine the narrative spotlight on Jesus, who travels briskly "throughout Galilee, proclaiming the message [literally, "word"; Greek: *logos*] in their synagogues and casting out demons" (Mark 1:39 NRSV; see 2:2). Once again, Jesus's message in Mark heralds God's coming reign more than his own messianic status. Yet even his exclusive proclamation of that message does not last long. For when Jesus warns the cleansed leper not to "say anything to anyone" (Mark 1:44), Mark says the man "went out and began to proclaim many things and to spread the message" (Mark 1:45 AT). Already, the good news that Jesus proclaims takes on a life of its own, since others announce it as well.

But it is not just the beneficiaries of Jesus's miracle working who declare the good news of God's sovereign power. For when Jesus gathers twelve disciples on a mountaintop, he commissions them to "be with him, to be sent out to preach" (Mark 3:14). Already, then, Jesus sends others out to announce his messianic message about God's coming kingdom. And this is just what they do. Mark reports, "They went out and preached in order that [people] might repent" (Mark 6:12 AT). Echoing Jesus's initial command to "repent and trust" (Mark 1:15 AT), the disciples deliver a message about God's coming kingdom that elicits a turning toward dependence on God as the one true king.

In Mark 4, Jesus highlights the disciples' role in spreading word about God's coming reign. This "parables chapter" begins with an illustrative story about a sower who scatters seed broadly, and with varying results (Mark 4:1-9). Puzzled about its meaning, Jesus's followers ask for an explanation. But before explaining the parable itself, he reminds them, "The *secret of God's kingdom* has been given to you, but to those outside everything comes in parables" (Mark 4:11, emphasis added). In other words, the disciples have been entrusted with the revelation of God's coming kingdom; they are thus bearers of its apocalyptic message. Like Jesus himself, they will sow the word (Mark 4:14). Since the outcome does not depend on them, they need not be troubled if the yields are not consistently robust. Thus the sower parable offers a word of encouragement to those who, like Jesus, meet with varying degrees of success as they promote his messianic message.

The teachings that follow make this point even clearer. First, the sayings about the lamp and measure (Mark 4:21-25) remind Jesus's hearers that the gift entrusted to them should be neither hidden nor safeguarded. Rather, the lamp belongs on the lampstand (Mark 4:21), and Jesus promises that "those who have will receive more" (Mark 4:25). In both cases, the messianic message is meant to be shared expansively. Finally, the parables about the seed growing secretly (Mark 4:26-29) and the mustard seed (Mark 4:30-32) offer a balanced word of assurance. As both Jesus and his followers broadcast the messianic message, they need not worry about results. Once scattered, the seed grows into plant and grain "by itself" (*automatē*; Mark 4:28)—that is, through divine, not human, activity. Ultimately, God's kingdom will flourish into a mustard bush (Mark 4:31-32), which is both hospitable to those who would take rest in it and, at the same time, a plant that is wild and resistant to domestication.

As Mark's story continues, Jesus's messianic message increasingly takes note of the sacrifice that accompanies loyalty to God's kingdom. Indeed, when Jesus first predicts his own suffering, Mark says he spoke "the word" clearly (Mark 8:32 AT). For Mark, the good news that God's reign has drawn near brings with it the harder news that those who align their lives with God's sovereign power will face hardship, even death. As Mark's Jesus puts it, "all who lose their lives because of me and because of the good news will save them" (Mark 8:35; see also 10:29). Notice that Mark distinguishes here between Jesus and his gospel message about God's kingdom. In Mark's story, the good news brings with it the violence that arises whenever the forces of life challenge the forces of death. But such violence is never the last word. Because God's victory is assured, so too is the salvation of those who have cast their allegiance with God's reign.

The Gospel's original ending[5] leaves the messianic message squarely in the hands of those to whom it has been given, even if the point is a subtle one. Notably, those entrusted with the good news about the empty tomb are not the disciples, who have fled in fear. It is the women, who remain "with him" to the end. For while the women arrive to honor a dead body, they find instead an angel who delivers the ultimate messianic message: "He has been raised. He isn't here" (Mark 16:6). In Mark, Jesus's resurrection only substantiates his message about God's coming kingdom. In this

---

5. Scholars widely agree that Mark 16:8 concludes the earliest version of the Gospel. Notably, even the Longer Ending of Mark (Mark 16:9-20)—added by scribes perhaps fifty years later—preserves Jesus's instruction to the disciples to "proclaim the good news" (Mark 16:15), without specifying Jesus's messianic identity as the content of their message.

ultimate victory over death, God's life-giving power has broken through the strongest lines of resistance, securing a permanent foothold on earth. The women's report is implicit rather than explicit, since the Gospel ends on a note of silence and fear (Mark 16:8). Yet the message, Mark suggests, ultimately makes its way from the angel, through the women, to the disciples. It is good news because it sheds dawn's first light on God's defeat of death in the messianic age. And because Jesus has promised to "[go] ahead of" the disciples (Mark 16:7), this message also secures the legacy of Jesus's life-giving presence, even after the resurrection.

The messianic message in Mark captures Jesus's own laserlike focus on God's coming kingdom as a relevant word for a beleaguered messianic community. For those caught in the social and political upheaval caused by the Jewish War, this Gospel offers an urgent message about God's coming reign that carries with it both challenge and comfort. For one thing, it summons them again to "turn and trust the good news" (Mark 1:15 AT) that God's power will finally prove victorious. Mark's story thus reminds them of their calling to "spread the seed" of God's power indiscriminately, regardless of its apparent effect. In this way, Jesus's messianic message emboldens Mark's community to proclaim "your God rules" (Isa 52:7).

Yet for Mark's community, the cost of such a calling was steep. They knew full well the possibility, even probability, of losing "their lives because of me and because of the good news" (Mark 8:35). They had likely "left house, brothers, sisters, mother, father, children, or farms" (Mark 10:29) for such devotion to God's coming kingdom. Thus this messianic message issues an apocalyptic word of hope, since the drama of God's redemption presses inexorably toward God's victory. Like Isaiah's exiles and the community beside the Dead Sea, Mark's community could rest assured that God's defeat of opposing forces was at hand. In Jesus the Christ, God had launched an incursion into the world that would culminate with life-affirming power over all the earth, even under threat of death itself. In the assurance that the risen Lord would "go ahead" of his followers, Mark affirms the enduring ties between Christ and community.

Messianic Message in Matthew: "God's Kingdom and God's Righteousness" (Matt 6:33)

In Matthew, Jesus's messianic message draws out end-time hopes for God's coming kingdom and enhances connections between Christ and community. As we have noted in chapter 1, Matthew uses Mark as a source, adding stories and sayings from Q and M to elaborate Mark's gospel message. As in Mark, Jesus is the "anointed one" who heralds God's coming kingdom. Yet Jesus also appears as an authoritative teacher whose messianic message concerns the righteousness that qualifies hearers for that kingdom. Thus Jesus's teachings prove foundational for Matthew's community, who in turn will carry forward his message to "all nations" (Matt 28:19).

What is the nature of Jesus's messianic message in Matthew? By noticing Matthew's editorial influence on underlying traditions, we can detect the distinctive aspects of that message as it appears in this Gospel. For instance, Matthew elaborates the story of Jesus's baptism to emphasize repentance in preparation for coming judgment. Using Mark's cryptic account as a narrative framework, Matthew adds John the Baptist's call to "produce fruit that shows you have changed your hearts and lives" (Matt 3:8; see also 3:11; Luke 3:8). What is more, this Q tradition points clearly to the eschatological harvest in which "a fire that can't be put out" will destroy the unrighteous (Matt 3:12). In a similar vein, Jesus's opening message reflects a subtle but significant change. Matthew captures Jesus's proclamation with these words: "repent, for the kingdom of heaven[6] has drawn near" (Matt 4:17 AT). By omitting the call to "trust this good news" (Mark 1:15), Matthew underscores the central role of repentance in relation to God's coming reign.

Jesus's messianic message in Matthew emerges over the course of the Gospel, as Jesus teaches repeatedly about God's righteous reign (Matt 5:1–7:27; 10:1-42; 13:1-52; 18:1-35; 24:1–25:46). In these discourses, Jesus's messianic message is communal in two respects. First, Jesus instructs his

---

6. Matthew often prefers the term *kingdom of heaven* to *kingdom of God*, perhaps due to Jewish prohibitions against pronouncing the name of God, but cf. Matt 6:33; 12:28; 19:24; 21:31, 43.

hearers to "desire first and foremost God's kingdom and God's righteous-ness" (Matt 6:33). Along the way, Matthew devotes significant attention to God's righteous ways as a pattern for human relationships. Second, he explicitly charges his disciples with the task of relaying his own messianic message, as both scribes and evangelists.

Several of Jesus's teachings prove vital to our understanding of the messianic message in Matthew. To begin with, the Sermon on the Mount (Matt 5:1–7:27) exposes both Jesus's way of righteousness and its roots in Jewish tradition, which he claims not "to do away with...but to fulfill" (Matt 5:17). In the Sermon's opening passage, the Beatitudes pronounce God's blessing on those who seem least rewarded in the present age: the poor in spirit, the meek, and those "harassed because they are righteous" (Matt 5:10), for instance. In each case, Jesus promises, the benefits of God's kingdom will accrue for those who reflect God's righteousness, even in the face of persecution. Already, Jesus highlights the righteous ways of God's kingdom.

Jesus's message also interprets Torah in a way that promotes a "greater" righteousness (see Matt 5:20). For one thing, Jesus addresses the ethical concerns of Jewish law (e.g., murder, divorce, and adultery: Matt 5:21-48) *before* turning to expressions of religious devotion (e.g., almsgiving, prayer, and fasting: Matt 6:1-18). Thus Matthew's Jesus reverses the or-der of the Ten Commandments (the Decalogue) to prioritize righteous human relationships. Even Jesus's message about religious devotion re-flects this concern. Jesus warns against "practicing your righteousness [*dikaiosynēn*] before others in order to be seen by them" (Matt 6:1 AT). Moreover, in Matthew, "whoever keeps these commands *and teaches people to keep them* will be called great in the kingdom of heaven" (Matt 5:19, emphasis added). Jesus's followers become teachers, and thus transmitters, of his own messianic message.

Jesus's second set of teachings in Matthew concern discipleship (Matt 10:1-42). Here, Matthew weaves disparate threads of Mark's story together to highlight the disciples' role in proclaiming Jesus's messianic message. For instance, Matthew links material that is thematically related, placing the story of their apostolic journey (Matt 10:5-15; see Mark 6:7-13) just after their mountaintop commissioning (Matt 10:1-4; see Mark 3:13-19). What is more, Matthew specifies the content of their message: "As you go, make this announcement: 'The kingdom of heaven has come near'" (Matt 10:7). Finally, to underscore the correlation between his own message and theirs, Matthew's Jesus adds these words: "Disciples aren't greater than their teacher [*didaskalon*].... It's enough for disciples to be like their teacher" (Matt 10:24-25).[7] Like the one who both proclaims and instructs others about the coming kingdom, then, the disciples assume a vital role in disseminating the messianic message.

A third set of teachings adopts and adapts Mark's parables chapter in ways that emphasize eschatological judgment and clarify the disciples' role as heirs to the messianic message (Matt 13:1-52). When the disciples ask Jesus to explain the parable of the weeds growing among the wheat—a story found only in Matthew—Jesus identifies the sower of good seed as the "Son of the Human" and the good seed as the "sons of the kingdom" (Matt 13:37-38 AT). As those "sown" in the world, Jesus's disciples bear witness to his messianic message even as others would thwart it. As if to confirm their active role in promulgating it, Matthew's Jesus concludes the chapter this way: "Therefore every legal expert who has been trained as a disciple for the kingdom of heaven is like the head of a household who brings old and new things out of their treasure chest" (Matt 13:52). Like Jesus himself, these scribes-in-training will carry forward the messianic message of God's kingdom, which both fulfills and renews God's righteousness.

Finally, the Great Commission that concludes this Gospel explicitly assigns Jesus's followers the task of proclaiming his messianic message. After Jesus has risen from the dead, he appears on a mountaintop in Galilee (cf. Mark 16:7) and delivers this charge to the remaining eleven disciples: "I've received all authority [*exousia*] in heaven and on earth. Therefore, go and make disciples of all nations, ... teaching them to obey everything that I've commanded you. Look, I myself will be with you every day until the end of this present age" (Matt 28:18-20). On the one hand, Matthew

---

7. But compare Matt 23:8-10, which distinguishes Jesus as the teacher and messiah in an exclusive sense.

begins by noting that Jesus's authority spans both heavenly and earthly realms. As he has wielded God's kingly power in his earthly career, now the risen Lord continues to exercise divine authority in the resurrection age. Yet his own sweeping authority extends, by design, to his disciples. Taking up his mantle of authority, they will "make disciples" by "teaching them to obey" Jesus's messianic message. Empowered by his persistent presence, they extend Jesus's authoritative, messianic message, to "all nations [*ethnē*]."

In sum, Matthew both adopts Mark's version of Jesus's messianic message and refashions it to promote a "way of righteousness" that leads to eschatological salvation. Such a message, of course, relates closely to Matthew's own community, which was forging a socioreligious identity of its own. Like the rabbis who gained influence after the temple's destruction in 70 CE, Matthew's Jesus emphasizes the importance of reflecting God's righteousness, as disclosed through Torah. And like the community at Qumran, his messianic message retains decidedly eschatological hopes for God's coming kingdom. What is more, Matthew highlights both the social implications of that righteousness—especially care for the "least of these"—and its expansive nature. Rather than a righteousness that inscribes ethnic or religious distinction, Jesus's messianic message in Matthew engenders righteousness among "all the nations" (Matt 25:32; see also 28:19).

For Matthew's post-resurrection community, Jesus's messianic message offers both a defining trait for their life together and marching orders as they carry it forth into the wider world. Along the way, Matthew assigns ultimate meaning to the righteousness it promotes. In its call to "desire first and foremost God's kingdom and God's righteousness" (Matt 6:33), Jesus's messianic message lays the groundwork for messianic community that will "display [God's] glory" (Isa 61:3 NRSV) for all the world to see.

Messianic Message in Luke: "God's Kingdom Is Already Among You" (Luke 17:21)

As many have noted, Luke tailors the gospel message in ways that both preserve its messianic roots—as part of Israel's unfolding story—and highlight motifs of social, political, and religious reversal. In addition, this Gospel accentuates the present, "realized" dimension of God's coming kingdom. Only Luke includes Jesus's claim that "God's kingdom is already among you [or "within you": *en hymin*]" (Luke 17:21); only Luke has Jesus state, "Today, salvation has come to this household" (Luke 19:9). Thus, Luke recounts a messianic message that heralds the good news that, in Jesus, God works to renew the present world order so that "a change of heart and life for the forgiveness of sins" become available "to all nations" (Luke 24:47).

The content of the gospel message in Luke is far from straightforward. On the one hand, Luke calls the birth of both John the Baptist and Jesus himself "good news" (Luke 1:19; 2:10). Elsewhere, Luke leaves unspecified the content of the gospel Jesus proclaims (e.g., Luke 4:43; 7:22; 8:1; 20:1). And both John the Baptist and Jesus's disciples deliver this "good news" as well (Luke 3:18; 9:6; 24:47). When Luke does indicate the content of the message, it can herald the coming kingdom of God (Luke 9:6; see also Luke 9:2) or the "forgiveness of sins... to all nations" (Luke 24:47) that reign entails. Moreover, Luke sometimes implies that this message supersedes, rather than fulfills, the earlier proclamation of "the Law and the Prophets" (Luke 16:16). What can we infer from this complex account of the gospel message?

Perhaps it goes without saying, but we should note first of all that the messianic message in Luke, as in Mark and Matthew, signals more than simply Jesus's identity as the Christ. To be sure, Jesus's messiahship lies at the heart of the message, a point underscored early in the Gospel, when the "Lord's angel" pronounces the "good news" to the shepherds that, "Your savior is born today in David's city. He is Christ the Lord" (Luke 2:9-11). Yet throughout Luke's first two chapters, the significance of Jesus's birth lies not as much in Jesus's identity per se as in the sweeping age of salvation he introduces, a salvation "prepared... in the presence of all peoples" (Luke 2:31). Thus the gospel message is messianic in the broader sense that it heralds the good news of God's unfolding redemption of the world.

Indeed, Luke highlights the inclusive scope of that redemption, which grows out of Israel's sacred tradition to encompass "all peoples." For one thing, Luke uses Jesus's inaugural sermon in his hometown synagogue to make this point. After his time in the wilderness, Jesus arrives in Nazareth and reads these words from the Isaiah scroll:

> *The Spirit of the Lord is upon me,*
> *because the Lord has anointed me.*
> *He has sent me to preach good news [*euangelisasthai*] to the poor,*
> *to proclaim release to the prisoners*
> *and recovery of sight to the blind,*
> *to liberate the oppressed,*
> *and to proclaim the year of the Lord's favor.* (Luke 4:18-19; see Isa
> 61:1-2).

When he claims that, "Today, this scripture has been fulfilled just as you heard it" (Luke 4:21), Jesus identifies himself with the anointed prophet, bringing a messianic message of release and restoration that accompanies God's coming reign. Thus Luke anchors that message in the rich scriptural traditions of Israel.

But Luke's Jesus also goes beyond the reversal of social order suggested in Isaiah 61 to invert the religious and ethnic order as well. As the passage unfolds, Jesus first predicts his rejection, since "no prophet is welcome in the prophet's hometown" (Luke 4:24) and then likens his own mission to that of Elijah and Elisha, who impart God's power to foreigners—a widow from Sidon (Luke 4:26; see 1 Kings 17:1, 8-16) and Naaman the Syrian (Luke 4:27; see 2 Kings 5:1-14). Rather paradoxically, Jesus's messianic message finds a precedent in *Israel's* archetypal prophets, who manifest God's redemption among the *Gentiles* (see Luke 2:32).

As the story progresses, Luke's Travel Narrative (Luke 9:51–19:27) expands this message of prophetic reversal and inclusion, often using traditions found only in this Gospel. For instance, in Luke 15, Jesus responds to charges that he "welcomes sinners and eats with them" (Luke 15:2) by telling three stories about a lost sheep, a lost coin, and a lost son. In each case, Jesus uses the parable to highlight both God's impulse toward restoration and the "joy in heaven" (Luke 15:7; see also 15:10; 15:32) it evokes. Notably, the stories suggest God's relentless pursuit of those who are "lost"; even the prodigal's father runs toward the returning son "while he was still a long way off" (Luke 15:20)—and *before* the son utters a word of repentance. In Luke's story, the charge that Jesus "welcomes sinners and eats with them" only confirms his status as one anointed by a God whose redemption is far-flung indeed.

A second passage from Luke's Travel Narrative sheds important light on Jesus's messianic message, since it tones down Mark's imminent sense of God's coming kingdom to account for its apparent delay. When the Pharisees ask about the timing of its arrival, Jesus replies, "God's kingdom isn't coming with signs that are easily noticed. Nor will people say, 'Look, here it is!' or 'There it is!' Don't you see? God's kingdom is already among you [*en hymin*]" (Luke 17:20-21). At first glance, this claim signals a shift toward "realized eschatology"—the taming of eschatological hopes into the present, and spiritualized, dimension of God's reign. Yet the passage that follows reaffirms the future expectation that the Son of the Human will yet come in judgment (Luke 17:22-27). In that night, Jesus twice says, there will be two and "one will be taken and the other left" (Luke 17:34-35). Read in context, then, Jesus's teaching about the kingdom that is "among you" may simply point to the early evidence of God's reign taking root on the earth even as it presses toward fullest expression in the age to come.

In many ways, the story of Zacchaeus, found only in Luke, draws together key elements of Jesus's messianic message in these two preceding passages. Though the shunned tax collector means only to watch Jesus "pass through" (Luke 19:4 AT), Jesus insists on staying "in your home today" (Luke 19:5). In response, Zacchaeus offers half of his wealth to the poor and fourfold repayment for his fraudulent gains (Luke 19:8). Jesus responds with these words: "Today salvation has come to this household because he too is a son of Abraham. The Human One came to seek and save the lost" (Luke 19:9-10). Once again, Luke suggests that the coming messianic age has dawned in the present, as "salvation" arrives "today." Yet this pithy statement captures several other dimensions of the messianic message in Luke. For one thing, Jesus pronounces Zacchaeus's salvation *after* he restores economic justice, a theme also evident in Luke's story of the rich man and Lazarus (Luke 16:19-31). In addition, Jesus affirms Zacchaeus's identity as a "son of Abraham"—that is, a full-fledged member of God's family rather than a reviled outcast. Finally, Jesus uses the story to reaffirm his messianic mission: "to seek and save the lost" (Luke 19:10). In all these ways, Jesus's messianic message in Luke heralds the salvation that arrives with the inclusive and just reign of God.

But besides the inclusive nature of Jesus's messianic message in Luke, this evangelist also expands earlier tradition to emphasize others' role in its proclamation. After Luke's Jesus charges twelve disciples "to proclaim God's kingdom" (Luke 9:2; see also 9:6), he sends seventy apostles as advance scouts for his own mission (Luke 10:1). Like Jesus, they proclaim, "God's kingdom has come upon you" (Luke 10:9; see 10:11). Rather than reporting *Jesus's* subsequent visit, though, Luke recounts his delight over *their* missionary success (Luke 10:18-20). Indeed, the passage concludes with Jesus both affirming his special status, since "my Father has handed all things over to me," and imparting this divine knowledge to "anyone to whom the Son wants" (Luke 10:22; see also Matt 11:25-27; 13:16-17). Thus Jesus's own messianic message, handed over to him by God, extends through him to others.

In all these ways, then, Luke tailors earlier traditions to highlight the expansive and inclusive nature of Jesus's messianic message—a message about God's coming kingdom that carried important implications for Luke's own community in the wider Greco-Roman world. For one thing, Luke probably wrote for an audience that was mostly, but not exclusively, made up of Gentiles. Thus Luke reiterates the deep roots of Jesus's messianic message in Israel's sacred traditions, providing common scriptural ground for a diverse group. At the same time, though, Luke uses Jewish scripture to highlight the inherently inclusive nature of God's coming kingdom.

This emphasis probably fits Luke's community on several levels. For one thing, such a religiously mixed community of Jews and Gentiles only confirms the dawn of the messianic age; God's inclusive reign takes root in their midst (see, e.g., Gal 3:27). But Luke's audience probably included a cross section of the wider socioeconomic world as well. Thus Jesus's messianic message offers an alternative to the stratified social order that was commonplace in the Greco-Roman world. What is more, Luke's message of repentance and forgiveness of sins reaches outward through the messianic community in ways that release the stranglehold of Satan, securing a salvation that affirms human dignity and wholeness for all people.

Messianic Message in John: "The Word Became Flesh" (John 1:14)

As we have noted, the Fourth Gospel depicts Jesus's messianic message in terms that differ starkly from the synoptic accounts. For one thing, John never uses the word *gospel* at all and only twice mentions "God's kingdom"—both times in a spiritual sense (John 3:3, 5). Moreover, when Jesus speaks, he often uses the phrase "I am" to designate his own significance or divine nature (see Exod 3:14; Isa 48:12) in ways that are unprecedented among the Gospels (see, e.g., John 4:26; 6:20; 6:48; 8:12; and so on). For many scholars, these observations lead to the view that, in John, the "proclaimer has become the proclaimed"[8]—that John's messianic message concerns Jesus's own christological identity in a narrow sense.

Yet careful attention to the Gospel itself, as well as its backdrop in Hellenistic Judaism, yields a more nuanced view of the messianic message than many recognize. Our discussion takes as a starting point John's depiction of Jesus as God's "word [*logos*] [that] became flesh" (John 1:14). In this claim, we find a helpful interpretive bridge from the Synoptic Gospels to John. On the one hand, the synoptic evangelists often use the term *logos* as shorthand for Jesus's messianic message. In their accounts, the sower broadcasts the "word" (Mark 4:14) or the "word about the kingdom" (Matt 13:19). And summary reports about Jesus's messianic mission often speak of Jesus spreading "the word" (Mark 1:45 NRSV; see also 2:2; 4:33). On the other hand, the Fourth Gospel expands this term to include but extend far beyond Jesus's own verbal proclamation. Thus, John takes

---

8. Rudolf Bultmann used this phrase to describe the transformation that happened between Jesus's historical ministry and the writing of the Gospels (*Theology of the New Testament* [Waco, TX: Baylor University Press, 2007], 1.33).

language familiar to Hellenistic Jews and casts it in a messianic light—as God's message takes on human form preeminently in Jesus and, through him, in believers who carry his word forward.

The term *logos* ("word" or "message") appears some forty times in John, almost always as a singular noun. As we shall see, this language captures in a focused way John's interest in Jesus's messianic message. The Gospel opens with this statement: "In the beginning was the Word, / and the Word was with God, / and the Word was God" (John 1:1). Already, the Fourth Gospel hints at the messianic significance of this *logos*. Just as God has called creation into being through the "word," so now that *logos* enters the created realm to establish the new age of "life [that] was the light for all people" (John 1:4). Indeed, in becoming flesh and living "among us" (John 1:14), God's *logos* shows forth divine glory in human form. Thus for John, Jesus the Christ both heralds and reflects the messianic age as the word-become-flesh.

Perhaps surprisingly, the Fourth Gospel assigns a wide range of meanings to the term *logos*. Sometimes, "God's word" refers to Jewish scripture (John 10:35), but elsewhere John distinguishes between "scripture and the word that Jesus had spoken" (John 2:22).[9] Notably, the Samaritans believe because of the "woman's word" (John 4:39)—presumably her report about her encounter with one she believes is the Christ. Often, John promotes a more mystical understanding of the *logos*. Jesus likens God's word to "truth," which sanctifies those who receive it (John 17:17), and speaks of its cleansing power (John 15:3). More than just the doctrinal claim that Jesus is the Christ, then, God's messianic "word" in John can be found not just in Jesus but also in those who believe in him.

Several facets of this message are worth noting. For one thing, Jesus makes clear that this *logos* originates with God: "The word that you hear isn't mine. It is the Father who sent me" (John 14:24; see 12:49). What is more, John's Jesus does not just *speak* God's word; rather, his knowledge of God means that he *keeps* that word (John 8:55). These examples show

---

9. This ambiguous relationship between Jesus's "word" and scripture is consistent with Sirach's view of wisdom, which resides in Jerusalem (Sir 24:10-11), among the people (Sir 24:12), and within Torah itself (Sir 24:23-24). Like this wisdom, the "word" can both be found in scripture and transcend it.

that, for John, Jesus both conveys and adheres to the messianic message entrusted to him.

In this role as messianic messenger, Jesus also opens the way for his hearers to share in his life with God. Often, that message secures eternal life. For instance, Jesus says that "whoever hears my word and believes in the one who sent me has eternal life and won't come under judgment but has passed from death into life" (John 5:24). Here, Jesus's messianic message inscribes a dividing line between those who trust God as its source and those who do not (see John 5:38).

John also underscores the messianic nature of Jesus's message by alluding to Jewish traditions about an anointed shepherd-king (see 1 Sam 16:11; *Psalms of Solomon* 17:40). When "the Jews" in Jerusalem ask if he is "the Christ" (John 10:24), Jesus explains their disbelief this way: "You don't belong to my sheep" (John 10:26). What is more, it is because his sheep hear his "voice" and "follow" that they receive eternal life (John 10:27-28). That is, his message both carries messianic authority and yields the messianic promise of new life.

In this Gospel, Jesus's messianic message plays a pivotal role in the training of disciples. He tells them, "If you remain in my word, you are truly my disciples" (John 8:31 AT). Elsewhere, he stresses the importance of "keeping" or "observing" the word. Just as Jesus himself keeps God's word, so too do the faithful both love him and keep his word (John 14:23, 24; 17:6).

But what does "keeping" Jesus's messianic message entail? Within the Gospel's Farewell Discourse (John 13–17), we draw near to the heart of that message—a message taught in Jewish scripture and fully disclosed in Jesus the Christ. This section begins with the story of Jesus washing his disciples' feet. Here, Jesus promotes a "new commandment: Love each other. Just as I have loved you, so you also must love each other" (John 13:34; 15:12). At first glance, Jesus seems to overstate the novelty of his message, since the Torah also commands the love of neighbor (see Lev 19:18). Yet John elaborates on this traditional command in at least two ways. First, because this teaching follows the story of his washing his disciples' feet, John underscores the self-giving nature of Jesus's love. Second,

John's Jesus forges a deliberate likeness between his own sacrificial love and the mutual love he promotes. Perhaps paradoxically, God's word-become-flesh enables his followers to manifest that word in their own self-giving love.

In this way, the messianic message ultimately draws the disciples into union with God. Jesus promises those who love him and keep his word that "my Father will love them, and we will come to them and make our home with them" (John 14:23). As a result, they too take up the task of sharing the message—a task that meets with mixed results. Indeed, Jesus issues this warning about their reception: "If the world harassed me, it will harass you too. If it kept my word, it will also keep yours" (John 15:20). Thus the disciples to whom Jesus has imparted God's word (John 17:14) continue to impart it to others, extending belief in the messianic message "because of their word" (John 17:20).

As we have seen, the messianic message—the *logos*—in John comes as part of God's new creation, enacted decisively in Jesus but also, through him, in those who gain eternal life. The message thus points to God as its source and to the messianic community Jesus establishes. As Irenaeus puts it, the *logos* "commenced afresh the long line of human beings, and furnished us, in a brief, comprehensive manner, with salvation; so that what we had lost in Adam—namely, to be according to the image and likeness of God—we might recover in Christ Jesus."[10]

In the Fourth Gospel, then, Jesus both embodies and proclaims the divine *logos* that in turn engenders eternal life. Read in its Hellenistic Jewish context, this word signals God's very presence in the world, disclosed in and through the word-become-flesh. If the notion that God's *logos* had entered the created order was familiar to many first-century Jews, the claim that it would take up residence in an anointed human figure was perhaps more jarring, even offensive. Indeed, in its present form, the Fourth Gospel probably addresses an audience that lived in tension with its native Jewish community. The depiction of Jesus's messianic message has, in this Gospel, grown more divisive: the resistance, persecution, and rejection it elicits intensify—likely mirroring the experience of John's community.

10. Irenaeus, *Against Heresies* 3.18.1.

Yet as God's word-become-flesh, Jesus does not back down from such conflict; rather, he continues to promote his messianic message as the reflection of God's word of life for the world that awaits redemption. At its core, that word is self-giving: not only has God given his Son for the salvation of the world (John 3:16-17), but Jesus too will "give up [his] life for [his] friends" (John 15:13). And because he has entrusted this word to his followers, they too will bear God's word of life to the world as they "love each other" and as they "testify" to him through the power of the spirit (John 15:17, 26).

Concluding Thoughts

As he stepped into the landscape of first-century Palestinian Judaism, Jesus took up the prophetic task of heralding the coming reign of God. Like the prophets and visionaries who had gone before, Jesus announced that God's heavenly sovereignty was breaking into the earthly realm. Indeed, it was this claim, at least in part, that led to his crucifixion by the powers that be. Yet the message about God's coming kingdom did not die with him; indeed, the Gospel witness to Jesus offers a vivid reminder that the message lived on in post-resurrection communities aligned with his mission.

In this chapter, we have noted important facets of Jesus's messianic message in all four Gospels. Together, the synoptic accounts emphasize the message's emphasis on the kingdom of God and its implications for human community. Yet even in the Fourth Gospel, where kingdom language is notably absent, Jesus's identity as the word-become-flesh anchors his messianic career in the message he bears to the world, a message that takes the form of sacrificial love and promises eternal life to those who keep it. In all four Gospels, then, the good news features Jesus as authoritative mediator of God's word of redemption; in the message of this Christ, each evangelist heralds the nature of God's sacrificial, life-giving power that is now loose in the world.

This survey of Jesus's messianic message in the Gospels has yielded another consistent finding. Despite the diverse accounts explored here, Jesus's role as authoritative herald consistently signals the inclusive nature of his message in two respects. First, the message itself is inherently communal, since it casts a sociopolitical vision based on biblical notions of righteousness, justice, and self-giving love. Even in John, the message promotes neither private religious observance nor doctrinal conformity. Discipleship—belonging to the messianic community Jesus gathers—hinges simply on this: "love each other just as I have loved you" (John 15:12). Jesus's messianic message, then, promotes the "incorporation" of Jesus's own life.

Second, despite—or perhaps, because of—its central place in his own mission, Jesus's messianic message extends, throughout the Gospels, to the community established in the post-resurrection era. As heirs to his message, his followers continue to affirm the same gospel about God's reign that Jesus had proclaimed or to pass along the same word he has entrusted to them. To be sure, their messianic message remains inextricably rooted in his messianic mission and enduring, post-resurrection presence. In all four Gospels, those who carry forward Jesus's messianic message speak as authorized agents rather than as autonomous voices. Even after the resurrection, his empowering presence remains with them, imparting his messianic message to them. Working together, the risen Lord and the faithful community perpetuate the gospel message wherever they cast a vision of restored human community anchored in God and enlivened by the world-tilting, life-giving power of God's reign.

Study Questions

1. Explain the connection between good news and God's coming kingdom in Isaiah and the Dead Sea Scrolls.

2. How was God's word understood in Hellenistic Judaism?

3. For each Gospel, identify one passage that helps explain the writer's portrait of Jesus's messianic message. Explain its significance.

4. How does each evangelist's portrait of Jesus's messianic message connect Christ and community?

For Further Reading

Allison, Dale C. *The New Moses: A Matthean Typology*. Minneapolis: Fortress, 1993.

Beasley-Murray, G. R. *Jesus and the Kingdom of God*. Grand Rapids: Eerdmans, 1986.

Beavis, Mary Ann. *Jesus and Utopia: Looking for the Kingdom of God in the Roman World*. Minneapolis: Fortress, 2006.

Dillon, Richard J. *From Eyewitnesses to Ministers of the Word*. Analecta biblica 82. Rome: Biblical Institute Press, 1978.

Koester, Craig R. *The Word of Life: A Theology of John's Gospel*. Grand Rapids: Eerdmans, 2008.

Marcus, Joel. *The Way of the Lord: Christological Exegesis of the Old Testament in the Gospel of Mark*. Louisville: Westminster John Knox, 1992.

Chapter Three
Messianic Power

"Authority over All the Power of the Enemy" (Luke 10:19)

If Jesus's messianic message lies at the heart of the Gospel witness to Jesus, his messianic power manifests in a tangible way the dawn of God's reign upon the earth. Even before the evangelists, the Apostle Paul says that "the kingdom of God [can be seen] not in word but in power" (1 Cor 4:20 AT). And as one scholar suggests, "the miracles worked by Jesus may contribute as much to [the Gospels'] implicit Christology as the authority of his teaching."[1] All four evangelists depict Jesus as the messiah who discloses God's reign in deed and word (Luke 24:19). Both his teachings and his miracles, then, contribute to their portrait of Jesus the Christ. As he heals the sick, casts out demons, feeds the hungry, and tames nature's chaotic forces, Jesus appears in the Gospels as an anointed agent of God's redemption unleashed in the world. In these deeds of power, Jesus triumphs over forces that would oppose God's coming reign and the human dignity and wholeness it promotes.

Despite the prominence of Jesus's messianic power in the Gospels, modern studies of NT Christology often downplay this dimension of his messianic mission. Focusing on motifs such as Jesus's divine Sonship and saving death, scholars often make scant mention of his miraculous powers. When they do, they sometimes separate his wonder working into two categories, according to their scientific plausibility. On the one hand, they

---

1. Eric Eve, *The Jewish Context of Jesus' Miracles*, Journal for the Study of the New Testament: Supplement Series 231 (London: Sheffield Academic Press, 2002), 386.

take healings and exorcisms more seriously, since they do not defy the laws of nature. On the other hand, stories that seem improbable to the modern reader—such as the feeding stories and the calming of the sea—recede into the background of academic study. The result of this reticence about Jesus's deeds of power leads many to overlook their vital part in the Gospel witness to Jesus.

Such reticence is, of course, understandable. For one thing, modern inquiry casts a skeptical light on stories that do not easily submit to rational explanation. As a result, interpreters have employed a range of approaches to the miracle stories. For instance, more than two hundred years ago, Thomas Jefferson used his scissors to cut out Gospel accounts at odds with a scientific worldview. Others explain the deeds of power in a reasonable light. For example, some suggest that the "miracle" in the feeding story came from the crowd sharing their own food with one another; others claim that, rather than walking on water, Jesus walked in the shallow surf at edge of the sea. Both approaches attempt to reconcile modern inquiry with ancient Gospel accounts. Along the way, they minimize the significance of the miracle stories for the Gospels themselves.

From a different angle, those who read the Gospels for evidence of Jesus's exclusive messianic status neglect his deeds of power because they do not distinguish him from other ancient figures. After all, stories of miracle workers from the Jewish and wider Hellenistic worlds seem to undermine the significance of his divine power. The Neo-Pythagorean Apollonius of Tyana reportedly worked miracles, and the first-century historian Josephus attributes similar powers to the Jewish figures Honi and Hanina. Against this backdrop, Jesus's deeds of power prove neither his divine origins nor his messianic status. Since they do not set Jesus apart, then, many push these stories to the sidelines as they consider the Gospel portrait of Jesus's messiahship.

Recent attention to Jesus's Jewish context, though, has reopened the question of Jesus's deeds of power. For once we view the miracle stories in light of Jesus's messianic landscape, they can be seen as a part of the wider horizon of God's reign taking root on earth. This allows us, in turn, to take seriously the Gospel witness to his power. The point is neither to confirm nor to deny the miracles' historical or scientific plausibility. Rather, we set aside questions that stem from dogmatic assumptions about both science and Christology and ask instead how the *evangelists* viewed Jesus's deeds of power against the backdrop of Jewish thought.

As we turn to the Gospel portrait of Jesus's messianic power, we find it to be both authoritative and shared. For all four evangelists, Jesus's wonder working constitutes a vital part of his messianic story. In the Synoptic Gospels, the miracles showcase Jesus's mission to bind "the strong person" (Mark 3:27). That is, Jesus wields God's power over evil to prepare for God's coming kingdom. And while observers often marvel at *Jesus's* abilities (e.g., Mark 4:41), he works miracles as part of *God's* restoration of the world, not as a magician who seeks his own acclaim. The Fourth Gospel includes fewer but more impressive miracles. There, they are "signs" that confirm Jesus's messiahship since they point to God's life-affirming power at work through him. In this chapter, then, we treat Jesus's deeds of power as they appear in the Gospels, exposing the evangelists' claims as part of their unfolding witness to his messianic mission.

But more than just Jesus's access to God's power, the Gospels also stress that Jesus imparts that power to others. As an inherent part of his messianic mission, Jesus's miracle working extends in turn to his disciples, either during his lifetime or in the post-resurrection age. Just as Jesus's followers carry forward his messianic message about God's coming kingdom, so too do they engage in messianic power sharing. Working alongside Jesus—both during his earthly career and after his death—*their* miracles disclose *his* messianic authority over the forces of evil. Christ and community are inextricably linked to each other, as both Jesus and those caught up in his mission participate in God's restoration of the world.

Deeds of Power in Jewish Tradition

As we turn to the question of Jewish context, we note from the outset that miracle working played no significant part in the mainstream Judaism of Jesus's day. Instead, the people of Israel found their religious focus in both the Jerusalem temple—with its priestly sacrifices—and the interpretation of Torah. Even those Jews who looked forward to a coming messiah did not generally expect that figure would perform such miraculous deeds as healing those in need.

At the same time, Jewish texts that promote a messianic *message* about God's coming kingdom often speak of its tangible *power* to restore physical and spiritual well-being. Thus we return in this section to the writings considered in the preceding chapter. There, we saw that the biblical book of Isaiah and the apocalyptic community at Qumran both announce that God's sovereignty in heaven will soon extend throughout the earth. Here, we find that these writers adduce palpable examples of the kind of human restoration that sovereignty will bring. Notably, those examples include motifs that mark Jesus's deeds of power in the Gospels: healings, miraculous feedings, and nature miracles.

As we shall see, Isaiah and the Dead Sea Scrolls offer two complementary insights about deeds of power that mark the messianic age. In the first place, the miracles themselves are divine, not human, in origin. The power they manifest emanates from the God whose heavenly reign is taking root on earth. Thus they bear witness to God's glory as it restores human life. But this leads to a second observation. In these texts, God imparts divine power to faithful humans, who perform divinely authorized acts on God's behalf. Thus, they act as advance agents of God's coming kingdom, defeating evil forces that would thwart human wholeness. Where messianic figures do appear, they mediate God's power to the community aligned with God's reign. In light of these texts, the deeds of power associated with God's coming kingdom signal the arrival of the messianic age more than they do the messianic identity of an anointed individual.

The Book of Isaiah

As noted earlier, the book of Isaiah exerted a strong influence on Jesus as well as the Gospel witness to his career. Already we have seen that the prophet's good news of God's coming reign lies behind Jesus's messianic message. Here, we find that Isaiah's oracles shed important light on the Gospel accounts of Jesus's messianic power as well. In what follows, we consider several key passages that signal the physical restoration associated with God's coming kingdom. In particular, Isaiah provides a conceptual framework for these Gospel motifs: sight for the blind, release for captives, power over chaotic waters, and food for the hungry.

The themes of blindness and sight work metaphorically in Isaiah to diagnose Israel's (temporary) recalcitrance and to pronounce prophetic hope for her restoration. In a stage-setting scene, Isaiah's heavenly vision suggests that, at least for the time being, God obscures Israel's clear sight and even prevents healing:

> Make the minds of this people dull.
> > Make their ears deaf and their eyes blind,
> > so that they can't see with their eyes
> > or hear with their ears,
> > or understand with their minds,
> > and turn, and be healed. (Isa 6:10)

Since the oracles found in Isaiah extend from the eighth to the sixth century BCE, this story of Isaiah's call to prophecy seems to take the "long view." Read in its canonical setting—as part of the compilation now called "Isaiah"—this "call" from the outset of the prophet's career in the "year of King Uzziah's death" (Isa 6:1) partly explains Israel's defeat by Babylon generations later. In any case, God promises that Isaiah's prophetic words of warning will fall on deaf ears, as part of God's unfolding plan.

But as we noted in the last chapter, Babylon's victory over Jerusalem is not the end of Israel's story in Isaiah. Later oracles coming from the time of exile and beyond use the motif of blindness and sight to herald Israel's coming redemption. For instance, the prophet writes, "On that day: The deaf will hear the words of a scroll and, freed from dimness and darkness, the eyes of the blind will see" (Isa 29:18). Elsewhere, we find a similar promise that deeds of power will accompany God's impending salvation:

> Then the eyes of the blind will be opened,
> > and the ears of the deaf will be cleared.
> The lame will leap like the deer,
> > and the tongue of the speechless will sing. (Isa 35:5-6)

Such dramatic reversal of fortune, says the prophet, will show the created world "the LORD's glory, / the splendor of our God" (Isa 35:2). In both passages, the miracles in view offer palpable evidence of creation restored to the state of wholeness intended from the beginning.

In Isaiah 40–66, God sometimes works through chosen agents who perform these mighty deeds of power. Second Isaiah's "Servant of Yahweh" is a prime example of such an authorized mediator of divine restoration. In the first Servant Song (Isa 42:1-9), Yahweh announces that a "servant, . . . / my chosen . . . [will] open blind eyes [and] lead the prisoners from prison, / and those who sit in darkness from the dungeon" (Isa 42:1, 7). But who is this servant? As many have noted, the individual figure named here designates the faithful community that serves collectively as staging ground for God's coming kingdom.[2] As a "light to the nations," the servant represents faithful Israel, who will together wield God's sovereign power in ways that bring wholeness and release (Isa 42:6). Yet these deeds of power glorify not the faithful community but their God. As Isaiah puts it, "I am the LORD; / that is my name; / I don't hand out my glory to others" (Isa 42:8). Any power the people exercise belongs to God. It is Yahweh who, through their deeds, subverts the present, oppressive world order and in turn wins widespread acclaim not for Israel but for her God.

Besides the motif of restored sight, Isaiah sometimes speaks of God's power over natural forces of chaos. Echoing the Exodus story, the prophet announces Yahweh's empowering presence as the people anticipate a new exodus from Babylon: "When you pass through the waters, I will be with you; / when through the rivers, they won't sweep over you" (Isa 43:2; see also 43:16; 51:10). These claims about God's triumph over "the waters" clearly echo traditions preserved not just in Exodus 15 but also in an array of psalms (e.g., 76:6-7; 104:7). In turn, this power over watery chaos provides convincing evidence, for Isaiah, of God's decisive defeat of evil

---

2. Of the twenty-one uses of the noun in Isa 40–55, *servant* refers to the people of God (sometimes through the name "Israel" or "Jacob") in at least sixteen cases. Such a clear designation sets these chapters apart from the rest of Isaiah, where *servant* refers to a generic social relationship (e.g., Isa 36:9, 11; 37:5, 24) or to a particular character (Isaiah, Isa 20:3; Eliakim, Isa 22:20; David, Isa 37:35). Outside Second Isaiah, where the noun refers to the faithful, it appears in plural form (Isa 56:6; 63:17; 65:8-15; 66:14).

(see Isa 44:27; 50:2). As the people themselves "pass through the waters," they participate in this dramatic display of a God "who makes a way in the sea / and a path in the mighty waters" (Isa 43:16) and thus bear active witness to God's defeat of evil.

Finally, Isaiah maintains that God's coming reign will ensure ample food in the face of human hunger. When the people come back from exile, for instance, God says, "The imprisoned ones will soon be released; / they won't die in the pit / or even lack bread" (Isa 51:14). The prophet even likens God's new world order to a lavish banquet:

> All of you who are thirsty, come to the water!
> Whoever has no money, come, buy food and eat!
> Without money, at no cost, buy wine and milk!
> . . . .
> Listen carefully to me and eat what is good;
>   enjoy the richest of feasts. (Isa 55:1-2)

These passages together suggest that God's coming reign on the earth institutes an economy of plenty. Indeed, this invitation to a divine banquet promises not just sufficiency but rich satisfaction and delight.

Elsewhere, Isaiah's vision about God's coming reign draws those who "acted righteously" (Isa 58:2) into the picture. When their lives reflect God's lordship, Isaiah says, the people heed God's call of "sharing your bread with the hungry, / and bringing the homeless poor into your house" (Isa 58:7). In these concrete acts of reconfigured power, Isaiah expects faithful human beings will participate in the new world order that displays God's triumph over the prevailing systems of injustice (Isa 58:6). Moreover, it serves as the basis on which God promises to "provide for you, even in parched places" (Isa 58:11). Those who remain loyal to God's reign play an active part in God's provision for those who lack basic resources.

Together, these images of God's renewal of the present age—with its blindness, captivity, chaos, and hunger—suggest that God's power is at work to unseat oppressive systems that prevail in the present. In these oracles, Isaiah offers glimpses of God's sovereign ways taking root on earth, as the human condition comes to reflect God's reign. But while God is both the source of that power and the object of the glory it elicits, Isaiah retains a consistent concern for the community that will manifest God's authority. Here, God enlists and empowers the faithful to embody God's coming kingdom in concrete ways. As a "light to the nations," faithful Israel will demonstrate divine power not for their own gain but for the glory of their God, and for the repair of the world.

The Dead Sea Scrolls

As we noted in the last chapter, the Scrolls found at Qumran expand Isaiah's vision for God's coming reign, framing it in a sharply apocalyptic light. Along the way, they find in that vision the foundation for their life together as a holy and righteous community. The Community Rule manifests the group's dualistic apocalyptic worldview. Attributing evil to "dominion of Belial" (1QS 1:17 and throughout), the Rule calls the faithful community to bear preliminary witness God's coming dominion as they "clear the LORD's way" (Isa 40:3). Though the Scrolls sometimes feature individual figures such as the Teacher of Righteousness (1QS 1:1, 18; and so on) and those designated as "messiahs," their overarching concern lies with the faithful community as those who establish in their life together a foothold for God's coming kingdom.

The fact that the Scrolls are, first and foremost, "community literature" can be seen in passages that concern the deeds of power associated with God's coming reign. One fragment in particular describes that messianic power in terms that resonate with the Gospel accounts. Called the Messianic Apocalypse because it mentions God's "anointed one" (4Q521 2:1), this excerpt says that the Lord, not the "messiah," will perform deeds of power in the messianic age. It reads, in part,

> For the Lord will consider the pious and call the righteous by name
> Over the poor his spirit will hover and will renew the faithful with
> his power.
> And he will glorify the pious on the throne of the eternal Kingdom.
> Liberating the captives, restoring sight to the blind, lifting up the
> b[ent] . . .

And the Lord will accomplish glorious things...
For he[3] will heal the wounded, and revive the dead and
bring good news to the poor. (4Q521 2:5-8, 11-12)[4]

Several details of this passage contribute to our understanding of messianic deeds of power. First, the "glorious things" mentioned here bear witness to God's "eternal Kingdom." Thus, in the messianic age, God's glory will be evident in ways that echo Isaiah's claims about the servant's deeds of power: restored sight and liberty for captives (see Isa 42:7). Moreover, it is "the Lord" who will perform these deeds of power. Yet also important for our purposes is the claim that this kingdom will take root among "the pious," "the righteous," and "the faithful." That is, they constitute the staging ground for God's deeds of power. Despite the excerpt's earlier mention of God's "anointed one," the figure serves mostly to signal the dawn of God's reign upon the earth. It is within this messianic age, the fragment suggests, that God's power will work to restore wholeness among the faithful. What is more, through these deeds of power, the Lord "will glorify the pious on the throne of the eternal Kingdom" (4Q521 2:7).

The War Scroll goes even further, attributing God's wonder-working power to the "holy ones" themselves. This document envisions a coming battle with God's opposition, the "Kittim" (the Romans), who serve as foot soldiers of evil. To be sure, the Scroll insists that God, not human warriors, will launch the first assault. Yet the Scroll provides marching orders for those who will be enlisted, equipped, and even accompanied by God. As a result, notice that the "holy ones" emerge as vessels of God's wonder-working power:

> [T]he second battalion will be equipped with a shield and a sword, to fell the dead by the judgment of God and to humiliate the enemy line by God's

---

3. The identity of the "he" in this translation is disputed. Some translators find a shift from the Lord's deeds to another (perhaps messianic) figure's accomplishments. See the discussion in Eve, *The Jewish Context of Jesus' Miracles*, 191–92, who finds such a reading "grammatically clumsy" and showing "suspicious signs of wanting the text to provide a 'disjunction' at this point."

4. This translation follows Geza Vermes, *The Dead Sea Scrolls in English*, 4th ed. (Sheffield: Sheffield Academic Press, 1995), 244–45.

might.... For kingship belongs to the God of Israel and with the holy ones of his nation he will work wonders. (1QM 6:5-6)

On the one hand, the kingship, judgment, and power belong to God. On the other hand, "God's might" empowers the group, who in turn perform deeds of God's power. Later, the War Scroll reinterprets the biblical claim that "Israel acts powerfully" (Num 24:18) to read, "Israel will work wonders" (1QM 11:7). Fighting on behalf of their divine ruler, faithful Israel will be endowed with the miraculous power that accompanies God's sovereign rule.

As they anticipate God's coming kingdom, both Isaiah and the Dead Sea Scrolls forge an intrinsic connection between God's sovereign power in heaven and the miraculous deeds that will substantiate it on earth. Significantly, the examples noted here emphasize God's role in those deeds of power in at least two ways. First, it is divine, not human, power that opens blind eyes, releases captives, tames waters, and feeds the hungry. Second, such deeds constitute evidence of the coming reign of God in and through the faithful. By trusting that God's eternal reign has dawned, the faithful participate actively in its disclosure not for their own notoriety, but to demonstrate God's renewal of the earth for all the world to see. Where individual figures—such as the "servant" and the "anointed"—appear, they function in dynamic relationship to the broader community aligned with God's coming reign.

Deeds of Power in the Gospels

The Gospels present Jesus's miracles as a vital part of his messianic mission. Indeed, these deeds of power work in tandem with his teachings to suggest that, in his earthly ministry, God's kingdom has drawn near. And though other early Christian writers focused on either his message (e.g., *Gospel of Thomas* and Q) or his deeds of power (e.g., *Infancy Gospel of Thomas*), the NT evangelists keep both in view. In light of the Jewish writings discussed above, this combination makes good sense as part of their messianic witness.

In this section, we consider each Gospel's depiction of Jesus's messianic deeds, as well as the ways in which his power extends to the faithful community it addresses. Like Isaiah and the Scrolls, both the Synoptic Gospels and John attribute Jesus's power to God. For instance, Jesus tells the Gerasene demoniac to report what "the Lord has done" for him (Mark 5:19), and John's Jesus speaks of the "works" that the Father "has given me . . . to do so that I might complete them" (John 5:36). Throughout all four accounts, Jesus appears, like the "pious" at Qumran, as an authorized agent of God's power. But those who focus on Jesus's exclusive messianic power overlook the reports of his power-sharing initiatives. In all four Gospels, Jesus both wields divine power and engages the faithful, who work in concert with him to mediate God's life-giving power for others. Moreover, the Gospels together maintain that God's power grows effective when humans trust that, in Jesus the Christ, God's redemptive purposes are taking root on the earth.

A preliminary word about the "messianic" nature of the miracle traditions will help anchor our study of the Gospels in the soil of Jewish thought. To begin with, Jesus's messianic deeds emerge as a by-product of his messianic message that God's kingdom has drawn near. Thus the miracle stories illustrate Jesus's access to divine authority over evil forces that would resist that coming reign. By "tying up the strong person" (Mark 3:27; see Matt 12:29; Luke 11:21), Jesus disarms Satan and gives advance notice that God's kingdom will soon prevail upon all the earth. Clearly, Gospel accounts of exorcisms fit within this framework, since they provide examples of Jesus's confrontation, and decisive defeat, of evil itself. Yet other kinds of "miracles" are also best understood as evidence of God's triumph over opposing powers. As we have seen in both Isaiah and the Dead Sea Scrolls, God's redemptive power appears wherever sight is restored, the oppressed are set free, "the waters" are tamed, or the hungry are fed. Moreover, these wonders testify to God's restoration of the world, in and through faithful human community. More than proving Jesus's messianic status per se, such deeds of power signal his messianic aim: to launch God's rule on the earth.

Seen in this light, it is perhaps not surprising that the canonical Gospels depict Jesus's extension of divine power to others—both in his own career and in the post-resurrection age. Though most studies of the miracle traditions emphasize Jesus's exclusive role as miracle worker, the Gospels themselves forge connection rather than distinction between Jesus's miracles and those of his followers. Perhaps paradoxically, what sets Jesus apart in these Gospels is not his access to divine power but his authoritative role—both before and after the passion—as mediator of that power to those who form a messianic community.

As we shall see, all four evangelists depict Jesus's deeds of power as both authoritative and expansive. On the one hand, they reveal his christological identity ("Who then is this?" in Mark 4:41) as God's anointed agent of divine power. On the other hand, this distinctive role entails his channeling of that power toward those whom he engages in his messianic mission. Rather than diminishing his christological significance, this power-sharing dynamic amplifies it beyond his own earthly career and into the messianic community that carries forward his mission. We turn attention, now, to the Gospel witness to such an inclusive view.

Messianic Power in Mark: "Tying Up the Strong Person" (Mark 3:27)

For decades, scholars have insisted that Mark sees Jesus's deeds of power as secondary to, or preparatory for, his messianic suffering. Some have even suggested that Mark portrays this dimension of Jesus's story in a negative light. To be sure, Mark's story moves from his miracles toward his sacrifice as the culminating disclosure of Jesus's messiahship. Yet to view his deeds of power as somehow separate from—even at odds with—Jesus's passion is to miss their intrinsic connection to his wider messianic mission. Once we read this Gospel in light of Jewish hopes for God's coming kingdom, we find that this Gospel represents miracle stories as early skirmishes in Jesus's battle against evil powers. Ultimately, that battle leads to the passion itself; in the cross and empty tomb, Mark insists that God's power prevails even over death. Thus for Mark, both Jesus's wonder working and his destiny bear witness to that divine victory.

What can we say about Jesus's messianic power in Mark? Among the miracle stories that dominate the Gospel's first half, Jesus's casting out of demons or unclean spirits occurs most often. For Mark, Jesus's exorcising power discloses the authority with which he announces God's coming reign; indeed, the crowd responds to his first deed of power by marveling, "What's this? A new teaching with authority! He even commands unclean spirits and they obey him" (Mark 1:27). In Mark's account, Jesus's word and deed operate together, as he manifests God's power on earth.

Indeed, Mark understands Jesus's miracles as part of an unfolding apocalyptic drama in which conflict escalates wherever God's power gains a foothold in creation. Sometimes, that conflict arises with religious leaders, who take issue with Jesus's commanding presence. This is the case early in the Gospel, as Jesus heals a paralytic (Mark 2:1-12), as well as a man with a withered hand (Mark 3:1-6). In these stories, onlookers question the forgiveness Jesus declares in the first instance and his "violation" of Sabbath observance in the second. But it is Jesus's reputation as an exorcist that inspires some "legal experts [who] came down from Jerusalem" to claim, "He's possessed by Beelzebul. He throws out demons with the authority of the ruler of demons" (Mark 3:22). Jesus responds first by noting that "a house torn apart by divisions will collapse" (Mark 3:25). In other words, he deploys force as Satan's opponent, not his ally. But Jesus goes further, spelling out the nature of his exorcising mission: "no one gets into the house of a strong person without first tying up the strong person" (Mark 3:27). Thus, Mark's Jesus exercises authority over evil as a first stage in God's reclamation of the world. As he subdues demons, he launches an early foray in an apocalyptic showdown against evil.

Notably, the miracle stories in Mark consistently cast Jesus's deeds of power in this messianic light. For one thing, the healings institute not just physical repair but spiritual and emotional health as well, signaling the holistic well-being associated with the reign of God. Mark's account often weaves together these aspects of wholeness. For instance, when four men set a paralytic before him, Jesus notes the friends' faith and then pronounces the man's forgiveness (Mark 2:1-12). In this story, to trust God's power unleashed through Jesus brings both spiritual and physical strength—and in just that order—where paralysis had prevailed. In a similar manner, when an ailing woman grasps for Jesus's power by touching the fringe of his garment, he responds, "Daughter, your faith has healed you [literally, "saved you"]; go in peace, healed from your disease" (Mark 5:34). Again, Jesus channels divine power that brings deliverance in place of debilitating suffering.

Besides exorcisms and healing stories, Jesus's other deeds of power in Mark often echo motifs we have detected in both Isaiah and the Dead Sea Scrolls. Mark's central section (Mark 8:27–10:45), built around three predictions of Jesus's suffering destiny, is flanked by stories in which Jesus restores sight to the blind (Mark 8:22-26; 10:46-52). In addition, it is often Jesus's clear sight that activates his divine power (e.g., Mark 2:5; 6:48). The theme of God's plenteous provision appears in this story as well. Mark includes not one but two feeding miracles (Mark 6:30-44; 8:1-10). Since they take place in Jewish and Gentile territory respectively, Mark seems to underscore the sweeping nature of God's power to feed the hungry. Finally, Mark twice highlights Jesus's divine triumph over the watery chaos. In the first story, Jesus's trustful repose signals the kind of faith the disciples do not yet exhibit, and they stir him to tackle the storm at sea head-on (Mark 4:35-41). In the second, though he has sent his followers out to sea without him, Jesus sees their struggle and responds by joining them and ultimately subduing the wind and waves (Mark 6:45-52). Taken together, then, Jesus's wonder working plays a vital role in this story of his messianic mission, as he wields the power of God's coming reign in palpable ways.

But it is not just Jesus who manifests that power, as his followers participate in this dimension of Jesus's messianic mission as well. To be sure, Mark offers a mixed review of the disciples, who often fail to comprehend Jesus and his messianic mission (see, e.g., Mark 6:52; 8:21). Some think this misunderstanding arises because they do not grasp Jesus's christological identity as God's anointed Son who must suffer. In this view, their lapses only accentuate Jesus's exalted status and forge a sharp distinction between Christ and community. But while the Gospel never *specifies* the nature of their misunderstanding, Mark *suggests* that it concerns not Jesus's identity in the narrow sense but his broader messianic mission, which carries important implications for his followers. Just as his disciples have been summoned to share in his messianic message, so too does Mark indicate that Jesus involves them in his messianic power.

Early in his ministry, Mark's Jesus deliberately engages his disciples in his active witness to God's coming reign. Already we have seen that, at their commissioning, the Twelve are called to be "with [Jesus], to be sent out to preach, and to have authority to throw out demons" (Mark 3:14-15). Notice that their being "with him" appears as the first part of their commission; as his collaborators, the disciples must rely on Jesus's presence for access to the divine power that discloses God's coming reign. Notice, too, that Mark depicts their calling in terms that follow the pattern of Jesus's own mission in Mark: like Jesus, they "preach"; like Jesus, they "have authority to throw out demons." From the outset of their apostolic career, then, the disciples are charged to participate in Jesus's Gospel witness, in word and deed.

As the story unfolds, the disciples do not always faithfully fulfill their calling. Indeed, they often appear as obtuse and even petty. Yet readers who stress only their lapses miss Mark's more nuanced blending of successes and failures. Perhaps surprisingly, even Jesus does not always "succeed" in his own miracle working in this Gospel. His work in Nazareth, for instance, is only partly effective. As Mark summarizes the episode, Jesus "did not have the power [*ouk edynato*] there to do any deed of power, except that he laid his hands on a few sick people and cured them" (Mark 6:5 AT). How does Mark explain this compromised power? The evangelist reports that Jesus was "appalled by their disbelief" (*apistis*; Mark 6:6). That is, the absence of *the people's* faith seems to short-circuit *Jesus's* access to power.

In the aftermath of this failure, Jesus sends his companions out to do deeds of power on his behalf: "He called for the Twelve and sent them out in pairs. He gave them authority over unclean spirits" (Mark 6:7). Here, Mark restates the divine authority over adversarial forces given to the disciples at their initial commissioning. Especially in contrast with Jesus's own results, they wield their power to striking effect. Mark reports, "They cast out many demons, and they anointed many sick people with olive oil and healed them" (Mark 6:13). And though Jesus sends them out with "authority over unclean spirits," Mark expands the impact of their power to include the healing of "many sick people."

Another story traditionally taken as evidence of Jesus's own messianic status sheds further light on the power-sharing dimension of his messianic mission. In the feeding of the five thousand (Mark 6:30-44), Jesus engages his disciples as participants in the abundant feast he provides as evidence of God's power to feed the hungry crowds. Though many readers focus on Jesus's miracle working in an exclusive sense, several details bring the disciples' role to light. First, though Jesus shows compassion for the crowd by teaching them "many things" (Mark 6:34), the disciples address the people's physical hunger, asking Jesus to "send them away" so they can "buy something to eat for themselves" (Mark 6:36). Jesus responds with a succinct command: "*You [hymeis]* give them something to eat" (Mark 6:37, emphasis added). Though the Greek verb *give* implies its subject, Mark adds the pronoun *you* for emphasis. Here Jesus undermines the disciples' emphasis on the crowd's self-sufficiency ("for themselves") by proposing a solution in line with God's kingdom, where the hungry are satisfied at a miraculous banquet "in parched places" (Isa 58:10-11; see Isa 55:1; Mark 6:35). In this command, Jesus calls on the disciples to mediate God's promised provision.

Initially, this biblical echo of divine abundance falls on deaf ears, as the disciples see human need through the lens of insufficiency: "Should we go off and buy bread without almost eight months' pay and give it to [the people] to eat?" (Mark 6:37). But though we might expect Jesus to step forward and accomplish the feeding through his own divine power, instead he continues to engage the disciples in the miracle. First, he asks them to supply the meal: "How many loaves do you have?" (Mark 6:38 AT). When they return with both loaves and fish, he involves them in the feeding. Just as Jesus "gave [*edidou*] them authority over unclean spirits" (Mark 6:7) earlier in the chapter, here he "gave [*edidou*] [the loaves] to the disciples to set before the people" (Mark 6:41). In the end, the feeding becomes a messianic meal. Though Jesus presides over the miracle, he does so by empowering his companions. Ultimately, he transforms both the crowd's hunger and the disciples' economy of scarcity into divine surplus. Mark summarizes the episode by noting, "Everyone ate until they were full. They filled twelve baskets with the leftover pieces of bread and fish" (Mark 6:42-43).

Finally, the story of a failed exorcism (Mark 9:14-29) bears witness, if only subtly, to the disciples' partnership in Jesus's messianic mission. Often, readers conclude that the disciples are at fault when a desperate father tells Jesus that his disciples "did not have the strength" (Mark 9:18 AT) to cast a demon out of his son. But other factors call this view into question. For one thing, the disciples' lack of (divine) strength recalls Jesus's own inability to do deeds of power in Nazareth (see previously, Mark 6:5). And notably, the lack of faith plays a role in both cases. Since Mark generally notes the faith of those who avail themselves of God's healing power (e.g., Mark 2:5; 5:34), Jesus's lament over the "faithless generation" (Mark 9:19) may concern a widespread lack of trust in God's kingly power more than the disciples' unbelief.

This view makes sense, too, in light of Jesus's explanation that "throwing this kind of spirit out requires prayer" (Mark 9:29). To what prayer does he refer? In this story, the only prayer Mark mentions is the father's plea, "I have faith; help my lack of faith" (Mark 9:24). This observation suggests that it may be his prayer—not Jesus's—that makes a way for God's healing power. In any case, to read this story carefully and in its literary context is to recognize the role that faith plays in Mark wherever God's power is at work—through both Christ and community—to stymie forces that oppose human wholeness.

For Mark's community, stories about Jesus's deeds of power offer evidence that, in him, the messianic age has dawned. By forging connections between Christ and community on this matter, Mark suggests that the divine power unleashed through Jesus continues unabated where the messianic community meets trust in God's coming reign. But such a promise likely brought a mixture of debilitating disbelief and revitalizing inspiration—the same mixture that characterizes the disciples in Mark. On some level, Mark's community probably identified themselves, at least in part, with what Jesus calls a "faithless generation." After all, the persecution they faced showed in living color that evil continued to work in the world, even after Jesus's defeat of death itself. Thus they may have looked to their risen Lord for salvation from evil's grip rather than power over it. Mark's Gospel thus offers a reminder that the faithful community had been charged and equipped to manifest God's dominion.

Yet Mark's story also makes it clear that Jesus's followers are not left to their own devices. From the outset, his disciples are commissioned to "be with him," and it is Jesus's empowering presence after the resurrection that may have inspired the community to continue as partners in his power-sharing messiahship. Thus Mark's portrait of the disciples, who both wield God's power and fail to do so, may capture the real-life tension of an audience convinced that Jesus is the Christ but still awaiting the full disclosure of God's sovereign power. To be sure, the disciples' participation in Jesus's deeds of power only increases in Matthew and Luke. Yet even for Mark, both Christ and community perform works that restore the well-being that manifests God's Lordship.

Messianic Power in Matthew: "Whatever You Bind on Earth" (Matt 18:18 NRSV)

As one of Mark's earliest interpreters, Matthew preserves both its portrait of Jesus's miraculous feats and the power-sharing relationship it depicts. Yet Matthew also reworks Mark and includes other traditions, crafting a story that portrays Jesus's messianic power in a distinctive light. For one thing, Matthew uses the miracle stories to enhance Jesus's own authority as God's Son and as the embodiment of God's wisdom. Thus interpreters sometimes speak of Matthew's heightened Christology. But this editorial elevation of Jesus's messianic identity goes hand in hand, in Matthew, with the disciples' expanded role in Jesus's miracle working.

We turn our attention, then, to the ways in which Matthew accentuates messianic deeds of power performed by both Christ and community. Notably, Matthew incorporates almost all of Mark's miracle stories, from healings to exorcisms to nature miracles. Indeed, Matthew explicitly interprets Jesus's therapeutic power in a messianic light, as evidence that

God is at work to redeem the world. Thus Matthew explains his deeds of power in these terms: "This happened so that what Isaiah the prophet said would be fulfilled: *He is the one who took our illnesses and carried away our diseases*" (Matt 8:17; see Isa 53:4). Here, Jesus takes on the role of Isaiah's "servant of the Lord," who bears human travails in order to redeem them.

In more subtle ways, too, Matthew revises Mark's account to accentuate Jesus's messianic power and authority. Even slight changes to Jesus's name demonstrate this tendency. Often, for instance, where people address Jesus as "teacher" or "rabbi" in Mark, Matthew changes the title to "Lord" (e.g., Matt 8:2, 25; 9:28; 20:33), suggesting Jesus's close kinship with the Father in heaven. Matthew also streamlines Mark's miracle stories to emphasize that Jesus is motivated more by his own (divine) initiative than by others' faithful gestures (e.g., Matt 9:18-19, 23-26; see Mark 5:22). In other cases, Matthew downplays Jesus's emotional response, emphasizing instead his magisterial command of the situation. For instance, Matthew omits Mark's claim that Jesus was "moved with compassion" before healing a leper (Mark 1:41 AT; see Matt 8:3).[5] Finally, Matthew leaves out Mark's perplexing story about Jesus's two-staged healing of a blind man (Mark 8:22-26), perhaps because it implies that Jesus failed in his first attempt. In all of these ways, Matthew portrays Jesus's deeds of power in ways that highlight his messianic agency.

On another level, though, Matthew reworks Mark's miracle stories to forge deeper connection between Jesus's christological authority and the authority of the messianic community. This is especially the case in stories where Jesus exerts command over nature. A small but significant change appears, for instance, in the feeding of the five thousand (Matt 14:13-20), where Matthew adds the clarifying explanation, "the disciples gave [the loaves] to the crowds" (Matt 14:19; see Mark 6:41). What is more, Matthew eliminates Mark's account of Jesus distributing the fish. As a result, Matthew's version of the story enhances the shared nature of this miraculous meal.

---

5. The Common English Bible follows the "minority" reading of Mark 1:41, which describes Jesus as "incensed."

A more dramatic example of this shift follows in the next passage. Here, Matthew faithfully repeats much of Mark's account of the storm at sea (Matt 14:22-33; see Mark 6:45-52). Jesus sends the disciples out on the water without him, and they struggle against an adverse wind for hours before Jesus approaches "his disciples, walking on the lake" (Matt 14:25; Mark 6:48). When the disciples cry out, Jesus reminds them of his identity and presence, uttering, "Be encouraged! It's me. Don't be afraid" (Matt 14:27; Mark 6:50). Despite these common contours, though, the Gospels end the episode in remarkably different ways. In place of Mark's statement about the disciples' misunderstanding (Mark 6:52), Matthew says Peter asks Jesus to "order me to come to you on the water" (Matt 14:28). Even in this request, Peter assumes that Jesus's power over the chaotic waters extends to those who, like him, trust God's sovereignty over evil. Indeed, Peter's assumption proves valid, as he "got out of the boat and was walking on the water toward Jesus" (Matt 14:29). Only when he sees the "strong wind" and becomes frightened does he begin to sink (Matt 14:30). What is more, it is Peter's plea for Jesus to save him that brings about both his rescue and a word of critique: "You of little faith! Why did you hesitate?" (Matt 14:31 AT). In "seeing" the adversarial wind rather than God's power over it, Peter fails to trust. Notably, it is not Jesus's power that he doubts—after all, his fear leads him to ask for Jesus's help; instead, he wavers on the matter of God's power over evil at work through him. Perhaps it is the chasm between Peter's faltering faith and Jesus's resolute trust that leads the disciples to affirm, "You must be God's Son" (Matt 14:33).

Matthew again connects Christ and community on the matter of messianic power in the story of Peter's confession at Caesarea Philippi (Matt 16:13-20). In this Gospel, not only does Peter call Jesus "the Christ" (see Mark 8:29), but he adds the epithet "Son of the living God" (Matt 16:16). Thus, Peter offers an enhanced christological claim. But Jesus's response departs strikingly from Mark's account. Here, Matthew includes Jesus's praise for Peter the "rock" as the foundation of "my church" (Matt 16:18). What is more, Jesus explains the nature of Peter's power in this way: "whatever you bind on earth will have been bound [*estai dedemenon*] in heaven, and whatever you loose on earth will have been loosed [*estai lelymenon*] in heaven" (Matt 16:19 AT; Matt 18:18). How are we to read such a claim?

The motif of "binding" (or "fastening," as the CEB translates the term) carries a range of implications elsewhere in Matthew, from physical binding (Matt 14:3; 21:2; 27:2) to the community's authority over sinners in their midst (implied in Matt 18:18). Some take this language to denote Peter's institutional authority in the early church. Yet elsewhere Matthew suggests that such authority derives from God's coming reign and so is inherently messianic. For one thing, Matthew thinks that the church itself will be the battleground where the kingdom of heaven will finally prevail against the power of Hades (see Matt 18:18-19).[6] Moreover, Matthew elsewhere uses language of fastening to imply the restraint of evil in at least two instances. In the first, Matthew writes of the binding of weeds growing among wheat in eschatological terms—that is, when they are being gathered for fiery judgment (Matt 13:30). In the second, Matthew adds to the parable of the wedding party (likely a Q tradition) this editorial conclusion: bind "his hands and feet and throw him into the farthest darkness" (Matt 22:13). More than just authority over church matters or Jewish law, then, the authority Jesus imparts to Peter proceeds from palpable power of God's dominion taking root on earth. For Peter, and thus Matthew's community (the "church"), the power over evil, first secured in the heavenly realm, becomes the hallmark of the messianic age.

By enhancing *both* Jesus's *and* the community's messianic authority, Matthew bears witness to Jesus for a community that was forming its identity around the belief that Jesus was the Jewish messiah. In Matthew, then, Jesus's deeds of power play a momentous and complementary role to his teachings. For if Jesus is a rabbi among rabbis, he is for Matthew also a vessel of the divine power that comes with the messianic age. Though wonder working in and of itself did not signal a figure's messianic status for first-century Jews, this Gospel sees in Jesus's exorcisms, healings, and nature miracles convincing proof that God's reign has indeed drawn near.

---

6. See Joel Marcus, "The Gates of Hades and the Keys of the Kingdom (Matt 16:18-19)," *Catholic Biblical Quarterly* 50 (1988): 443–55.

Yet the community's authority works, for Matthew, in concert with Jesus's. When his followers trust the power of God he manifests through his words and deeds, they become its agents. Thus, Peter walks *with Jesus* on the water. And Jesus assigns him the power to "bind and loose" when he sees that *in Jesus*, the messianic age has dawned. In this way, Matthew merges the messianic power of Christ with those like Peter who find themselves swept up in Christ's own faith. More than just shoring up church authority, as some have suggested, Matthew fosters the audience's identity by locating them within the dawning messianic age, where they derive power from God and from the one "anointed" to share it. Like the Qumran covenanters, then, they participate in the first glimpses of God's coming kingdom and the authoritative power it brings. As Matthew both elevates Mark's christological portrait of Jesus and accentuates the community's access to that power, this Gospel casts a vision for messianic community that manifests God's heavenly reign spreading relentlessly toward the "end of this present age" (Matt 28:20).

Messianic Power in Luke: "Authority over All the Power of the Enemy" (Luke 10:19)

The Gospel of Luke amplifies both Jesus's deeds of power and the community's miracle-working capacity. Though it was probably written for a mostly Gentile audience, this Gospel casts those mighty acts in a decidedly Jewish and messianic light. Indeed, many scholars think this is because Luke wants to distinguish Jesus from "magicians," who were often viewed with suspicion in the Greco-Roman world. Like his messianic message, this dimension of Jesus's messianic mission grows out of Jewish hopes for the redemption of the whole world. And like his messianic message, Jesus's messianic power is prophetic in nature. As Luke connects Jesus's deeds of power with those done by Moses, Elijah, and Elisha, Jesus's miracles consistently challenge social, religious, and ethnic boundaries to manifest the inclusive nature of God's saving acts. Through Jesus, messianic power flows relentlessly outward, "to the end of the earth" (Acts 1:8).

In Luke, messianic deeds of power occur even before Jesus is born. First, God opens the womb of a barren woman named Elizabeth; soon thereafter, the angel Gabriel announces to Mary that she will bear a son through the "power of the Most High" (Luke 1:35). Indeed, "the Lord God will give him the throne of David his father...and there will be no end to his kingdom" (Luke 1:32-33). This messianic promise comes from a God who "has shown strength with his arm" (Luke 1:51). Luke's birth story, then, is shot full with divine power that is messianic in nature. As such, this power already signals prophetic reversal, as God has "filled the hungry with good things / and sent the rich away empty-handed" (Luke 1:53).

In turn, Luke's Jesus performs deeds of power that fit well within this messianic and prophetic framework. After situating his own career within that of the "anointed" prophet of Isaiah 61 (see Luke 4:18-21), Jesus points out that the prophets Elijah and Elisha deployed their divine power in service to Gentiles. Already, he both identifies himself as a prophet and stirs the ire of "insiders" who resist such a reversal of God's favor (Luke 4:25-28). Indeed, Luke includes episodes from Jesus's messianic mission that echo the biblical account of these prophets' miraculous deeds (e.g., Luke 7:1-16). In a similar way, a story found only in Luke further underscores that "foreigners" benefit from Jesus's healing power. In this passage, Jesus moves along the margins of Israel, "between Samaria and Galilee" (Luke 17:11). When he cleanses ten lepers, only one turns back, "prais[ing] God with a loud voice" (Luke 17:15), and he was a Samaritan. In true prophetic fashion, Jesus wields God's power without regard to ethnic and religious distinction; what is more, a non-Israelite bears authentic witness to that power.

Besides highlighting the messianic and prophetic nature of Jesus's power, Luke devotes increased attention to his followers' role in displaying that power. Luke's account of the first call to discipleship (Luke 5:1-11) makes this point subtly, since it emphasizes from the outset of his mission both Jesus's miracle working and his empowerment of others. As in Mark and Matthew, Jesus recruits a group of fishers. But in Luke, instead of ordering them to "follow me" (Mark 1:17; Matt 4:19), he tells them to "row out farther, into the deep water, and drop your nets for a catch" (Luke 5:4). After a mild protest, they follow his instruction and, as a result, "their catch was so huge that their nets were splitting" (Luke 5:6). Such an encounter offers an important snapshot of Luke's Christology and its implications for community. On the one hand, this story offers a compelling glimpse of Jesus's empowering presence, which leads to a reversal in fortune for the fishers. On the other hand, by trusting his command, the fishers themselves haul in the catch. In the end, Luke's Jesus interprets the episode this way: "From now on, you will be fishing for people" (Luke 5:10). Thus Jesus's own miracle working engages his first followers in the display of God's power.

In a similar vein, the sending of seventy(-two) apostles (Luke 10:1-20) expands others' participation in Jesus's messianic career. Though Luke includes the sending of the twelve found in Mark and Matthew (Luke 9:1-6), the appointment of "seventy-two others" (Luke 10:1) extends the scope of Jesus's mission. For Luke, this venture remains closely connected to Jesus's ministry in many respects. First, Jesus sends this group "to every city and place he was about to go" (Luke 10:1). In other words, they will serve as advance scouts for *Jesus's* messianic mission. In this role, Jesus says, they will "heal the sick who are there, and say to them, 'God's kingdom has come upon you'" (Luke 10:9). Like Jesus's deeds of power, theirs are messianic in nature, in that they confirm the approach of God's reign. As one interpreter puts it, their deeds of power signal "the invasion of God's kingdom and part of the rolling back of Satan's empire."[7] The outcome of their mission only confirms that their power is derived from Jesus: "Lord, even the demons submit themselves to us in your name" (Luke 10:17). Thus the missionaries bear witness to his messianic mission by displaying God's power on Jesus's behalf. In response, Jesus marvels that he "saw Satan fall from heaven like lightning" (Luke 10:18; see Isa 14:13). As his designated agents, the missionaries wield Jesus's own "authority over all the power of the enemy" (Luke 10:19).

Though the NT book of Acts falls outside the bounds of this study, its account of miracle working in the early church only confirms the tendencies found in Luke's Gospel. Once endowed with a "power [from] the Holy Spirit" (Acts 1:8), Luke says the apostles perform "wonders and

---

7. Richard B. Vinson, *Luke* (Macon, GA: Smyth & Helwys, 2008), 329.

signs" (Acts 2:43; see also 4:30; 5:12) that bear witness to the messianic age. As many have noted, Luke includes miracle stories in this sequel that follow the pattern of Jesus's own deeds of power in the Gospel itself. For instance, Peter heals a crippled man, telling him to "rise up and walk" (Acts 3:6; see Luke 5:24). Throughout Acts, though, the apostles perform such deeds "in the name of Jesus Christ" (Acts 3:6; see also 4:10, 30).

Writing for those who live in the wider Greco-Roman world, Luke takes care both to preserve synoptic accounts of Jesus's divine power and to distinguish it from the magical manipulation of nature. In Luke's account, Jesus's miracles remain closely associated with his messianic mission, in that they manifest God's redemptive power unleashed on earth. As God's anointed, Jesus deploys that power to combat the forces of Satan wherever they threaten human dignity and wholeness. Besides enacting Isaiah's promise of restored sight for the blind and release for those held captive by this "enemy," Luke's Jesus deliberately reaches beyond the bounds of Israel to extend that saving power to Gentiles.

But that expansive vision also means that Jesus's messianic power, for Luke, also reaches out through the messianic community he establishes. Both within Jesus's earthly career and in the post-resurrection age, his followers continue to perform the "wonders and signs" that have characterized his messianic mission. Importantly, Luke retains the connection between miracles and the defeat of evil associated with God's coming reign. Just as Jesus has authoritatively established a foothold for that kingdom, its incursion continues through those whom he equips with its power. For Luke's audience, such active display of God's reign only lends credence to the expansive, inclusive nature of the reign of Israel's God.

Messianic Power in John: "Life in His Name" (John 20:31)

As we have seen, Jesus's messianic mission in John departs in significant ways from the synoptic accounts. Already, we have noted that his messianic message more closely identifies Jesus as the one in whom God's "word" now resides (John 1:1-18); indeed, John's Jesus goes so far as to claim that "I and the Father are one" (John 10:30). Perhaps not surprisingly, then, Jesus's deeds of power in John elicit not just faith in God but explicit belief in Jesus the Christ as well. What is more, Jesus's followers often appear as passive witnesses to Jesus's ministry of "signs," sometimes even serving as literary foils to Jesus's messianic power. Yet, this christological focus on Jesus does not diminish the community's access to God's life-giving power. They will, Jesus says, do "greater works than these" (John 14:12).

Jesus's deeds of power in John are both less frequent and more impressive than in the other Gospels. Specifically called "signs" in the Fourth Gospel, their significance for John's story is hard to overstate. John summarizes the account this way: "Then Jesus did many other miraculous signs in his disciples' presence, signs that aren't recorded in this scroll. But these things are written so that you will believe that Jesus is the Christ, God's Son, and that believing, you will have life in his name" (John 20:30-31). Throughout the Gospel, then, Jesus's deeds of power work to convince the audience that Jesus is the Christ and thus offer access to the life he brings. As evidence that the messianic age has dawned in Jesus's own career, the signs thus point to Jesus—but also through him, toward the life-giving power of God.

Indeed, all of the signs in John bear witness, if only symbolically, to God's life-giving presence at work in Jesus. For example, John uses the wedding at Cana to suggest that, in Jesus, God has "kept the good wine until now" (John 2:10). Thus Jesus's spontaneous and gracious provision of "good wine," John says, "revealed his [divine] glory, and his disciples believed in him" (John 2:11). Likewise, Nicodemus attributes Jesus's reputation for signs to his divine origins, since "no one can do these miraculous signs that you do unless God is with him" (John 3:2).

Other signs in John point even more overtly to the life available through this wonder-working messiah for those who believe. When he heals the official's son, who was "about to die" (John 4:47), Jesus tells the father, "your son lives" (John 4:50). Indeed, such restored life leads in turn to the father's belief in Jesus as its agent (John 4:53).

John also interprets the feeding of the five thousand (John 6:1-14) in a way that both accentuates Jesus's role and associates this sign with life. In contrast to the synoptic account, the disciples play a diminished role in John: Jesus, not the disciples, attends to the crowd's physical hunger; he also distributes the loaves provided by an unnamed boy (John 6:9) without mention of his disciples (John 6:11). Thus John adds this fitting conclusion: "When the people saw that he had done a miraculous sign, they said, 'This is truly the prophet who is coming into the world'" (John 6:14). What is more, John's Jesus interprets the deed as metaphor for the life he provides: "I am the bread of life. . . . I am the living bread that came down from heaven" (John 6:48, 51).

Finally, the last sign in John's Gospel highlights Jesus's role as the one sent to disclose God's life-giving power. For one thing, in raising Lazarus from the dead, Jesus draws attention to the "God's glory" such new life attests (John 11:40). What is more, he says the sign engenders belief that he is God's earthly agent of power (John 11:42). Finally, when Lazarus walks out of the tomb, Jesus says, "Untie him and let him go" (John 11:44). On one level, Jesus's command undoes the traditional Jewish burial rites of binding and wrapping. But read through a messianic lens, John suggests that, in this ultimate sign, Jesus the Christ brings deliverance even from the captivity of the grave.

In all these ways, then, Jesus's signs bear witness in this Gospel to the life available to those who trust that, in him, the messianic age has dawned. To be sure, they engender belief in Jesus's messiahship. But more than just belief, they ultimately point the way to the eternal life unleashed through it. The signs are thus christological in two respects: they testify to Jesus as the messiah who manifests God's presence, and they illustrate the life-giving power his messiahship brings to those who are "born anew" (John 3:3).

But how does Jesus's messianic power relate to the community he establishes in this Gospel? As with his messianic message in John, Jesus imparts his messianic power to his followers only as his earthly mission draws to a close. Thus we turn again to the Farewell Discourse, where Jesus fosters enduring messianic community among "his own." Here we find vital clues to the ways in which Jesus channels his divine power to his followers. After Jesus tells his disciples about the "the place I'm going" (John 14:4), he says that he is the "way" (or "path"; Greek: *hodos*) to the Father (John 14:6). Just as Isaiah promises that God makes a "way" for the faithful people (Isa 62:10), here Jesus becomes that way to God for those who believe in him.

Indeed, when Philip asks Jesus to "show us the Father" (John 14:8), Jesus replies, "Don't you believe that I am in the Father and the Father is in me?" (John 14:10). It is through this indwelling of the Father that Jesus performs messianic deeds of power: "the Father who dwells in me does his works" (John 14:10). But belief in this divine indwelling is not, for John's Jesus, an end in and of itself. Jesus offers this staggering promise: "I assure you that whoever believes in me will do the works that I do. They will do even greater works than there because I am going to the Father" (John 14:12). That is, the divine power that has marked Jesus's mission will become, in the wake of his departure, available to those who seek access to that power in his "name" (John 14:13-14).

John's vision of messianic community perhaps grows clearest in the so-called high-priestly prayer found in John 17. Though the chapter mentions neither Jesus's "works" nor deeds of power, the evangelist combines claims that the Father has "sent" Jesus (John 17:8, 18, 21, 23) with Jesus's "sending" of his own. "As you sent me into the world," John's Jesus says, "so I have sent them into the world" (John 17:18). Already we have seen that, for John, believing in Jesus means trusting that God has "sent" him into the world (e.g., John 5:24; 6:29; 7:16; 8:16; 11:42); indeed, Jesus says that "these works I do" confirm that "the Father sent me" (John 5:36). In turn, those whom Jesus sends into the world will carry forward his deeds of power, indeed "greater works" (John 14:12). As a result, they too will inspire belief that in him, the messianic age offers "life to the fullest" (John 10:10).

In its portrait of messianic power, the Fourth Gospel assigns momentous value to Jesus's signs as testimony to the presence of God in the world. Together, Jesus's deeds of power constitute for John, as for the Synoptics, evidence that the Father enters the human realm to release it from the power of death itself. For John's community, this story works partly to confirm Jesus's messianic status in a setting where such a view was hotly disputed. But more than just his status alone, John consistently affirms the life-giving nature of Jesus's messianic power as evidence of the "new creation" he begins. For an audience that found itself at odds with those who looked askance at the notion of a crucified messiah, this christological point is an important one. For this Gospel, Jesus performs miracles that affirm and renew the life—and the life eternal—available under God's sway.

Beyond reassurance that belief in Jesus's messiahship secures eternal destiny, John's Gospel also presents that messiahship—and the power that accompanies it—as unfinished business. After all, John's Jesus takes a long view with respect not just to the heavenly afterlife but also to the group gathered in his name. Those who believe in him continue to impart the message about the messianic age and do the works, and greater ones, that testify to it. While John's community may be sectarian in that it is cut off from mainstream Judaism, this Gospel casts a wide vision of its witness as those "sent into the world" (John 17:18). For them, the "way" to the Father that Jesus reveals (John 14:6) promises access not just to the "place" where he dwells but also to the divine life that is available to them in his name.

Concluding Thoughts

Despite their wide range of settings, the Gospels together bear witness to a persistent link between Jesus as miracle worker and his christological identity. True, key differences remain. While the synoptic writers portray Jesus's miracles as evidence of messianic power unleashed in the world, John thinks Jesus's signs manifest God's messianic—and life-giving—presence. And while the synoptic writers include the disciples in Jesus's wonder-working mission, John's Jesus promises that their "greater works" will be part of the post-resurrection era.

Yet despite these differences, the evangelists share common features worth noting. First, all four Gospels agree that Jesus's own deeds of power are inherently messianic because they derive from Jesus's special status as God's anointed one. In his deeds, God's power is at work in a way that is authoritative, authentic, and ultimately life giving—and in ways that echo and amplify Jewish hopes for the messianic age. Second, the evangelists concur on this point: Jesus's power is not his own; it comes from God, and it glorifies God (see Mark 5:19; John 14:13). Even the Fourth Gospel emphasizes the divine source of Jesus' mission and the divine glory it discloses (John 11:40). Finally, in all four Gospels, messianic power channels through Jesus outward, to the faithful community established in his wake. The Gospel witness to Jesus's messianic power thus suggests it is more inclusive than exclusive. Three concluding observations help frame the inclusive impulse of the Gospels with respect to this palpable witness to God's power.

First, the evangelists together forge a complex relationship between messianic power and faith, trust, and belief (Greek: *pistis*). In the Synoptic Gospels, trust is operative where God's wholeness breaks in to restore human life (e.g., Mark 5:34). At times, both Jesus's and the disciples' power is compromised by others failing to trust in it (*apistiaein*; Mark 6:6a; see 9:24). For its part, the Fourth Gospel suggests that belief in Jesus's messiahship leads in turn to deeds of power on the believers' part (John 14:12).

To be sure, such a connection between miracles and faith introduces profound theological and pastoral dangers. Though the intent of this chapter is to describe the inclusive contours of messianic miracle working, modern readers do well to exercise caution about assessing the "faith"—or lack thereof—in relation to healing today. To consider the complex and nuanced witness of the four NT Gospels is to affirm that they belie any human attempt to view healing and faith in formulaic terms.

A second observation follows from the first. Both Jesus's and his followers' deeds of power are messianic in nature in that they point ultimately not to their agents but to God alone. Such an orientation is striking especially in the Fourth Gospel, so noted for its high Christology; there, too, Jesus affirms that he operates not on his own but through the power of the one who has "sent" him. Thus, throughout the Gospels, messianic deeds of power fit squarely within their Jewish context as evidence of God's decisive defeat of evil and renewal of the earth.

Finally, the Gospel portrait of messianic power sharing establishes a persistent connection between Christ and community. In Jesus's earthly career, the evangelists find convincing evidence that God's victory over evil has found a way into the created order; in his death and resurrection, they affirm his enduring presence for the community established in his wake. Thus despite their varying settings and emphases, the Gospels consistently suggest that, to follow him, to remain in him, is to be gathered into his own pattern of trust in God's coming kingdom. Jesus's messianic power, then, extends to Gospel audiences across time and space wherever God's palpable, life-giving ways work to thwart the powers of blindness, captivity, hunger, and chaos.

Study Questions

1. What is the relationship between the message about God's coming kingdom and deeds of power in Jewish background texts?

2. Explain an example of messianic "power sharing" in the Synoptic Gospels.

3. How does John's Gospel differ from the synoptic portrait of Jesus's messianic power?

4. Discuss the relationship between faith/trust/belief and messianic power in the Gospels.

For Further Reading

Eve, Eric. *The Jewish Context of Jesus' Miracles*. Journal for the Study of the New Testament: Supplement Series 231. London: Sheffield Academic Press, 2002.

Garrett, Susan R. *The Demise of the Devil: Magic and the Demonic in Luke's Writings*. Minneapolis: Fortress, 1989.

Meier, John P. *Mentor, Message, and Miracles*. Vol. 2 of *A Marginal Jew: Rethinking the Historical Jesus*, 109–1038. New York: Doubleday, 1994.

Myers, Ched. *The Binding of the Strong Man: A Political Reading of Mark's Story of Jesus*. Maryknoll, NY: Orbis, 1988.

Twelftree, Graham H. *Jesus the Miracle-Worker: A Historical and Theological Study*. Downers Grove, IL: InterVarsity, 1999.

Wenham, David, and Craig Blomberg, eds. *The Miracles of Jesus*. Vol. 6 of *Gospel Perspectives*. Eugene, OR: Wipf & Stock, 2003.

Chapter Four
Messianic Sacrifice

"To Give Up One's Life" (John 15:13)

While the Gospel witness to Jesus begins with his messianic message and power, his sacrificial death proves to be the hallmark of his messiahship in at least two respects. First, Jewish writings generally agree that the "anointed one" would decisively defeat the forces opposed to God's reign, not suffer at their hands. This puts Jesus's death on a Roman cross at odds with Jewish messianic expectation. As a result, Paul calls Jesus's messianic death a "scandal" to Jews (1 Cor 1:23), and a second-century writer characterizes the Jewish understanding of Jesus's messiahship this way: "This so-called Christ of yours was dishonorable and inglorious, so much that the last curse contained in the law of God fell on him, for he was crucified."[1] Jesus's passion thus sets his messianic mission apart since it departs from prevailing thoughts about "the messiah."

To highlight the difference between Jesus's destiny and Jewish messianic expectation leads to a second distinctive element of his messianic suffering. For rather than minimizing Jesus's humiliating death, all four Gospels treat the Passion Narrative as the culmination of his messianic mission. In a more positive sense, then, his messianic death plays a pivotal role in the Gospel witness to Jesus the Christ. While his resurrection and reign will point to his decisive vindication, all four evangelists assign redemptive significance to Jesus's messianic sacrifice.

---

1. Justin Martyr, *Dialogue with Trypho*, 32:1, in vol. 1 of *The Ante-Nicene Fathers*, ed. Alexander Roberts and James Donaldson (Peabody, MA: Hendrickson, 1994).

In this chapter, we consider the Gospel witness to Jesus's sacrificial death. As we shall see, the evangelists view Jesus's suffering destiny as messianic in this respect: it arises from the conflict between the waning powers of the world and the dawn of God's reign. As God's anointed, Jesus the Christ makes himself vulnerable to the full force of the opposition. Yet even in that vulnerability, he triumphs decisively over death, thus loosening its destructive grip on the world. As one scholar puts it, "The opposition has been overcome and humanity restored."[2] In a paradoxical twist, Jesus's apparent defeat has ushered in God's promised kingdom and with it, new life.

But while Jesus's sacrificial death is both historically distinctive and central to Gospel Christology, this messianic destiny is not unique to him. Rather, in all four Gospels, Jesus's sacrificial suffering becomes paradigmatic for his disciples. As his "followers," they will "take up their cross" (Mark 8:34; see Matt 10:38; Luke 14:27); like him, they are called to "give up [their] life" for others (John 15:13; see 10:11). In so doing, they participate in the new world order established by Jesus the Christ, as they bear witness to the messianic age that has dawned.

Once again, this connection between Christ and community reflects the first-century settings the evangelists addressed. Though the Gospels share much common ground in their depiction of Jesus's messianic sacrifice, each accentuates details that connect his story to the concerns of its audience. For instance, since Mark's community lives in a time of social and religious turmoil, Mark draws out the apocalyptic dimensions of Jesus's death. Matthew highlights Jesus's righteousness, as well as the eschatological import of Jesus's suffering. Luke stresses its divine necessity as a part of God's sweeping plan of salvation. And John portrays the cross as the full expression of divine glory. Across the board, though, the Gospels establish the contours of Jesus's messianic sacrifice as model for his followers. As they carry forward his messianic mission, their suffering too plays a part in God's unfolding redemption of the world.

---

2. Joel Marcus, "Identity and Ambiguity in Markan Christology," in *Seeking the Identity of Jesus: A Pilgrimage*, ed. Beverly Roberts Gaventa and Richard B. Hays (Grand Rapids: Eerdmans, 2008), 133–147 (147).

Messianic Sacrifice in Jewish Tradition

While no known Jewish text asserts that the "messiah" will suffer, the theme is far from absent in the writings that provide the conceptual and religious backdrop for our study. Indeed, Jewish writers repeatedly address the question of suffering in light of God's sovereign Lordship. As we shall see, they often attribute righteous suffering to the power of evil in the world. But they also depict suffering as both prelude to and instrument of God's coming victory over evil. Here we consider texts that are messianic in a broad sense. Though they make no mention of a messiah per se, they look forward to the establishment of God's reign on earth. And while individual figures sometimes herald that coming dominion, the traditions in question emphasize the people's role as its collective embodiment.

Suffering in Exile

When early Christians wanted to understand Jesus's death, they found in Second Isaiah's fourth Servant Song (Isa 52:13–53:12) a hopeful claim about the redemption that comes through faithful suffering. For there, the prophet writes of God's servant, "He was pierced because of our rebellions / and crushed because of our crimes. / He bore the punishment that made us whole; / by his wounds we are healed" (Isa 53:5). On the one hand, this verse attributes the servant's unwarranted suffering to "our rebellions... [and] crimes." On the other hand, it credits his suffering with the power to restore health and wholeness. It is no wonder that, over time, readers of the Passion Narratives came to emphasize Jesus's death as a "once for all" sacrifice that had secured forgiveness for the faithful.[3] Yet such an exclusive view of Jesus's messianic suffering leaves out of account important Gospel claims about its implications for the faithful community.[4]

---

3. Gospel passages adduced in support of "substitutionary atonement" include Mark 10:45; Matt 20:28; John 19:36; Luke 24:21. As we shall see below, these passages themselves point to a more inclusive view of messianic suffering than is often noted.

4. This connection between Christ and community apparently persisted for a while. Early accounts of martyrs found in Acts (the stoning of Stephen: Acts 7:54-60) and the second-century CE *Martyrdom of Polycarp* tell of the suffering of the faithful in ways that echo the Gospel accounts of Jesus's death.

To read this "suffering servant" song in its own context provides important interpretive leverage as we approach the question of Jesus's messianic suffering in the Gospels. As we have noted, Isaiah 40–55 (Second Isaiah) addresses a faithful community that grapples with the questions raised by their anguished plight. Written during the Babylonian Exile, these oracles generally cast faithful Israel in the role of Yahweh's "servant." Notably, this subverts their earthly status as "slave[s] of rulers" (Isa 49:7), maintaining *God's* sovereignty in the face of oppression at the hands of such rulers. And while the prophet often attributes the people's suffering to Israel's unfaithfulness (e.g., Isa 43:28; 47:6; 50:1; 53:5-6), Second Isaiah has even more to say about their coming rescue by a God who reigns (e.g., Isa 41:8-10; 43:19; 44:24-28; 52:9-10).

Besides these literary and historical observations, careful attention to this Servant Song in its context yields further clues about the "suffering servant" in relation to both God and God's people. For one thing, the surrounding passages underscore the collective identity of the "servant." In the oracle that precedes the Servant Song, the prophet laments the "captive Daughter Zion / . . . taken away for nothing" (Isa 52:2, 5); this servant "was oppressed [and] . . . / due to an unjust ruling he was taken away" (Isa 53:7-8). Likewise, the passage that follows addresses the "suffering one" (Isa 54:11) with this message: "don't be dismayed, / because you won't be disgraced. / You will forget the shame of your youth" (Isa 54:4). It is to faithful Israel, then, that God says, "For a brief moment I abandoned you, / but with great mercy I will bring you back" (Isa 54:7).

Likewise, this Servant Song promises that, despite present suffering, the "servant will succeed" (Isa 52:13) through the redemptive power of God and for the benefit of the wider world. When "Yahweh has bared his holy arm / before the eyes of all the nations" (Isa 52:10 AT), the servant Israel's exaltation will "astonish many nations" (Isa 52:15). True, Israel has withstood Babylonian oppression, as the servant "has borne our infirmities / and carried our diseases" (Isa 53:4 NRSV) and was "struck dead because of my people's rebellion" (Isa 53:8). Read in context, the servant figure appears less as a replacement or substitute for the people than the one who embodies their collective plight. In a remarkable twist, though, this anguish presses inexorably toward their coming redemption. In accepting the burden of exile, the servant Israel is "offered as restitution" (Isa 53:10) that will restore the faithful people to their God and ultimately to their land. In the end, the servant "will make many righteous" (Isa 53:11). Just as a sinful legacy has led to exile, so too will Israel's righteousness extend across "all the earth" (see Isa 54:5). In this way, the Servant Song employs an individual figure to depict the experience of faithful people, whose suffering plays a redemptive role as God's kingdom takes root on the earth.

Suffering during the Maccabean Era

In many respects, the book of Daniel applies Second Isaiah's view of righteous suffering to a later setting. As "prophecy" written centuries after the exile, Daniel 7–12 purports to predict events related to Israel's plight in Babylon and beyond. But most scholars agree that these chapters were written in the second century BCE, not the sixth. The oppression addressed here comes not from Babylon but from the Syrian ruler Antiochus IV Epiphanes, whose occupying forces undermined Jewish practice and identity at every turn. For instance, they placed a statue of Zeus on the temple's altar (the "desolating monstrosities" of Dan 9:27; see also 1 Macc 1:54-59) and made keeping some Jewish customs, including dietary laws, punishable by death. Like Second Isaiah, this writer attributes Israel's oppression to rampant forces of evil, including the people's own sinful ways. And like Second Isaiah, Daniel looks forward to deliverance that will accompany God's coming reign.

In terms of literary style, Daniel offers a visionary, even apocalyptic, account of Israel's plight. For instance, the prophet gains heavenly insight into the earthly conflict at hand, seeing it as a cosmic battle in which successive "beasts" ultimately "devour the entire earth, trample it, crush it" (Dan 7:23). But while the vision decries the beasts as villainous and inhumane, Daniel's own prayer blames the calamity at least in part on the people's unfaithfulness: "We have sinned and done wrong. We have brought guilt on ourselves and rebelled" (Dan 9:5; see 9:13). Yet, as in Second Isaiah, it is not just the sinful who suffer these consequences. As the vision unfolds, the "teachers...will fall by sword and by flame, by captivity and by plunder" (Dan 11:33). That is, the faithful will not escape the coming anguish, since their righteousness makes them vulnerable to its destructive forces. Still, as with Isaiah's oracles, their suffering does not ultimately prevail. In an echo of the Servant Song, Daniel's vision promises that the wise will "lead many to righteousness" (Dan 12:3; see Isa 53:11). Their utter loyalty to God's covenant in the face of such opposition only brings their righteousness to light, as they "shine like the sky...like the stars forever and always" (Dan 12:3).

Another work from the same era also offers a helpful example of redemptive suffering in Jewish thought. In this instance, 2 Maccabees interprets a family's martyrdom at the hands of Antiochus IV in light of God's unfolding plan of redemption. Like Second Isaiah and Daniel, this account explains the Hebrews' persecution partly in terms of God's "rebuke and discipline" (2 Macc 7:33). Yet the youngest among seven brothers explains his sacrifice this way: "I give up both body and life for the ancestral laws. I call upon God to be merciful to the nation without delay, and to make you confess, after you suffer trials and diseases, that only he is God" (2 Macc 7:37-38). The brothers' suffering is redemptive in at least two respects. First, their allegiance to the "ancestral laws" only strengthens the case for God's exclusive sovereignty even among God's most hardened opponents. At the same time, their sacrificial devotion to God turns the tide of God's just rebuke and ushers in the moment when God "will again be reconciled with [God's] own servants" (2 Macc 7:33).

In sum, the examples considered here depict a complex view of suffering in relation to God's sovereignty. On the one hand, we find the prophetic view that suffering comes as a just consequence of collective unfaithfulness. On the other hand, the writers portray the suffering of the righteous as both unjust and redemptive—unjust because the oppressors become the agents of evil and redemptive because righteous suffering ushers in God's decisive reign. While not messianic in a technical sense, these texts dare to peer through the crisis at hand and affirm God's sovereign power to renew Israel and, through her, the whole world.

Messianic Sacrifice in the Gospels

When they turn to the question of Jesus's messianic suffering, the evangelists likewise interpret his destiny in relation to God's coming reign. And while each Gospel depicts Jesus's sacrificial death in ways that address its particular setting, together the four accounts affirm that, in Jesus's death on a Roman cross, God's sovereign power is strikingly evident in vulnerable human faithfulness. As a result, his messianic sacrifice constitutes a turning point as God's reign dawns on the earth. In turn, those who, like Jesus, trust in the coming kingdom of God will reflect that power through their redemptive suffering as well.

Messianic Sacrifice in Mark: "Say No to Themselves" (Mark 8:34)

Of all the Gospels, Mark devotes the most narrative attention to Jesus's messianic sacrifice. Sometimes called a "passion narrative with an extended introduction,"[5] the earliest Gospel has much to say about the way of the cross that characterizes Jesus's messiahship as well as the plight of those who come after him. Early on, the Gospel hints at mounting conflict (Mark 2:6-7; 3:6), but Jesus's first passion prediction (Mark 8:31; see also 9:31; 10:33-34) focuses more squarely on his impending death and its implications for discipleship. Moreover, as Jesus's sacrificial destiny takes center stage in the Gospel, his messianic identity grows clearer; when the high priest asks, "Are you the Christ, the Son of the blessed one?" Jesus replies, "I am" (Mark 14:61-62). It is this affirmation, in turn, that leads to his death (Mark 14:64).

What, then, is the nature of messianic sacrifice in Mark? In the first place, Jesus's suffering stems organically from his apocalyptic mission. Beginning with the claim that God's kingdom has drawn near (Mark 1:14-15), we have seen that Mark's Jesus wields messianic power over cosmic forces of evil such as disease, demon-possession, and hunger. Along the way, this frontal assault on the present world order—this "tying up the strong person" (Mark 3:27)—meets resistance, fear, and unbelief. Indeed,

---

5. Martin Kähler, *The So-Called Historical Jesus and the Historic Biblical Christ*, trans. Carl E. Braaten (Philadelphia: Fortress, 1964), 80n11. He calls this a "provocative" statement that applies to all the Gospel passion narratives.

such early skirmishes between divine and evil powers escalate in the Gospel's second half, where Jesus faces the forces of death as he trusts in God's sovereign power.

But on the way to Golgotha, Mark's central section (Mark 8:27–10:45) forges close ties between Christ and community when it comes to messianic sacrifice. On the one hand, it is here that his own passion comes into view as a vital part of his messianic mission. Just after Peter calls him the messiah, Jesus announces that "the Son of the Human must suffer many things" (Mark 8:31 AT), including rejection by religious leaders and, ultimately, death. Thus he suggests the inevitability of the story's outcome: the low-grade resistance that has been festering during his Galilean ministry will lead to a violent end.

Yet after predicting his own messianic sacrifice, Jesus spells out its implication for his followers. Turning to "the crowd together with his disciples," Jesus says, "All who want to come after me must say no to themselves, take up their cross, and follow me" (Mark 8:34). What will discipleship entail? In the first place, his followers will "lose their lives because of me and because of the good news" (Mark 8:35).[6] Rather than self-interest or self-preservation, their devotion to the gospel—the good news of God's in-breaking power—becomes the defining trait of messianic community. In Mark, to align oneself with Jesus's messianic mission is to challenge the prevailing world order, and thus to tangle with the forces of death.

After predicting his own death a second time (Mark 9:30-32), Jesus has more to say about the cost of discipleship. For one thing, when his followers debate their own greatness, Jesus says, "Whoever wants to be first must be least of all and the servant of all" (Mark 9:35). For Mark, this pattern of servanthood applies not just to Jesus but to his disciples as well. Likewise, the Gospel's third and final passion prediction (Mark 10:33-34) leads into another discussion of the servant nature of messianic power. After James and John ask, "Allow one of us to sit on your right and the other on your left when you enter your glory" (Mark 10:37), Jesus contrasts the presumed "lordship" of Gentile rulers, which brings subjuga-

---

6. A few early textual witnesses omit the phrase "because of me" (D and Origen among them). But since the phrase is likely original, Mark's Jesus distinguishes between himself and the "gospel," which in Mark does not yet equate with Jesus's messianic identity per se.

tion and tyranny (Mark 10:42), with authentic greatness: "But that's not the way it will be with you. Whoever wants to be great among you will be your servant. Whoever wants to be first among you will be the slave of all, for [*gar*] the Human One [or the Son of the Human] didn't come to be served but rather to serve and to give his life to liberate [or as ransom for] many people" (Mark 10:43-45). While the servant dimension of Jesus's messianic sacrifice lies at the heart of this passage, Jesus applies this model in turn to his disciples (the "you" of Mark 10:43). To manifest true power, they too must be both servants and slaves; they too must forfeit their very lives as they "liberate many people."

To be sure, readers generally assume that this phrase alludes to Jesus's atoning death in an isolated, exclusive sense. That is, they find saving power in Jesus's sacrifice, but not in the suffering of his followers. Yet the text itself forges connection rather than distinction between Christ and community. Not only do Jesus's own passion predictions lead to teachings about discipleship, but the explanatory conjunction "for" (*gar*) in Mark 10:45 casts Jesus's sacrifice as a paradigm for his followers. But in what sense might they join in Jesus's redemptive suffering? Though the Greek word *lytron* ("ransom") appears rarely in the NT, the LXX often uses it for the price required to secure a slave's freedom (e.g., Exod 30:12; Lev 19:20). Like Isaiah's suffering servant, Jesus and his disciples secure freedom by becoming "slave of all" (Mark 10:44) since they thereby disempower the "seeming rulers" (Mark 10:42 AT) and so disclose the liberating force of God's coming reign.

Jesus's apocalyptic teaching in Mark 13 provides an important transition from the Gospel's central section to the Passion Narrative itself. Without explicitly mentioning Jesus's death, the discourse explains the community's suffering in terms of unfolding apocalyptic conflict. Beginning with the prediction that "not even one stone [of the temple precinct] will be left upon another" (Mark 13:2; cf. Jer 26:6; Mic 3:12), Jesus provides a detailed account of the affliction (*thlipsis*, Mark 13:19, 24) his disciples will soon face. In many respects, this chapter reveals the inclusive nature of messianic suffering in Mark.

To begin with, Jesus notes the cosmic conflict that will precede the coming end: "wars and reports of wars] ... earthquakes and famines in all sorts of places" (Mark 13:7-8). Echoing Israel's prophets, Jesus calls these events the "beginning of the sufferings" (Mark 13:8; see Rom 8:22)—evidence that God's reign on earth is dawning. What is more, Jesus subtly links his followers' suffering to his own. Like him, they will be handed over "to councils ... beaten in the synagogues ... [and stood] before governors and kings because of me" (Mark 13:9; see Mark 9:31; 10:33; 14:10-11). That is, they will face both religious and political trials (see Mark 14:53-64; 15:1-15). Further, this suffering comes, he says, "on account of me, as a witness to them" (Mark 13:9 AT). As they carry forward Jesus's gospel message that God's kingdom has drawn near (Mark 13:10; see Mark 1:14-15), Jesus's followers will find themselves in the midst of sacrificial, righteous suffering. Situated between the "way of the cross" instructions and the Passion Narrative itself, then, Mark 13 connects Christ and community through the shared destiny of messianic sacrifice that accompanies the dawn of God's reign.

Of course, Mark's portrait of messianic suffering culminates with Jesus's own sacrifice in his trial, torture, and death. The conflict that first appeared in the Gospel's earliest chapters now presses toward the cross itself, where we find a graphic disclosure of God's power unleashed in the messianic age. Both his trial before the Sanhedrin (Mark 14:53-65) and the account of his crucifixion and death (Mark 15:21-41) depict Jesus's suffering as intrinsically messianic, as this "anointed one" presides over the dawn of God's reign.

What do these passages contribute to Mark's view of messianic sacrifice? First, when the high priest asks, "Are you the Christ, the Son of the blessed one?" (Mark 14:61), Jesus utters his first overt claims to messiahship in this Gospel. On the one hand, he affirms his messianic identity with a simple "I am," possibly alluding to and identifying with God's own name (see Exod 3:14; Isa 43:25 LXX). What is more, he heralds the "Son of the Human from the right hand seated in power coming with clouds of heaven" (Mark 14:62 AT). Here, Jesus invokes Daniel's apocalyptic vision of God's decisive reclamation of the world. That such a claim warrants a death sentence in the high priest's eyes only confirms its messianic nature, since by it Jesus threatens the very basis of existing religious and political power.

Jesus's messianic challenge to both religious and political power persists throughout Mark's passion story. For one thing, Mark connects Jesus's messianic destiny with the imminent demise of the Jerusalem temple (Mark 14:58; 15:29). Thus Jesus's messianic sacrifice in part institutes the renewal of corrupt religious practice. In the story's climax, Mark only underscores this point. When Jesus takes his last breath, Mark reports two related events. First, in the claim that "the curtain of the temple was torn apart [*eschisthē*]" (Mark 15:38 AT), Mark uses standard apocalyptic language to suggest that, in Jesus's death, the chasm between heaven and earth has been eclipsed (see Isa 64:1; Mark 1:10); the presence of God safeguarded by religious institution has, in his messianic death, been set loose in the world. And when the Roman centurion identifies the crucified Jesus as "a son of God" (Mark 15:39 AT), Mark implies that even Rome's minions now see, in living color, the nature of true power.

The messianic sacrifice depicted in Mark exhibits many important connections with suffering in the background texts considered above. As we have seen, like Second Isaiah, Mark takes the servant motif in an inclusive, rather than exclusive, sense. Moreover, this Gospel portrays both the willing sacrifice of this innocent servant as well as its redemptive purpose in ways that connect with both Isaiah and 2 Maccabees. As in Daniel, the theme of increasingly violent resistance fits well with an apocalyptic worldview in which the wise suffer the brunt of oppressive tactics as they await the salvation that arrives when they endure "until the end" (Mark 13:13). As Jesus faces his destiny, then, he models a way of faithfulness that brings sacrifice and, through it, redemption for the world.

Of course, Mark's emphasis on messianic sacrifice offers a fitting message for a persecuted community. If Mark writes for those affected by the Jewish War and the turmoil surrounding it, this Gospel's view of Jesus's suffering both explains their plight and assigns it saving significance. On the one hand, those aligned with the dawning messianic age follow their Christ into the matrix of religious and political power. Taking their cues from Jesus's own story, they cast their loyalty with One who promotes self-sacrifice in place of self-promotion, servanthood in place of status. In this way, their witness to his messiahship means they subvert entrenched social and religious hierarchy. At the same time, Mark's view of messianic suffering also sounds a clarion call to participate in God's salvation of the world, begun in Jesus's own messianic death but continued in the community that takes its bearings from this "suffering servant." As they suffer "because of [him] and because of the good news" (Mark 8:35), their witness brings apocalyptic disclosure of God's vulnerable power; in turn, they play a part in the release from oppression that God's coming reign will secure.

Messianic Sacrifice in Matthew: "Because They Are Righteous" (Matt 5:10)

As is true for both Jesus's messianic message and power, Matthew makes faithful use of Mark as a source in bearing witness to Jesus's messianic sacrifice. At the same time, this Gospel adapts Mark's account to reflect its audience's social and religious setting. Thus Matthew underscores the righteous dimension of messianic suffering—both Jesus's and the community's. For Matthew, Jesus's righteous standing before God brings the same kind of persecution to him that Israel's prophets endure throughout scripture. Like the "wise" in Daniel and the Maccabean martyrs, Jesus suffers partly as a result of his own faithfulness. But Matthew also draws out the hope of eschatological judgment, where the righteous who suffer in the short-term find their promised vindication. In Matthew, then, the sacrifice of both Christ and community plays a vital part in the redemption of the world.

From start to finish, Jesus's suffering in Matthew is decidedly messianic since it grows out of his status as an anointed leader. Already the birth stories point not just to his messianic origins and birth (Matt 1:1-25) but also to the hostility his messiahship elicits. After all, when Herod hears of this child born "king of the Jews" (Matt 2:2), the earthly ruler sets out to "search for the child in order to kill him" (Matt 2:13). Though the foreign magi are eager to honor this newborn "king," the native king, who serves as Rome's client, would eliminate him.

As the story progresses, opposition to Jesus's messianic mission only intensifies. And though Mark partly explains this resistance by hinting at Jesus's ties with the servant of Second Isaiah, Matthew draws the connection more explicitly. Thus, after "the Pharisees went out and met in order to find a way to destroy Jesus" (Matt 12:14), Matthew uses a "fulfillment citation" to introduce this passage from Isaiah's first Servant Song:

> *Look, my Servant whom I chose,*
> *the one I love, in whom I find great pleasure.*
> *I'll put my Spirit upon him,*
> *and he'll announce judgment to the Gentiles.*
> *He won't argue or shout,*
> *and nobody will hear his voice in the streets.*
> *He won't break a bent stalk,*
> *and he won't snuff out a smoldering wick,*
> *until he makes justice win.*
> *And the Gentiles will put their hope in his name.* (Matt 12:18-21; see
> Isa 42:1-4)

Though Isaiah's figure is not called a "messiah," the oracle's concern with "judgment to the Gentiles" (Matt 12:18) frames Jesus's suffering destiny as part of his messianic mission, more broadly understood. God's righteous reign, both Isaiah and Matthew affirm, transcends religious and ethnic boundaries. By noting the scriptural basis for Jesus's mission to the Gentiles, Matthew also suggests that the Pharisees' antagonism arises as a natural by-product of it.

Matthew's Passion Narrative, too, relates Jesus's sacrificial destiny explicitly to his messianic mission. Notably, while Jesus's opponents identify him as "the Christ, God's Son" (Matt 26:63-64), Jesus affirms the dawn of the messianic age, inaugurated by the coming Son of the Human (Matt 26:65-66). Thus Matthew's Jesus shifts attention from his own status toward the dawn of God's reign on earth. Still, the scribes and elders accuse him of blasphemy even as they mockingly name him "you Messiah" (Matt 26:68 NRSV). And as in Mark, Jesus hangs on a Roman cross under the banner, "This is Jesus, the king of the Jews" (Matt 27:37).

Besides establishing the messianic nature of Jesus's sacrificial death, Matthew also draws Jesus's righteousness into view. Only in Matthew does Pilate's wife call Jesus "this righteous one" (Matt 27:19 AT), an identification the Roman governor accepts. Once Pilate declares his own innocence in the matter, the crowd responds, "Let his blood be on us and on our children!" (Matt 27:25).[7] Here, Matthew signals the judgment that awaits those who preside over the death of a righteous man.

Matthew's account further accentuates the eschatological nature of Jesus's destiny by adding details not found in the other Gospels. Matthew alone includes the cataclysmic events that accompany Jesus's death: "The earth shook, and the rocks were split. The tombs also were opened, and many bodies of the holy ones [*hagiōn*] who had fallen asleep were raised. After his resurrection they came out of the tombs and entered the holy city and appeared to many" (Matt 27:51-53 AT). In Matthew, Jesus's death as a righteous messiah ushers in a new era of postmortem vindication— for both Jesus and other "holy ones" who have died. Thus Matthew goes beyond Mark's claim about the apocalyptic tearing of the temple veil to insist that Jesus's death inaugurates the resurrection that leads to judgment and salvation for the "holy ones."

Momentous as Jesus's own messianic sacrifice is in Matthew, the dynamics that give rise to it are not unique to his story. Like Mark, Matthew presents Jesus's persecution as a pattern for those who would follow him. Indeed, Matthew only enhances this connection between Christ and community. Early in the Gospel, the Beatitudes expand traditional Jewish blessings by addressing those who are persecuted both "because they are righteous" (Matt 5:10) and "on my behalf" (Matt 5:11 AT). A suffering destiny, Jesus says, awaits those who bear witness to God's righteous ways—both Jesus and his followers—since "in the same way, people harassed the prophets who came before you" (Matt 5:12). Later in the Ser-

---

7. It goes without saying that the interpretive legacy of this verse has had catastrophic repercussions. The anti-Semitic tone it strikes quickly gained traction in early Christian thought (see e.g., the second-century CE *Gospel of Peter*). Tragically, it led to systemic violence against the Jewish people across time and place. Only in the wake of the Holocaust has Christianity begun to reassess, in a serious and deliberate way, the implications of the view of the Jews as "Christ killers."

mon on the Mount, Matthew forges a subtle connection between Jesus's and his followers' suffering. Teaching them not to "oppose those who want to hurt [them]" (Matt 5:39; see also 5:11), Jesus commands his hearers to "turn the left cheek to them as well" and to "let them have your coat too" (Matt 5:39-40)—possible allusions to his being "whipped" (Matt 27:26) and "stripped" (Matt 27:28). In any case, the Sermon promotes an ethic of righteousness that both derives from God's own righteous ways and leads inexorably toward sacrifice.

Matthew also reworks Mark's traditions about the disciples' missionary journey in ways that highlight the persecution they will face. For one thing, Matthew 10 combines their commissioning (Matt 10:1-4; see Mark 3:13-19) with their evangelistic journey (Matt 10:5-15; see Mark 6:7-13). But Matthew adds a warning about their rejection (Matt 10:16-25; see Mark 13:9-13) and explains the cost of discipleship in sacrificial terms (Matt 10:34-36; see Mark 8:34-35). In doing so, Matthew highlights the torment to which their mission will lead. Sending them to the "lost sheep, the people of Israel" (Matt 10:6), Jesus charges the disciples: "make this announcement, 'The kingdom of heaven has come near.' Heal the sick, raise the dead, cleanse those with skin diseases and throw out demons'" (Matt 10:7-8; see Mark 6:7). Yet, he warns that they go "as sheep among wolves" (Matt 10:16); Israel's own "councils" and "synagogues" will serve as the place of judgment against them (Matt 10:17). In this way, Matthew's Jesus notes that "the disciples [will] be like their teacher" (Matt 10:25): Jesus's followers share the same destiny of persecution that he does.

But that persecution is not the end of the story—either for Christ or for the community. Indeed just as Jesus's death signals eschatological judgment and the vindication it brings, Matthew draws that coming judgment into view for the disciples as well. Thus Matthew adds to the cost of discipleship (Matt 16:24-26) this promise: "The [Son of the Human] is about to come with the majesty of his Father with his angels. And then he will repay each one for what that person has done" (Matt 16:27). In Matthew's account, messianic sacrifice will soon find its just reward.

As Matthew's Jesus makes his way to Jerusalem—and to the heart of religious and political power—the resistance to his messianic mission only hardens. In Matthew 23, for instance, Jesus calls the "legal experts and Pharisees" the "children of those who murdered the prophets" (Matt 23:29, 31). The "murder" in view here surely encompasses Jesus's impending death, but he also alludes to the wider community who will likewise suffer: "Therefore, look, I'm sending you prophets, wise people, and legal experts. Some of them you will kill and crucify. And some you will beat in your synagogues and chase from city to city" (Matt 23:34). And in Jesus's lament over Jerusalem (a Q tradition—see Luke 13:34-35), Matthew makes a similar point. Jerusalem, Jesus says, is the city that "kill[s] the prophets and stone[s] those who were sent to [it]" (Matt 23:37). In its context, this saying points both to Jesus's coming rejection and to the similar suffering his disciples will face as they carry forward his prophetic mission.

Like Mark, Matthew draws heavily on Jewish tradition to elaborate the nature of messianic sacrifice. But while Mark emphasizes the cosmic conflict associated with the apocalyptic reign of God, Matthew develops the motif of suffering as inherent to the role of the righteous prophet within the story of Israel itself. Moreover, Matthew adds to Mark's account of messianic suffering the promise of eschatological judgment. Both Jesus and his followers will be rejected by their own. Yet Jesus frames that rejection in light of coming end-time justice; those who suffer "because they are righteous" in the meantime will find vindication and new life.

In many respects, this portrait of messianic suffering fits well with widely held views about Matthew's community. Written mainly for Jews who affirmed Jesus's messianic status, for instance, this Gospel interprets Jesus's sacrifice in familiar terms: as God's anointed prophets had suffered, so too did this herald of God's reign. But Jesus's messianic suffering also brings the promise of eschatological vindication. Jesus's messianic death is not the last word; beyond the cross lies new life for this righteous one.

More than just Jesus's suffering, though, Matthew addresses the community's own plight as they negotiated their relationship to rabbinic Judaism. Most scholars think Matthew's audience was forging a social and religious identity that put them at odds with many Jewish leaders. For one thing, the calamity of the temple's destruction had shaken Palestinian Judaism at its foundation. In the shift toward Torah, the rabbis found a way to promote religious purity apart from the sacrificial system. Especially the aspects of Jewish law that promoted a righteous Jewish identity gained central importance for the covenant people. But Matthew's community took a different tack. Upholding traditions about Jesus's interpretation of Torah meant downplaying religious and ethnic distinction in favor of a more sweeping vision of righteousness. If such competing visions of righteousness evoked persecution for Matthew's community, this Gospel may offer a word of solace, purpose, and hope. Like Jesus the messiah, the messianic community defined by allegiance to God's reign would suffer in the meantime but could rest assured that the eschatological script was unfolding in a way that would bring vindication—both his and theirs.

Messianic Sacrifice in Luke: "Wasn't It Necessary?" (Luke 24:26)

As the risen Jesus walks with disenchanted followers on the road to Emmaus, he asks, "Wasn't it necessary for the Christ to suffer these things and then enter into his glory?" (Luke 24:26). This question sheds important light on Luke's portrait of messianic sacrifice. Luke moves beyond Matthew's view that Jesus's destiny was the inevitable outcome of his prophetic and righteous witness. For Luke, messianic suffering is indispensable to God's unfolding plan for the salvation of the world. Thus Luke accounts for the anomaly of a crucified Christ by framing Jesus's sacrificial destiny as a purposeful part of God's sweeping story of redemption.

Luke's emphasis on divine necessity relates closely to the Gospel's messianic message of prophetic reversal, especially its interest in the inclusion of Gentiles within Israel's unfolding story. Early in the Gospel, Luke combines these motifs in Simeon's song (Luke 2:29-32). After Simeon names the infant Jesus the "Lord's Christ" (Luke 2:26), this "righteous" man praises God for sending "a light for revelation to the Gentiles / and a glory for your people Israel" (Luke 2:32). This reversal—that is, naming the Gentiles first and Israel second—leads in turn to the more ominous claim that Jesus "is assigned to be the cause of the falling and rising of many in Israel and to be a sign that generates opposition so that the inner thoughts of many will be revealed" (Luke 2:34-35). Such opposition from his own people, in Luke's account, is necessary for the inclusion of outsiders (see Rom 11:25).

Indeed, Jesus's opening proclamation in his hometown synagogue (Luke 4:16-30) builds the case for necessary suffering by combining his prophetic witness and the conflict it inspires. Already we have seen that Luke places Jesus's rejection at Nazareth at the outset of Jesus's public ministry. What is more, Luke embellishes Mark's account to signal Jesus's messianic sacrifice from the outset of his public ministry (cf. Mark 6:1-6). After reading from the Isaiah scroll, Jesus says, "this scripture has been fulfilled just as you heard it" (Luke 4:21). He even goes so far as to provoke his receptive audience by pronouncing that "no prophet is welcome in the prophet's hometown" (Luke 4:24). As we have seen, Jesus then reminds them that Elijah and Elisha's missions brought God's power not to Israel but to outsiders. As a result, "everyone in the synagogue was filled with anger" (Luke 4:28). Early in the story, then, Luke's Jesus not only expects his destiny of rejection but also deliberately promotes it.

Not surprisingly, the prelude to Jesus's journey to Jerusalem establishes the divine purpose and necessity of his messianic sacrifice. For one thing, Luke's Jesus predicts his suffering and betrayal twice, in short order. In the first instance, Jesus says that the "[Son of the Human] *must* suffer many things" (Luke 9:22, emphasis added). Suffering thus awaits as an essential part of his messiahship. As if to underscore the point, Jesus says, "Take these words to heart: the [Son of the Human] is about to be delivered into human hands" (Luke 9:44). Here, Jesus both anticipates his disciples' resistance to his destiny and insists his rejection has already been determined.

Between these two predictions, Luke uses the story of Jesus's transfiguration (Luke 9:28-36) to cast his sacrificial destiny as the fulfillment of God's unfolding plan. As in the other Synoptic Gospels, Peter, James, and John join Jesus on a mountaintop. Here, too, they behold both his divine aura and the conversation he holds with Moses and Elijah. But only in Luke do these prophetic predecessors speak of Jesus's "departure [*exodos*], which he was about to fulfill [*plēroun*] at Jerusalem" (Luke 9:31 AT). Thus Luke depicts Jesus's destiny as a "new exodus" that accomplishes God's release of the world from the powers that enslave it. Luke sounds a similar note in the verse that many take to be the Gospel's narrative hinge: "As the time approached when Jesus was *to be taken up into heaven*, he determined to go to Jerusalem" (Luke 9:51, emphasis added). Using a construction called a "divine passive," Luke implies that it is God who will take Jesus up in Jerusalem. Thus Jesus determines "to go" headlong toward messianic sacrifice in resolute compliance with the divine plan.

Along the way, Luke's Jesus approaches his impending end as the fulfillment of his mission. For instance, when the Pharisees alert him to Herod Antipas's opposition, Jesus responds, "I'm throwing out demons and healing people today and tomorrow, and on the third day I will complete (*teleioumai*) my work. However, it's necessary for me to travel today, tomorrow, and the next day because it's impossible for a prophet to be killed outside of Jerusalem" (Luke 13:32-33). Though he laments Jerusalem as the city that "kill[s] the prophets and stone[s] those who were sent to" it (Luke 13:34), Luke's Jesus also draws near to his "end" as one wholly devoted to God's plan.

Once Jesus enters the holy city, he again weeps over Jerusalem (Luke 13:31-35; see Matt 23:37-39), this time adding dire predictions of the city's fate (Luke 19:41-44; 23:29-30). According to Jesus, Jerusalem has failed to pursue peace (Luke 19:42) and to recognize divine visitation (Luke 19:44); as a result, enemies will "crush you to the ground" (Luke 19:43 AT). As the seat of religious authority, then, Jerusalem itself plays a part in the dawn of the messianic age, meting out violence and, in turn, suffering the birth pangs of God's coming reign (see, e.g., Isa 29:3-10; Jer 6:6-20; Ezek 4:1-3).

Within the Passion Narrative, Luke downplays Jesus's agony in contrast to Mark and Matthew, emphasizing instead both his righteousness and his equanimity in service to God's unfolding plan. For instance, the scene on the Mount of Olives probably omits any reference to Jesus's anguish; the only grief Luke notes belongs to the disciples (Luke 22:45).[8] Though Jesus asks God to "take this cup" (Luke 22:42), Luke adds the phrase "if it's your will" to indicate acquiescence on Jesus's part. Jesus's

---

8. Luke 23:43-44 is likely a later scribal addition to the Gospel's original account, perhaps to emphasize Jesus's human suffering.

last words on the cross, too, change dramatically in Luke from the other synoptic accounts. In both Mark and Matthew, Jesus cites Psalm 22:1: "My God, my God, why have you left me?" (Mark 15:34; Matt 27:46). But Luke replaces this cry of dereliction with the words "into your hands I commit my spirit" (Luke 23:46 AT; see Ps 31:5). In all these ways, Luke's Jesus faces his suffering and death in a manner that affirms, at least indirectly, his willing sacrifice.

Luke also emphasizes Jesus's innocence, or righteousness, in at least two ways that point to the divine necessity of that sacrifice. In terms of earthly justice, Luke points out Jesus's innocence from a legal standpoint. Both Mark and Matthew convey Pilate's disquiet with Jesus's condemnation when he asks, "What wrong has he done?" (Mark 15:14; Matt 27:23). But Luke makes his exoneration patently clear; Pilate finds no "legal basis for action against" Jesus (Luke 23:4). Luke also adds a trial before Herod (Luke 23:6-12) to underscore Jesus's innocence. In light of Pilate's and Herod's vindication of Jesus, his death on a Roman cross can only be the work of God. The crucifixion itself elicits two more confessions of Jesus's innocence. First, the convicted criminal hanging alongside Jesus at Golgotha distinguishes between his just conviction and "this man [who] has done nothing wrong" (Luke 23:41). And while the centurion in Mark affirms that "this man was certainly God's Son" (Mark 15:39), in Luke he claims, "Certainly this man was innocent" (Luke 23:47 NRSV). Jesus's messianic sacrifice, then, occurs not through his culpability but despite it.

In another sense, though, the centurion's statement probably carries connotations of Jesus's righteousness in a way that supports the necessity of his suffering for the salvation of the world. More than just "innocence" in a judicial sense, Luke uses the term to designate Jesus's reflection of God's righteousness, even in the face of injustice. Like other righteous figures throughout Jewish tradition (see, e.g., Wisdom 2:10-20; 4:16-20; Pss 7:4; 69:4; 109:3), Jesus thus bears witness to God's ways in an unjust world. And like the Isaianic servant, Daniel's "wise ones," and the Maccabean martyrs, the suffering of the righteous emerges as part of God's unfolding plan of salvation.

In all these respects, though, Luke's portrait of Jesus's sacrifice applies not just to Jesus, nor even just to his twelve closest companions, but to the broader community that this prophetic figure engages in his messianic mission. As one writer puts it, "Luke's portrayal of Jesus as the Leader, the first among many, in death as in resurrection, is an essential element in his *theologia crucis* [theology of the cross]."[9] We turn attention, now, to the many in Luke who carry forward this motif of messianic suffering.

After he "sets his face toward Jerusalem" (Luke 9:51 AT), Luke's Jesus stresses not just his own messianic destiny but also its implications for his followers. First, Jesus sends "messengers . . . [to] a Samaritan village to prepare for his arrival, but the Samaritan villagers refused to welcome him" (Luke 9:52). As the story unfolds, Jesus only reiterates the persecution that attends those aligned with his prophetic mission. For instance, he assails the Pharisees with these words: "You built memorials to the prophets, whom your ancestors killed. . . . Therefore, God's wisdom has said, 'I will send prophets and apostles to them and they will harass and kill some of them'" (Luke 11:47, 49; see Matt 23:34). Attributing this destiny to "God's wisdom," Luke's Jesus detects deliberate purpose, even necessity, in the opposition and death that await both Jesus and his prophetic successors. And perhaps addressing his own community, Luke includes Jesus's encouragement to his "friends" not to fear "those who can kill the body" (Luke 12:4; see also Matt 10:28). Such repeated attention to his followers' inevitable persecution (see Luke 12:11) draws a close correlation between the opposition Jesus faces and the opposition of those who follow him.

Finally, while our focus lies with the Gospel itself, the story's sequel in Acts deliberately links Jesus's sacrifice with the suffering of those who bear witness to his messiahship. For instance, Luke applies details from Jesus's own story to the account of Stephen's stoning (Acts 7:54-60): like Jesus, he is filled with the Holy Spirit, his death takes place outside the city, and he prays both for his spirit to be received and for the forgiveness of those who kill him. And though Acts does not report Paul's death, the resistance, rejection, and interrogation he faces certainly echo Jesus's own

---

9. Peter Doble, *The Paradox of Salvation: Luke's Theology of the Cross*, Society for New Testament Studies Monograph Series 87 (Cambridge: Cambridge University Press, 1996), 231.

messianic destiny in Luke. As many have noted, in the book of Acts such "doubling" patterns work to narrate the early church's experience against the backdrop of Jesus' story.[10]

What then can we say about messianic sacrifice in Luke? For one thing, as we have seen throughout this study, conflict arises in Luke as an inevitable part of the dawn of the messianic age. Whenever God's power enters the earthly force field tyrannized by evil, the resulting showdown introduces a cosmic clash within the prevailing social order. In Luke, this conflict revolves especially around the inclusion of the Gentiles and others designated as outsiders from a religious standpoint. But for Luke, the suffering that accompanies the messianic age is more than just an inevitable result of prophetic challenge. More than the other Gospels, Luke portrays Jesus's messianic sacrifice as part of God's deliberate plan, a plan that moves ultimately through that suffering toward universal salvation.

The motif of divine necessity goes a long way, for Luke, toward solving the problem of Christ crucified. In many respects, this explanation fits well with what we know about Luke's audience. For one thing, Luke makes it clear that Jesus's messianic sacrifice belongs to God's saving purposes at work through history: from Israel's story, through Jesus's story, and into the account, in Acts, of the age of the spirit. Thus the rejection and violence that meet God's anointed prophet play an inherent part in the extension of salvation to the whole world.

Drawing on a range of Jewish traditions, from prophecy to apocalypse to wisdom, Luke interprets Jesus's suffering destiny in ways that confirm the Jewish roots of his movement and its universal scope. Like prophetic figures who have gone before, Jesus faces rejection as a result of his commitment to God's inclusive plan of salvation. For Luke, Jesus's destiny is neither tragedy nor defeat; instead, it emerges as part of God's calculated, purposeful redemption of the world. But it is not just Jesus who participates in this unfolding plan. Luke crafts his story about Jesus as a pattern for the messianic community that will, like him, bear righteous witness to God's redemption in ways that stir opposition, hostility, and division. For

---

10. On this motif, see especially the seminal work of Charles H. Talbert, *Literary Patterns, Theological Themes, and the Genre of Luke-Acts*, Society of Biblical Literature Monograph Series 20 (Missoula, MT: SBL Press, 1974).

Luke, though, such messianic sacrifice is not the end of the story; like his own, the followers' devotion to God's messianic mission will ultimately sweep them into active participation in God's reign (Luke 22:28-30).

Messianic Sacrifice in John: "When I Am Lifted Up" (John 12:32)

"It is completed" (John 19:30). For the Fourth Gospel, Jesus's final words portray his messianic sacrifice as the fulfillment of his mission. From his appearance as the "Lamb of God" (John 1:29) to his death on the Day of Preparation (John 19:14, 31, 42), Jesus appears in John as one who will give up his life for others (John 10:18). Thus John underscores, in an unprecedented way, the sacrificial dimension of Jesus's suffering; it is the end, the *telos*, to which the Gospel story presses (John 13:1; 17:4; 19:28). Yet, just as Isaiah's servant "will succeed. / He will be exalted and lifted very high" (Isa 52:13), so too will John's Jesus, this Son of the Human, "be lifted up" (John 3:14). Here, God's project of incarnation in Jesus reaches its climax as the motifs of sacrifice and exaltation converge on the cross. Yet even this lofty view of Jesus's saving death carries important implications for the beloved community this Gospel addresses.

How does John understand Jesus's messianic destiny? To begin with, the Fourth Gospel repeatedly frames Jesus's death in light of the Jewish story of the Passover. Only in John, for instance, does Jesus's death occur on the Day of Preparation, when the Passover lamb was traditionally slaughtered for the sacred feast (John 19:14). Both John the Baptist's identification of Jesus as the "Lamb of God" (John 1:29)[11] and the evangelist's report that "they didn't break his legs" (John 19:33; see Exod 12:46; Num 9:12) accentuates this motif. In addition, the use of hyssop to deliver the sponge full of wine to Jesus's lips echoes the role of that shrub in the Passover liturgy (Exod 12:22). In all these ways, John depicts Jesus's suffering in terms that portray him as the sacrificial Passover lamb.

This identification of Jesus as the Passover sacrifice carries important implications for this Gospel's view of his messianic death. For one thing,

---

11. John adds the clause, "who takes away the sin of the world"—a function not typically associated with the Passover lamb. See below for a discussion of Jesus's judgment against the powers of death in relation to this claim.

like the Passover lamb's, Jesus's blood provides a safeguard against the angel of death (see Exod 12:7, 23). In Exodus, houses that bear the lamb's blood over the doorpost stand under God's protection from the Pharaoh's power of death. In a similar way, those who align their lives with Jesus's messianic sacrifice will benefit from his death as, in it, "this world's ruler will be thrown out" (John 12:31; see also 14:30; 16:11). In this sense, then, the power that activates the "sin of the world" (John 1:29) is defeated in this Passover sacrifice.

But John's portrait of Jesus's messianic sacrifice extends beyond his defeat of "this world's ruler." Even more than the lamb shared at the Passover meal, Jesus's own flesh and blood nourish those who partake of it and so find "eternal life" (John 6:54). In his sacrifice, Jesus gives access to the same life he shares with God: "As the living Father sent me, and I live because of the Father, so whoever eats me lives because of me" (John 6:57). In this allusion to early Christian practice, the Eucharist moves beyond a meal commemorating *Jesus's* sacrifice to involve its *participants* in his very life with God. By partaking of his flesh and blood, the faithful community becomes, in Paul's language, the "body of Christ" (1 Cor 12:12-31; see Rom 12:4-5).

Besides viewing Jesus's messianic sacrifice in light of the Passover, John also emphasizes Jesus's deliberate self-offering for the sake of others. In the Good Shepherd discourse (John 10:11-18), for instance, Jesus interprets his impending sacrifice as a willingness to "give up [his] life for the sheep" (John 10:15). While threat and danger might make the "hired hand" run away (John 10:13), Jesus says, "I give up my life for the sheep" (John 10:15). Notably, this commitment grows out of the intimate relationship forged with his "sheep": "I know my own sheep and they know me" (John 10:14). What is more, even this sacrifice discloses his true power "to give it up, and...to take it up again" (John 10:18). Jesus's self-giving for others, in John's view, constitutes the fullest expression of his divine authority (see John 3:16).

If John casts Jesus's willing sacrifice as the defeat of death's power for others, this Gospel also echoes the Servant Song discussed earlier by affirming that Jesus's suffering ultimately brings not defeat but exaltation and glorification. Paradoxically, the crucifixion becomes, for John more than any other Gospel, the evidence of God's power unleashed in the world through Jesus and those devoted to him. More than the death of a righteous martyr, then, Jesus's being "lifted up" in death both negates the evil that causes it and reveals God's glory.

Early in the Gospel, Jesus explains his destiny to Nicodemus this way: "Just as Moses lifted up the snake in the wilderness, so must the [Son of the] Human One be lifted up" (John 3:14). Here, Jesus alludes to a biblical story in which God sends poisonous serpents as punishment for sin (Num 21:4-9). When the people repent, God commands Moses to "make a poisonous snake and place it on a pole [so that] whoever is bitten can look at it and live" (Num 21:8). In serpent's image, the people face their sin head on and find life. Indeed, later Jewish reflection on the story found in the Wisdom of Solomon calls the serpent "the sign of their salvation as a reminder of the command of your Law. Those who turned to that sign were saved not by what they saw but by you, the savior of all because your mercy traveled along with them and healed them" (Wisdom 16:6-7, 10).[12] Thus John depicts Jesus's crucifixion as an iconic embodiment of human sin that brings mercy, healing, and life.

Building on this theme, Jesus provides this explanation to "the Jews": "When the [Son of the] Human One is lifted up, then you will know that I Am [*egō eimi*]" (John 8:28). In this case, John signals that Jesus's death on the cross will expose the divine nature of Jesus's mission, as well as his intimacy with the Father. In his earthly deeds and in his death, Jesus claims, "He who sent me is with me" (John 8:29). All who "look at" Jesus's exaltation on the cross, John suggests, will perceive his divine power. Elsewhere, John's Jesus suggests the sweeping impact of that power: "When I am lifted up from the earth, I will draw everyone[13] to me" (John 12:32). Fulfilling a role that the Wisdom of Solomon ascribes to "savior of all" (Wisdom 16:7), John's Jesus sees his destiny as a means of God's restoration of all creation.

---

12. See also Philo, *Allegorical Interpretation* 2.81; *Rosh HaShanah* 3.8.

13. Some significant manuscripts read "all things," reflecting the sweeping nature of the apocalyptic redemption associated with Jesus's passion, especially in Paul (see e.g., Rom 11:36; Gal 3:22).

Closely linked to these claims about Jesus's exaltation is this Gospel's sense that Jesus's death constitutes his glorification. While Jesus's earthly signs offer early glimpses of his glory (e.g., John 2:11; 11:4), John depicts his sacrificial death as its fullest manifestation (e.g., John 7:39; 12:16). Notably, this divine glory (John 5:41; 7:18) provides evidence that God is at work in Jesus. As his mission draws to a close, Jesus claims, "the [Son of the] Human One has been glorified, and God has been glorified in him" (John 13:31). Yet anticipating his destiny, Jesus adds, "If God has been glorified in him, God will also glorify [him] in himself and will glorify him immediately" (John 13:32). Just as he bears God's glory through his work in the world, Jesus moves toward the coming moment when he will reflect that glory in his death.

But is it not just Jesus, in John's Gospel, who will both embody sacrificial love and reflect divine glory. Here, too, Jesus's companions emerge as heirs and successors to Jesus's messianic mission. In the Farewell Discourse, for instance, Jesus applies the sacrificial pattern of his own career to those who would observe his new commandment: "This is my commandment: love each other just as I have loved you. No one has greater love than to give up one's life for one's friends. You are my friends if you do what I command you" (John 15:12-14). As Jesus prepares to face death, he instructs his followers about the sacrificial nature of their life together (John 13:34). Just as Jesus has "loved his own who were in the world" (John 13:1), he now depicts their love for one another as a witness to his mission. Like him, they will exhibit servanthood as they "wash each other's feet" (John 13:14). Like him, too, they will "give up" life for one another. His sacrificial death constitutes a model for their own self-giving love.

The divine glorification of Jesus's messianic destiny extends to the community as well. For John's Jesus, this theme emerges as part of the legacy he envisions for his followers. Thus he begins his prayer for his disciples by asking, "Father, the time has come. Glorify your Son, so that the Son can glorify you" (John 17:1; see also 17:10). Yet as the prayer progresses, its scope expands exponentially, as Jesus petitions God both on behalf of his disciples and "also for those who believe in me through their word" (John 17:20). Of such a widening circle of believers, Jesus says, "I've given them the glory that you gave me so that they can be one just as we are one" (John 17:22). Thus Jesus imparts the divine glory entrusted to him—even the glory "like that of a father's only son" (John 1:14). Once again, Jesus's unique christological role entails a paradoxically inclusive and expansive mediation of his divine glory to those who trust in him.

In the Gospel's concluding chapter, probably added at the last stages of composition, the writer applies this glorification specifically to the death of Simon Peter, an event probably known to John's community. In an interpretive aside, the narrator explains the risen Jesus's prediction of Peter's destiny this way: "He said this to show the kind of death by which Peter would glorify God" (John 21:19). Like Jesus's death, Peter's death will glorify God (John 12:33; 18:32).

In sum, John portrays Jesus's messianic sacrifice in richly nuanced terms. Drawing heavily on Jewish traditions about the Passover, Israel's wilderness story, and the suffering servant, John depicts Jesus as a sacrificial lamb whose death brings life for others; as he is "lifted up," he bears the sin of the world in a way that brings messianic redemption and renewal. What is more, Jesus's passion manifests the fullest expression of God's radiant presence.

For John's community, such a decisive display of God's glory was vital to their view that Jesus was indeed God's anointed one. In the face of the mounting resistance and rejection, these sweeping claims about Christ's cosmic reversal of evil through self-sacrifice offer a clear biblical framework for their messianic views. What is more, this destiny—both the suffering and the glorification it brought—provides a lens through which their own witness carries forward God's self-disclosure. For everyone who "hears [the] word and believes" (John 5:24), John's Jesus embodies life-giving sacrifice and charges his followers to do so as well; he reflects God's glory and imparts it to others, including Peter, who will join in its disclosure. Even this Gospel, so focused on promoting Jesus's messianic status, depicts his messianic sacrifice as the way to the Father—the path that the community will take as they radiate God's glory to the world.

Concluding Thoughts

Despite their differing emphases, the Gospels together affirm the messianic nature of Jesus's crucifixion. As he wields God's kingly power on the earth, Jesus the Christ attracts first the attention, and then the outright opposition, of the ruling powers that conspire against his very life. The Gospels also affirm, on this score, a close connection between Christ and community. Like Jesus, his followers will face persecution and even death as they bear witness to God's power unleashed on earth. This common interest in Jesus's messianic sacrifice leads to several observations about Christ and community.

First, in all four Gospels, messianic suffering occurs as a direct result not of God's will in a specific sense but of the conflict that unfolds when Jesus inaugurates the messianic age of God's reign. On the one hand, the Gospels identify prevailing earthly forces—natural, political, and religious—with the forces of chaos, destruction, and death. On the other hand, Jesus challenges these powers, by bringing physical, social, and spiritual wholeness. As a result, he elicits the kind of opposition and violent resistance that characterize earthly power. Messianic suffering, then, both signals the coming kingdom of God and intensifies as it grows imminent. Ultimately, Jesus's humiliating death on a Roman cross both exposes the full measure of human sin and, in turn, strips it of its power. As Paul puts it, *"Where is your victory, Death? / Where is your sting, Death?"* (1 Cor 15:55).

Second, the Gospels consistently depict the suffering of both Christ and community as an organic outgrowth of their loyalty to God's coming reign. Notably, the Gospel message about costly discipleship does not promote suffering for its own sake, nor does it glorify human degradation in any form. While Christians throughout the ages have often read Jesus's summons to self-denial as encouragement to accept abuse and scorn, the Gospels issue no such call. Instead, they promote an active rather than passive stance toward the forces of earthly evil. Understood as part of their broader vision for messianic community, the motif of sacrificial suffering emerges as a by-product of full-throttle trust in the power of God unleashed in the world—first by Jesus and, through him, by those who incorporate his christological mission.

Third, even before the empty tomb, the gospel story of messianic sacrifice affirms that devotion to God's coming reign brings life out of death. Redemption is no "dream deferred," since the crucifixion itself constitutes the "lifting up" of the one who has shown the way of life. Those who participate in the new world order established by Jesus the Christ carry forward this way whenever they forfeit self-interest, self-promotion, and self-preservation.

Together, then, the Gospels offer a robust portrait not just of Jesus's messianic sacrifice but also of its implications for the communities they address. While Western Christianity has often isolated Jesus's death as a uniquely redemptive act, the Gospels themselves draw on Jewish tradition to forge important ties between Jesus and his followers on even this most essential element of his story. The call to "take up [the] cross" and follow him echoes throughout the Gospels, summoning disciples in the first century and beyond to live lives that challenge forces of chaos, destruction, and death in every age.

Study Questions

1. In what ways is Jesus's sacrificial suffering a departure from Jewish messianic thought? In what ways does it fit this worldview?

2. What claims about righteous suffering in Jewish traditions are most helpful for understanding the Gospel witness to messianic sacrifice?

3. Explain one dimension of Jesus's messianic sacrifice that each evangelist highlights.

4. Discuss the similarities and differences between Jesus's messianic sacrifice and the sacrifice he promotes among his followers.

For Further Reading

Bellinger, William H., Jr., and William R. Farmer, eds. *Jesus and the Suffering Servant: Isaiah 53 and Christian Origins*. Harrisburg, PA: Trinity Press International, 1998.

Best, Ernest. *Following Jesus: Discipleship in the Gospel of Mark*. Journal for the Study of the New Testament: Supplemental Series 4. Sheffield: JSOT Press, 1981.

Brown, Raymond E. *The Death of the Messiah*. 2 vols. New York: Doubleday, 1994.

Carroll, John T., and Joel B. Green. *The Death of Jesus in Early Christianity*. Peabody, MA: Hendrickson, 1995.

Doble, Peter. *The Paradox of Salvation: Luke's Theology of the Cross*. Society for New Testament Studies Monograph Series 87. Cambridge: Cambridge University Press, 1996.

Hengel, Martin. *Crucifixion: In the Ancient World and the Folly of the Message of the Cross*. Translated by John Bowden. Philadelphia: Fortress, 1977.

Senior, Donald. *The Passion of Jesus in the Gospel of Matthew*. Wilmington, DE: Michael Glazier, 1985.

Chapter Five
Messianic Resurrection and Reign

"Inherit the Kingdom" (Matt 25:34)

When Paul asks, *"Where is your victory, Death?"* (1 Cor 15:55), he does so confident that Jesus's crucifixion did not end the story of his messianic career. In the Gospel accounts of the empty tomb, all four evangelists emphatically herald the messiah's physical defeat of death itself. For them, Jesus's resurrection bears witness to the life-giving power of God unleashed on earth at the dawn of the messianic age, an age characterized in turn by divine justice. Thus, the Gospels connect messianic resurrection with messianic reign. After rising from the dead, the anointed one presides over the judgment that reign brings—a judgment that leads, in John's words, to—either "resurrection of life" or "resurrection of judgment" (John 5:29 NRSV). As is the case in the wider Jewish landscape, for the Gospel writers, resurrection and reign "hang together like Siamese twins."[1] For the Gospels, then, Jesus's resurrection goes hand in hand with his exaltation to a heavenly throne, from which he presides in judgment.

The Gospel witness to Jesus's messianic mission thus reaches its climax in his resurrection and reign. But that witness extends beyond Jesus's own messianic story to encompass the destiny of the faithful community as well. In this chapter, we explore the Gospel accounts of resurrection and

---

1. Harold W. Attridge, "From Discord Rises Meaning: Resurrection Motifs in the Fourth Gospel," in *The Resurrection of Jesus in the Gospel of John*, ed. Craig R. Koester and Reimund Bieringer (Tübingen: Mohr Siebeck, 2008), 1–20 (5).

reign as they apply to both Christ and community. Indeed, Jewish texts that look forward to God's coming kingdom often anticipate resurrection and reign as part of the renewal it brings. Against this backdrop, the Gospels cast Jesus's own resurrection and reign in this broadly messianic light. Yet, as with every other dimension of Jesus's messianic career, in this case too the Gospel witness to Jesus carries vital implications for those who call him Christ and Lord; they too will be raised by God's power to play a part in his coming reign.

Each Gospel, of course, highlights dimensions of messianic resurrection and reign that relate to its original audience. Mark's apocalyptic story includes a mysterious, open-ended empty tomb account (Mark 16:8) and incorporates Daniel's apocalyptic vision of the heavenly throne room (Mark 13:26; see Dan 7:13-14). Matthew sketches the broader, and decidedly eschatological, contours of both resurrection (Matt 27:52) and judging authority (Matt 19:28). Luke consistently points to the divine necessity of Jesus's resurrection (Luke 24:46) and confers post-resurrection power on the community (Luke 12:32). Finally, John affirms both present and future dimensions of Jesus's resurrection and reign in glory, linking them with the "life" his messiahship promises those who believe in him (John 5:28-29; 17:22). Despite their distinct depictions of resurrection and reign, though, the Gospels together view these motifs as part of God's decisive defeat over the cosmic forces of death, a defeat that leads to the just reign of God upon the earth. Both Christ and community, it turns out, bear witness to the messianic age in which death has, indeed, lost its sting (see 1 Thess 4:13).

Resurrection and Reign in Jewish Tradition

Perhaps no element of the gospel story of Jesus's messiahship has profited more from attention to Jewish background literature than the motifs of resurrection and reign. For while Western Christianity has long forged sharp distinction between Christ and community on this matter, the communal dimension of this aspect of Jesus's messianic career grows clearer in light of Jewish hopes for God's coming reign. While interest in any form of afterlife developed late in Second Temple Judaism, a range of messianic texts from this period—writings that look forward to God's decisive defeat of evil—introduce the motifs of resurrection and reign as part of that unfolding scheme.

Hints of resurrection appear from the time of exile, if at first only in a metaphorical sense. For instance, Ezekiel's vision of the valley of the dry bones provides an evocative image of life out of death that influenced later writers. When God promises, "I am about to put breath in you, and you will live again" (Ezek 37:5), the prophet brings a message of restoration for the "dead" people of Israel in exile. While this tradition predates any fully developed belief in the afterlife, it lays conceptual groundwork for the notion that God has the power to bring life even out of death. Indeed, later Jewish and Christian interpreters took Ezekiel's image to anticipate a general resurrection of the dead, though this was not the text's original sense.

Some of Isaiah's later oracles also hint at future resurrection, at least in a symbolic sense. When the prophet wants to reconcile the people's loyalty to Yahweh (Isa 26:13) with their stunning lack of "victories on earth" (Isa 26:18), the answer proves to be a matter of timing; in the future, the prophet says, "Your dead will live, their corpses will rise, / and those who dwell in the dust will shout for joy. / Your shadow is a shadow of light, / but you will bring down the ghosts into the underworld" (Isa 26:19). As part of the Isaianic Apocalypse (Isa 24–27), this passage affirms God's lordship, even over death itself, in the face of the people's defeat. In a similar way, Second Isaiah anticipates the "raising up" of Israel after the exile as a result of God's sovereign reign. Though the prophet promises that the Babylonians "cannot rise up" (Isa 43:17 AT), Jerusalem will do just that: "Rise up; sit enthroned, Jerusalem. Loose the bonds from your neck, / captive Daughter Zion!" (Isa 52:2; see also 51:17). In Isaiah's oracles, Israel's suffering will give way to her vindication, her "rising up" as part of the "new thing" God is doing in her midst (Isa 43:19). Even if Isaiah does not anticipate resurrection per se, these texts speak of God's redemptive impulse to bring life out of death.[2] Together, then, both sets of writings

---

2. Many who take Isa 26 as a late addition to the collection think that it does. Since the book of Isaiah includes oracles that span centuries, this hypothesis is entirely plausible.

refract the present experience of exile through the prism of God's power to renew and restore human life.

While Ezekiel and Isaiah affirm God's power over death, Daniel's vision situates the twin motifs of resurrection and reign explicitly within the apocalyptic drama of God's coming kingdom. Daniel's final chapter, for instance, looks toward the resurrection and reign that will occur when "Michael the great leader who guards your people will take his stand" (Dan 12:1). In this time, "many of those who sleep in the dusty land will wake up—some to eternal life, others to shame and eternal disgrace. Those skilled in wisdom will shine like the sky. Those who lead many to righteousness will shine like the stars forever and always" (Dan 12:2-3). Notice the passage's eschatological timetable. In the midst of the people's suffering (Dan 12:1), God's messenger will "rise up" to set in motion their deliverance from anguish. Though not called "messiah," Michael plays a leading messianic role: first he rises; then so do those "who sleep in the dusty land." Daniel thus heralds a general resurrection, as the rising of one leads toward the rising of many.

But in Daniel's account, the resurrection itself leads beyond resuscitation to judgment, as those who awake meet their respective destinies: either "eternal life" or "eternal disgrace." Here Daniel sets apart "those skilled in wisdom," along with "those who lead many to righteousness," as the faithful recipients of life (Dan 12:2-3). To understand this judgment, we reach back to the vision of Daniel 7, where final judgment *in heaven* has already taken place. There, Daniel has spied a series of increasingly oppressive "beasts" who continue to threaten God's people Israel. Chief among them is the "horn," which scholars recognize as the tyrannical ruler Antiochus IV Epiphanes. But in Daniel's vision, the power of both Antiochus and the "remaining beasts" has already been stripped away in the heavenly realm (Dan 7:11-12). Though their oppressive tactics still reign on earth, Daniel ensures that their end has already been determined.

Indeed, just after these inhumane rulers have been disempowered, "one like a human being" arrives in heaven. This humanlike figure apparently joins God ("the Ancient of Days") on one of the "thrones set in place" (Dan 7:9 AT). This latecomer to the heavenly throne room thus assumes the place of dominion that has been denied the beasts and, as a result, presides "in judgment" (Dan 7:26 NRSV) over the fourth beast's reign. Though Daniel does not call this figure a "messiah,"[3] at least some first-century rabbis understood the passage to designate the Davidic messiah.[4] But in Daniel's vision, both the reign and its accompanying judgment extend to the "people, / the holy ones of the Most High" who will inherit an "everlasting" kingdom (Dan 7:27). This messianic vision thus discloses a binding verdict against the evil forces animating the beast-like earthly rulers. That judgment proceeds from God, through a humanlike co-ruler, and ultimately to the "people of the holy ones" who inhabit the messianic age. It is they who "shine like the stars forever and ever" (Dan 12:3 AT) as they bear the light of God's righteousness to the world.

Probably under Daniel's influence, the Dead Sea Scrolls feature several references to resurrection and reign in conjunction with the disclosure of God's sovereign power on earth. For instance, the Messianic Apocalypse (4Q521) discussed earlier promises that, in the coming messianic age (cf. Frag 2, 2:1), God's deeds of power in this era will include resurrection: "the Lord...will make the dead live" (Frag 2, 2:11). What is more, the faithful play a role in God's reign, as the Lord "will honor the pious upon the throne of an eternal kingdom" (Frag 2, 2:7). Likewise, the Community Rule (1QS) assigns the "chosen" ones a role in the coming judgment; they will serve as "true witnesses for the judgment...[and those who] render the wicked their retribution" (1QS 8:5). Like the "wise ones" in Daniel, the righteous ones "shall shine to all the edges of the earth" (1QM 1:8), reflecting God's light of "peace and blessing, glory and joy" (1QM 1:9; see also 1QS 4:6-8). That is, the messianic community will radiate the aura of God's kingly reign.

Other Jewish texts from the Second Temple era also look toward resurrection, and the judgment to which it leads, as delayed delivery of divine justice. In the story of the Maccabean martyrs, for instance, the third brother approaches suffering and death fearlessly, freely offering his

---

3. The "anointed one" mentioned in Dan 9:25-26 seems to be a different figure—a human who reigns on earth.

4. See, e.g., *b. Hagigah* 14a.

tormentors his tongue and hands with this explanation: "I have received these limbs from heaven, and . . . I hope to recover them from God again" (2 Macc 7:11). The fourth brother, in turn, also affirms "the hope that God gives of being raised by him," adding this warning: "But for you there will be no resurrection to life" (2 Macc 7:14). Together, these texts express the hope that God's life-giving power will bring resurrection and, with it, the final establishment of God's righteousness. Indeed, despite their present suffering, the righteous can look forward to ultimate deliverance even from death. In many cases, their resurrection leads not just to new life but also to an active part in God's reign. Even texts that anticipate spiritual rather than physical resurrection help to set the stage for the Gospel witness to Jesus's resurrection and reign.

Resurrection and Reign in the Gospels

Given the wide range of Jewish writings that link life-giving power with God's righteous kingdom, it is not surprising that all four Gospels present Jesus's resurrection and reign as the crowning event of his messianic career. As God's "anointed one," Jesus manifests God's victory over death and so offers a compelling witness to the dawn of the messianic age. And if in his life and death, Jesus the Christ exposes the nature of God's kingly power, his resurrection constitutes the "first crop" of the new age gaining a foothold on earth through the faithful communities they address (see 1 Cor 15:20). Ultimately, even Jesus's heavenly reign extends, in the Gospels, to those who inherit and inhabit God's coming kingdom.

Messianic Resurrection and Reign in Mark: "He Isn't the God of the Dead but of the Living" (Mark 12:27)

Among the Gospels, Mark offers the most subtle and allusive account of Jesus's messianic resurrection and reign. The earliest version of this Gospel ends with the women's fearful, stunned response rather than any sightings of the risen Lord. As a story noted for its "way of the cross" drumbeat, Mark heralds Jesus's resurrection, as well as the reign to which it leads, in ways that are more evocative than explicit. Despite this reticence, though,

Mark views Jesus's resurrection and reign in a decidedly messianic light. In turn, this Gospel draws on Jewish tradition to indicate that the faithful, too, will be raised up to join Christ in the "glory" of his exalted reign.

Even the three passion predictions all announce that the suffering Son of the Human "will rise up" or "rise again" (Mark 8:31; 9:31; 10:34). In each case, Mark's Jesus both identifies with the messianic figure found in Daniel (the "one like a human being," Dan 7:13) and looks forward to the new life Isaiah associates with God's coming deliverance. With these and other traditions as conceptual backdrop, the short-term reality of messianic suffering and humiliation gives way to redemption and life. Because God's kingdom has come near (Mark 1:15), its life-affirming force will, Mark insists, prevail even in the face of death itself.

As Mark's story moves from passion prediction to the cross itself, resurrection and the reign to which it leads remain faintly in view. For one thing, Jesus's response to a hypothetical question about resurrection reveals, at least indirectly, Mark's apocalyptic understanding of the motif. The question comes from some Sadducees, a Jewish group who denied any interest in life after death (see Acts 23:8).[5] As if to set a rhetorical trap for Jesus, they inquire about a woman married to several brothers in her lifetime, due to Levirate marriage: "At the resurrection, when they all rise up, whose wife will she be?" (Mark 12:23). First, Jesus attributes their question to ignorance, saying they know neither "the scriptures nor God's power" (Mark 12:24). On one level, he implies that God's life-giving power has already been disclosed in scripture.

In the response that follows, Mark's Jesus exposes the apocalyptic nature of resurrection and then explains that it reveals the very nature of God. First, he says, "when people rise from the dead, they won't marry nor will they be given in marriage. Instead they will be like God's angels" (Mark 12:25). God's power over death endows the risen ones with a kind of embodied life—they are "like God's angels"—that transcends marital status or sexuality. Such a transposed bodily existence, of course, fits well with the renewal of creation that marks the messianic age (see, e.g., 1 Cor 15:35-45). But Jesus takes the discussion further. Once he has affirmed

---

5. See also Josephus, *Jewish War* 2.165.

the coming resurrection, Jesus adds that God is not "God of the dead but of the living" (Mark 12:27). For evidence, Jesus cites Moses's encounter with Yahweh at the burning bush: "*I am the God of Abraham, the God of Isaac, and the God of Jacob*" (Mark 12:26; see Exod 3:6). In this reply, Jesus uses the query to draw into focus the life-giving activity of God that accompanies the coming kingdom he heralds *in the present*. Thus, Mark's Jesus both assumes Jewish apocalyptic hopes for a general resurrection and insists that God's renewal of creation is already at work in his own messianic mission.

The apocalyptic teachings found in Mark 13 echo Daniel's vision as they assign the risen Lord a pivotal role in establishing God's kingdom upon the earth. In this chapter, Mark's Jesus explains the community's coming suffering as "birth pangs" (Mark 13:8 NRSV) that lead inexorably toward God's decisive defeat of evil. Indeed, that suffering—both communal and cosmic (see Isa 13:10; 34:4; 50:2-3; Ezek 32:7-8; Joel 2:10, 31)—gives way at this decisive turning point: "*Then* they will see the Son of the Human coming in clouds in great power and glory" (Mark 13:26 AT, emphasis added). As in Daniel, the Son's arrival coincides with the dawn of God's reign on earth. Most scholars think Mark reverses Daniel's vision, where the humanlike one travels to heaven from an earthly origin (see Dan 7:13). Thus, Mark assures a post-resurrection audience that the risen Christ will soon return *from heaven* to establish God's kingdom on earth.[6] Already, Jesus's messianic reign engages the faithful in its disclosure.

These hints about resurrection and reign provide a narrative backdrop for Mark's empty tomb story, where the women find stunning evidence for God's resurrection power over the present evil age. While Mark's apocalyptic sensibilities make the story fraught with mystery (e.g., Mark 4:10), several details point to the cosmic renewal this messiah's resurrection signals. Indeed, even the setting suggests that the new creation has dawned. In the report that the women visit the tomb "very early on the

---

6. A few interpreters, including N. T. Wright, think that Mark preserves Daniel's direction to indicate that the Son travels from earth to heaven. In this reading, the saying would herald his "coming in the clouds" (Mark 13:26) as his exaltation at the resurrection, after the suffering. This reading is more problematic, since for Mark's community—still in the midst of the "birth pangs"—the risen Lord has ostensibly already taken a seat in the heavenly throne room.

first day of the week, just after sunrise" (Mark 16:2), Mark recalls the Genesis creation story, where God establishes light on the "first day" (Gen 1:3-5). In addition, the sun's rising forges thematic ties with two important messianic traditions.[7] First, the LXX likens God's "raising up" of David as the "anointed one" to the rising of the sun in the morning (2 Sam 23:1, 4). Second, in a passage widely read in a messianic light, Numbers 24:17 looks toward a "star" that "arises from Israel" as a messianic sign. Thus God's activity in the anointed one coincides with God's activity in the cosmos: Jesus's resurrection constitutes a rising, a first light—indeed, a new creation.

Besides the timing, Mark depicts the messenger who greets the women as a standard character in apocalyptic literature. To say he is "in a white robe" (Mark 16:5) identifies him with angelic figures who shuttle between the heavenly and earthly realms (see, e.g., Dan 8:15-16; 9:21). When he appears in place of Jesus's corpse, the angel brings word of Jesus's resurrection as well as a reminder of his promise to go "ahead of" them (Mark 16:7). Jesus's messianic mission in Mark, then, continues unabated, even after the messiah dies on a Roman cross. In the word that "he has been raised" (Mark 16:6), the angel assures the women—and thus Mark's community—that God's reign has indeed triumphed over the power of death.

In all these ways, Jesus's resurrection and reign appear in Mark as signposts marking the power of God at work to reclaim the earth. But for Mark, God's defeat of death and reign in glory extend in turn to the community dedicated to Jesus's messiahship. To begin with, just as Jesus instructs his followers about their required messianic sacrifice, so too does he promise their messianic vindication. After the first passion prediction, Jesus says, "all who lose their lives because of me and because of the good news will save them" (Mark 8:35). The salvation in view here is apocalyptic salvation—that is, the eternal life they will secure when God's reign ushers in the final judgment (see Mark 8:38). As is the case for the Son of the Human, their loyalty to God's reign may well bring their death, but it will ultimately bring salvation, and life anew.

---

7. See Joel Marcus, *Mark 8–16*, Anchor Bible (New Haven, CT: Yale University Press, 2009), 1084.

But along with this possibility for life out of death, Mark portrays the disciples as participants in Jesus's coming reign. Notably, James and John assume the shared nature of Jesus's post-resurrection authority when they ask him, "allow one of us to sit on your right and the other on your left when you enter your glory" (Mark 10:37). Jesus says their request "isn't mine to give" (Mark 10:40), but he does not question their premise. Indeed, he affirms that his reign will be shared by "those for whom it has been prepared" (Mark 10:40) and that others will join him in the heavenly throne room. To make this point, he spells out the nature of their lordship. Unlike earthly rulers who dominate and oppress (see, e.g., Dan 7:23), those who manifest God's sovereign power do so by forfeiting self-interest in service to the liberation of others (Mark 10:41-45).

Jesus's response to the Sadducees' question about resurrection, too, suggests its broadly inclusive nature. Since those who "rise from the dead" will be like "God's angels" (Mark 12:25), Jesus implies that the resurrection will lead to participation in God's restorative purposes. Mark makes this point even more emphatically in Jesus's teachings about the coming "Son of the Human" (Mark 13:26 AT). First, since Daniel's vision promises that "authority . . . shall be given to the people, the holy ones" (Dan 7:27), the Son's arrival "with great power and splendor" (Mark 13:26) also implies that the faithful will soon share that reign. What is more, Mark's Jesus adds this promise: "Then he will send the angels and gather together his chosen people from the four corners of the earth, from the end of the earth to the end of heaven" (Mark 13:27). For one thing, the angels' mission fits widespread biblical hopes for Israel's restoration as part of the messianic age (see Isa 11:11, 16; Jer 16:16-21; Ezek 39:25-29; Zech 10:6-12). Like the disciples whom Jesus "sends" during his earthly ministry (Mark 3:14; 6:7), the angels (or "messengers"; Greek: *angelous*) play an active role in the ingathering of the faithful to reside in God's kingdom. What is more, the angels' journey "from the end of the earth to the end of heaven" (Mark 13:27) indicates that this cosmic assembly includes both the living (from earth) and the dead (from heaven). If this is the case, Mark again hints at the resurrection this kind of ingathering for judgment necessarily entails. At any rate, Mark's Gospel both assumes end-time resurrection and implies that those who are raised will play an active role in establishing God's just rule upon the earth.

Even if its message of apocalyptic travails often looms large, Mark's story of messianic resurrection and reign offers a hopeful message to a community located in the throes of that suffering. For besides promoting endurance in the face of trial, Mark's Jesus promises readers that on the other side of conflict and chaos lie life, restoration, and glory. To affirm the resurrection and reign of Jesus is to affirm, like Daniel, that the destructive powers of the earth have already met their match. But it is not just the end of oppression that Jesus's messianic destiny brings; it is the hope that a new kind of lordship will be firmly established on the earth.

Through allegiance to another "kingdom" and another "lord," Mark's audience likely made themselves vulnerable to the religious and political powers that held sway in the first-century Greco-Roman world. As a result, their costly devotion may have brought a crisis of identity and loyalty. This story of Jesus's messianic resurrection and reign, then, offers an apocalyptic word of assurance: in the midst of chaos and oppression lies the imminent hope for a dawning messianic age that reflects God's "great power and splendor" (Mark 13:26). As the community that inhabits that new age, Mark's audience probably found in this Gospel not just redemptive meaning for their suffering but also a glimpse into the heavenly throne room, where the risen Lord already wields divine authority—an authority that would soon be imparted to those "for whom it has been prepared" (Mark 10:40). In Jesus's messianic resurrection and reign lies both hope for the future and purpose in the meantime.

Messianic Resurrection and Reign in Matthew: "To Sift the Wheat from the Husks" (Matt 3:12)

In portraying Jesus's messianic resurrection and reign, Matthew both affirms Mark's apocalyptic framework and draws out the theme of eschatological judgment. Thus for Matthew, too, Jesus's resurrection constitutes evidence of God's kingly power over death. For Matthew, too, it ushers in the "new creation, when the Son of the Human is seated on the throne of his glory" (Matt 19:28 AT) as righteous judge (see Matt 25:31-46). Yet this judging aspect of Jesus's messianic mission plays a more prominent role in Matthew. What is more, Jesus's own resurrection and reign bear witness to the wider "righteous road" this Gospel message promotes (Matt 21:32; see Matt 3:15). As the Christ, Matthew's Jesus presides over God's righteous kingdom and transmits his judging authority to the faithful as well.

Throughout this Gospel, God gives life by raising up those associated with the new creation. Sometimes, the verb *raise up* (literally, "wake up"; Greek: *egeirein*) signals Jesus's own resurrection (e.g., Matt 16:21; 17:23; 20:19). But elsewhere, Matthew uses the same language to speak of God's life-giving force at work more broadly. Early in the story, John the Baptist claims that "God is able to raise up Abraham's children from these stones" (Matt 3:9)—that is, to animate even inanimate objects. Elsewhere, both Jesus and his followers exercise divine power to "raise the dead" (Matt 10:8; see 11:5)—a power that Matthew identifies with God's reign taking root on the earth. Already, then, we see that resurrection power extends beyond Jesus's own story to showcase God's sovereign authority wherever life arises out of death.

Even the passion story itself in Matthew illustrates this inclusive view of resurrection. Only in Matthew do we find that, at the moment of Jesus's death, "the bodies of many holy people who had died were raised" (Matt 27:52). Notably, the resurrection of the saints (literally, "holy ones"; Greek: *hagiōn*; see 1 Thess 4:16) *precedes* Jesus's own resurrection. At his death, Matthew suggests, the righteous one unleashes God's revitalizing force in the world. The tombs of the righteous are emptied when death has lost its grip on creation. Even before Jesus himself, the holy ones constitute the "first crop" of the resurrection of the dead (cf. 1 Cor 15:23).

In a sense, resurrection in Matthew—both Jesus's and the saints'—serves as a hinge on which God's redemption swings toward messianic reign, along with the universal judgment it will bring. And in this Gospel, that judgment is in view early on. As we have seen, Matthew expands Mark's cryptic account of the baptism with a Q tradition about the coming judgment. After calling hearers to "repent, for the kingdom of heaven has drawn near" (Matt 3:2 AT), the Baptist heralds his successor with these words:

> I baptize with water those of you who have changed your hearts and lives. The one who is coming after me is stronger than I am. I'm not worthy to carry his sandals. He will baptize you with the Holy Spirit and with fire. The shovel he uses to sift the wheat from the husks is in his hands. He will clean out his threshing area and bring the wheat into his barn. But he will burn the husks with a fire that can't be put out. (Matt 3:11-12)

From the outset, John identifies Jesus as the righteous one who will preside over the "sifting" that end-time judgment entails.

The theme of eschatological judgment, meted out on the basis of righteousness, recurs throughout Matthew. For instance, in a Q tradition, Jesus both condemns the unrepentant cities Bethsaida and Chorazin (Matt 11:20-24; cf. Luke 10:13-16) and points toward "Judgment Day," when they will face eternal destruction. Their condemnation in the present only anticipates the decisive moment of final judgment that awaits. Indeed, this emphasis on coming judgment can be seen in the parable of the weeds among the wheat, which only Matthew includes. Here, Jesus encourages his hearers to leave the separation of good from evil to the harvest. He explains the parable this way: "The harvest is the end of the present age. The harvesters are the angels. . . . The [Son of the] Human One will send his angels, and they will gather out of his kingdom all things that cause people to fall away and all people who sin. He will throw them into a burning furnace. . . . Then the righteous will shine like the sun in their Father's kingdom" (Matt 13:39, 41-43). Reworking the tradition about the angels' mission discussed above (see Mark 13:27), Matthew adds a sharp distinction between "people who sin" and the "righteous." And though Matthew does not mention resurrection, the saying seems to presume it. Indeed, Matthew both extends this kingdom to the living and the dead and alludes to Daniel's vision of the resurrection, in which the "righteous will shine like the sun" (Dan 12:3 AT). To drive the point home, Matthew adds a parable of the "net that people threw into the lake" (Matt 13:47-50), where angels "separate the evil people from the righteous people"

(Matt 13:49). As both of these parables imply, Jesus's messianic resurrection and reign will establish God's expansive righteousness on earth.

In many respects, Matthew's story of the judgment of the "nations" (literally, "peoples"; Greek: *ethnē*; Matt 25:31-46) draws together many facets of this Gospel's witness to messianic resurrection and reign. For one thing, this passage casts the Son of the Human as the one who arrives "in his majesty" to exercise judging authority. That is, the judging task falls to the one who, like the figure in Daniel, has taken a seat upon a heavenly throne. Matthew also specifies that the coming judgment brings the separation of "people one from another" (Matt 25:32 NRSV) according to their righteous deeds. What does that righteousness involve? The story defines righteousness not as religious doctrine or observance (see Matt 6:1-18), but as concrete acts that manifest God's concern for the vulnerable: care for the hungry, thirsty, outcast, and imprisoned (Matt 25:35-36; see also Isa 58:6-7; 61:1, 5). Finally, though interpreters often overlook the detail, the Son of the Human assumes his throne of judgment not alone, but accompanied by "all his angels...with him" (Matt 25:31), implying the shared nature of the task. Thus messianic judgment is inclusive in two respects: "all the nations" will face accountability for their righteous deeds, not just Israel; and the messianic judge will be joined by the "angels" who bear witness to this way of righteousness.

Elsewhere, Matthew uses another Q tradition to highlight the sweeping nature of messianic resurrection and reign. Here, Jesus responds to a Pharisee's request for a "sign" by invoking biblical traditions about outsiders: "The citizens of Nineveh will stand up at the judgment with this generation and condemn it as guilty, because they changed their hearts and lives in response to Jonah's preaching. And look, someone greater than Jonah is here. The queen of the South will be raised up by God at the judgment with this generation and condemn it because she came from a distant land to hear Solomon's wisdom. And look, someone greater than Solomon is here" (Matt 12:41-42; see Luke 11:29-32). On the one hand, both the Ninevites and the queen will "be raised up . . . with this generation"; the messianic resurrection, and the judgment to which it leads, extends once again beyond the bounds of the people of Israel. What is more, these ethnic and religious "strangers" will also "condemn" (literally, "judge against"; Greek: *katakrinein*) "this generation" at the resurrection. Deemed righteous because they have aligned their ways with God's, they play an active part in the eschatological judgment.

Yet another Q saying presents an even clearer account of the inclusive nature of messianic reign in judgment. When Peter asks about the gain in following Jesus, which has required leaving "everything," Jesus responds, "I assure you who have followed me that, when everything is made new, when the [Son of the] Human One sits on his magnificent throne, you also will sit on twelve thrones overseeing the twelve tribes of Israel" (Matt 19:28; see Luke 22:28-30). This apocalyptic vision of the renewal of all things fits well with the dawn of the messianic age in which God's power extends to all creation. But here, Matthew expands Daniel's heavenly vision of "thrones" for the Ancient of Days and the Son of the Human (Dan 7:9) to include thrones for Jesus's twelve original followers. With their reign in heaven comes the task of pronouncing judgment upon "the twelve tribes of Israel."

Finally, messianic reign extends through Christ to a wider community in a more general sense throughout this Gospel. For one thing, Matthew notes that the righteous will "inherit" God's kingdom. Like Daniel's "people, the holy ones" (Dan 7:27) and the Qumran community, those who embody God's righteousness will lay claim to God's dominion on the earth. In the Beatitudes, Jesus pronounces that the "hopeless," as well as those "harassed because they are righteous," will inherit the "kingdom of heaven" (Matt 5:3, 10). Even among the nations judged by the Son of the Human, those who have reflected God's righteous ways "inherit the kingdom that was prepared for [them] before the world began" (Matt 25:34).

Like Mark, Matthew's Gospel casts Jesus's resurrection and reign in a decidedly messianic light. Indeed, the life-giving power associated with God's coming reign has triumphed over death, both in Jesus's ministry and in the empty tomb. Through this messiah, God's resurrection power will extend to "all the nations" (Matt 25:32). In turn, it brings sweeping judgment according to the scales of God's righteousness. Thus Matthew's Gospel identifies righteousness as the dividing line that separates those who will inherit God's kingdom from those who will be thrown "into a burning furnace" (Matt 13:42; see 3:12). Such a view sets aside ethnic or religious credentials in favor of a sweeping vision of a "greater" righteousness (see Matt 5:20).

Such a thematic emphasis makes sense in light of Matthew's setting. As we have seen, the Gospel's audience was devoted to Torah and the righteousness it promotes. But their devotion to Jesus's messianic interpretation of that righteousness drew critique and scorn. As a result, Matthew underscores the future implications of the coming resurrection, as well as the vindication to which it leads. For Matthew, Jesus's resurrection belongs to the wider landscape of God's life-giving power set loose on earth. In turn, his reign in heaven will be expansive in scope. Though the rabbis had not yet dismissed messianic hopes entirely, Matthew's community seems to have placed greater emphasis on the coming day of the Lord and the judgment it would bring.

Matthew responds to this setting by bearing witness to Jesus's messiahship in ways that forge connection rather than distinction with the messianic community. For Matthew, neither those who affirm sacred tradition for its own sake nor those who belong to one ethnic or religious group will "inherit the kingdom" (Matt 25:34). It is, instead, those who live righteously toward others—showing mercy, suffering for the cause of justice, and reorienting their lives toward God's reign. That they, like Jesus the righteous one, will be raised means in turn that they, like Jesus the righteous one, will reign in judgment as the new age dawns. For those likely living in tension with their own ethnic and religious communities, this message of messianic resurrection and reign must have conveyed good news indeed.

Messianic Resurrection and Reign in Luke: "Children of the Resurrection" (Luke 20:36 NRSV)

In some respects, Luke parts company from both Mark and Matthew when it comes to the resurrection and reign of Christ and community. For one thing, while Luke includes traditional material found in the other two synoptic accounts, this Gospel generally softens their Jewish apocalyptic and eschatological tones,[8] emphasizing instead the divine necessity of resurrection and reign as part of God's plan for universal redemption. In addition, Luke stresses the *bodily* nature of Jesus's resurrection as a remarkable work of God. Yet this sharper focus on Jesus's resurrection and reign still carries significant implications for the community that affirms his Lordship.

From the outset, Luke presents the destiny of a Jewish messiah named Jesus as the fulfillment of divine purposes for the whole world. The opening verse of Luke's prologue makes clear the writer's intent to provide "an account of the events that *have been fulfilled* among us" (Luke 1:1, emphasis added). Indeed, the theme of fulfillment spans this Gospel account, where both tragedy and triumph proceed from divine necessity as part of God's plan (*boulē*) and will (*thelēma*). Jesus's resurrection, then, takes its place within this divinely orchestrated scheme.

Luke's narrative makes this clear in several places. For instance, the Gospel's first passion prediction underscores God's activity in the resurrection through the grammatical use of a divine passive verb: "and *be raised* on the third day" (Luke 9:22, emphasis added; cf. Mark 8:31). Luke thus stresses that God is in charge of the story's outcome. Likewise, in the transfiguration story, we find Moses and Elijah "speaking of [Jesus's] departure [*exodus*], which he was about to fulfill [*plēroun*] in Jerusalem" (Luke 9:31 AT). Already, we have seen that Luke sees Jesus's death (his "departure" from earthly ministry) in terms of God's redemptive purposes. But his resurrection (his "departure" from realm of death itself) is probably in view as well. This two-tiered understanding of Jesus's exodus only grows clearer in the verse on which the Gospel story hinges: "When the days were completely fulfilled [*symplērousthai*] for him to *be taken up*, [Jesus] set his face to Jerusalem" (Luke 9:51 AT). Once again, Luke signals that Jesus's destiny lies squarely in God's hands; in Jerusalem, God's plans for the world will be finally fulfilled in Jesus's resurrection.

Luke's view that Jesus's resurrection reflects God's command over history itself can be seen near the Gospel's end in the stories of both the

---

8. The fact that Luke incorporates Q, which includes many apocalyptic sayings, means the themes are far from absent in Luke.

empty tomb and the risen Lord's post-resurrection appearances. While the women respond in fear to the angelic messengers, these "men . . . in gleaming bright clothing" (Luke 24:4) seem just as surprised by the women's reaction and remind them of Jesus's declaration "that the [Son of the] Human One must be [*dei*] handed over to sinners, be crucified, and on the third day rise again" (Luke 24:7). The risen Jesus makes this same point to two men on the road to Emmaus, posing this rhetorical question while still *incognito*: "Wasn't it necessary [*edei*] for the Christ to suffer these things and then enter into his glory?" (Luke 24:26). Notably, the necessity presses beyond resurrection toward messianic reign, where the messiah enters "into his glory." In a final encounter, Jesus casts the events as part of the unfolding scriptural story. He tells his companions, "This is what is written: the Christ will suffer and rise from the dead on the third day" (Luke 24:46). Luke's Gospel has come full circle, then, from promising to narrate the fulfillment of events to their culmination in his defeat of death itself. Along the way, every element of Jesus's story has occurred in conjunction with God's active participation and plan.

Besides insisting that Jesus's resurrection fulfills God's unfolding purposes, Luke also underscores the bodily nature of the resurrection. In the Hellenistic world, claims about resurrected figures were generally dismissed with some degree of scorn, and many Greek philosophers (especially Plato) taught that only the soul, not the body, lived on after death. Perhaps responding to such views, Luke goes to great lengths to stress the corporeal nature of Jesus's resurrection. This emphasis can be seen, for instance, in the contrast between what the women did find ("the stone rolled away") and what they did not ("the body," Luke 24:2-3). For his part, Peter discovers "only the linen cloth" (Luke 24:12), a detail that highlights the absence of the body they had covered. When the risen Lord joins his followers later, Luke mentions their meal of bread and "a piece of baked fish" (Luke 24:42), as if to stress that they ate real food. Such narrative features seem calculated to belie the notion that only Jesus's spirit or soul lived on.

If Jesus's bodily resurrection belongs to the divine plan, it is because it sets in motion the whole world's salvation. Like fulfillment, the motif of universal deliverance appears from the Gospel's outset and, in the end, helps frame the resurrection. In the birth story, Zechariah praises God, who has "raised up a horn of salvation for us" (Luke 1:69 AT), and Simeon marvels at the infant Jesus, in whom he recognizes God's "salvation" prepared "in the presence of all peoples. / It's a light for revelation to the Gentiles / and a glory for your people Israel" (Luke 2:30-32). And, in his final encounter with the disciples, Jesus explains the purposes toward which his messianic career presses, saying that "a change of heart and life for the forgiveness of sins must be preached in his name to all nations, beginning from Jerusalem" (Luke 24:47). From start to finish, then, the salvation at work through Jesus extends through Israel for the whole world. In this way, his resurrection ushers in an age in which "all nations" might turn toward God in a relationship of salvation and restoration.

What, though, does Luke make of Jesus's messianic reign? Despite the Gospel's tendency to diminish eschatological elements found in Mark and Matthew, Luke does preserve the expectation that Jesus's reign reaches its culmination after the resurrection. On some level, of course, that reign is already established in his earthly ministry. Though the language is notoriously imprecise, we have noted earlier that only in Luke Jesus says, "God's kingdom is already among you [or, "within you"; Greek: *en hymin*]" (Luke 17:21). Regardless of the translation, the saying stresses the present dimension of God's reign. In a similar vein, the birth narrative includes this promise to Mary about Jesus's reign: "The Lord God will give him the throne of David his father. He will rule over Jacob's house forever, and there will be no end to his kingdom" (Luke 1:32-33; see 2 Sam 7:14; Dan 7:14). And at their last meal together, Jesus tells his disciples that "the Father has conferred on me a kingdom" (Luke 22:29 AT). Again, Luke's Jesus suggests that he already shares a divinely appointed reign.

But even if these examples suggest that God's kingdom, and Jesus's reign within it, have dawned, Luke elsewhere looks toward its full arrival. For instance, Jesus promises his disciples that they will "eat and drink at my table in my kingdom" (Luke 22:30). Luke's account of the crucifixion, too, includes a conversation with criminals who imply that Jesus is the messiah (Luke 23:39) who yet will ascend to his throne. One implores

135

him, "Jesus, remember me when you come into your kingdom" (Luke 23:42). And Luke emphasizes that, when Jesus "enter[s] into his glory" (Luke 24:26), his reign will open the way for messianic salvation.

In Luke, then, Jesus's messianic resurrection and reign constitute a pivotal moment in God's unfolding redemption. On the one hand, all of scripture points toward this event; on the other hand, Luke devotes more attention than any other evangelist to what lies on the other side of it: the witness to Jesus's messianic mission through the life of the church. In the Gospel's sequel, the book of Acts, the messianic community perpetuates the salvation that Jesus's story unleashes. Yet even in the Gospel itself, Luke points toward the inclusive nature of Jesus's resurrection and reign. Already in Jesus's earthly ministry, Luke indicates that Jesus's followers participate in this culminating dimension of Jesus's christological career.

As noted above, Luke rarely refers to the general, eschatological resurrection so taken for granted in Matthew. For instance, while Luke includes the saying about the Son of the Human "'coming on a cloud' with power and great glory" (Luke 21:27), this Gospel leaves out the angels' ingathering of the elect that follows in both synoptic accounts (see Mark 13:27; Matt 24:31). Luke also modifies Jesus's response to the Sadducees in this way: "People who belong to this age marry and are given in marriage. But those who are considered worthy to participate in that age, that is, in the age of the resurrection from the dead, won't marry nor will they be given in marriage. They can no longer die, because they are like angels and are God's children since they share in the resurrection" (Luke 20:34-36). In this rather puzzling saying, Luke's Jesus implies that only those deemed "worthy to participate in that age" will be raised (Luke 20:35). Moreover, the present tense verbs suggest that their resurrection is more spiritual than eschatological. In any case, those who are "children of the resurrection" belong to "that age," which is characterized by God's life-giving power (Luke 20:35-36 NRSV).

Luke's communal concern grows clearer when it comes to Jesus's messianic reign. For instance, Luke includes the Q tradition that promotes striving for "[God's] kingdom" (Luke 12:31; see Matt 6:33) but adds this word of explicit reassurance: "Don't be afraid, little flock, because your Father delights in giving you the kingdom" (Luke 12:32). Like the "people, the holy ones" in Daniel (Dan 7:27), those who pursue the promise of God's reign share in its rewards as well.

In a similar vein, Luke uses the story of Jesus's last meal with his disciples to signal the shared nature of the messianic reign that is dawning. First, Jesus somberly announces that he "won't drink from the fruit of the vine until God's kingdom has come" (Luke 22:18), suggesting the imminent-but-still-future dawn of God's reign. Then Luke includes the Q tradition, discussed above, about the disciples sitting on throne in judgment (Luke 22:29-30; see Matt 19:28). More than Matthew, then, Luke thus stresses the connection between the reign Jesus inherits at death and the reign in which his disciples will participate.

In a way, Jesus's messianic resurrection and reign constitute for Luke a decisive turning point in God's plan of salvation for the world. On the one hand, this Gospel portrays Jesus's messianic destiny as the fulfillment of God's will, disclosed in Jewish scripture. Once again, Luke establishes the deep biblical roots of Christ and community. In light of their location in the Greco-Roman world, such an interpretive impulse is vital to Luke's witness to one whose followers were convinced he had been raised from the dead.

Yet, besides the Jewish basis for Jesus's messianic—and bodily—resurrection, Luke highlights the ways in which his messianic reign extends to the community. After Jesus's own ascension, when his followers have been "furnished with heavenly power" (Luke 24:49), the messianic community will bear witness to his resurrection and reign and the messianic age it ushers in. As Luke and his community claim their identity as "children of the resurrection," then, they participate in God's unfolding redemption of the whole world, the "salvation" that grows available through Jesus's own messianic resurrection and reign (Luke 20:36 NRSV). As they share in God's coming kingdom, Luke's audience become "like angels and are God's children" (Luke 20:36).

Messianic Resurrection and Reign in John: "Life in His Name" (John 20:31)

Already we have noted that, in important ways, Jesus's crucifixion in John brings the culmination of his messianic career. Indeed, his exaltation on the cross accomplishes God's saving purposes for the world. As the Passover lamb, his death for others brings deliverance and restoration. Thus, many have agreed with Bultmann's claim that for John, Jesus's resurrection "cannot be an event of special significance."[9]

Yet far from omitting or downplaying Jesus's resurrection and reign, the Fourth Gospel expands both the empty tomb story and the post-resurrection appearances to make them the most elaborate accounts among the Gospels. Tellingly, the motif of resurrection works its way back into the earthly ministry of Jesus through both his teachings and his raising of Lazarus. It turns out, then, that resurrection and reign do bear special significance for Jesus's messianic career, even in the Fourth Gospel. If John tells a story designed to convince its audience that "Jesus is the Christ" (John 20:31), his resurrection and reign prove vital to that story.

How might we understand resurrection and reign in John? For one thing, this Gospel goes beyond Luke to collapse future messianic expectation into the present. Thus, John includes statements such as these: "I *am* the resurrection and the life" (John 11:25, emphasis added); "*Now* is the time for judgment of this world" (John 12:31, emphasis added); "*Now* the Son of the Human *has been glorified*" (John 13:31 AT, emphasis added). In many instances, John indicates that Jesus's resurrection and the reign it brings have already occurred—even within his earthly ministry.

At first glance, John's emphasis on the present, spiritual dimension of resurrection and reign seems at odds with Jewish notions of messiahship we have considered in this study. Yet more than any other Gospel, this story is crafted for the express purpose of convincing its audience to "believe that Jesus is the Christ, God's Son" (John 20:31). How then might we read John's diminished end-time hopes in relation to the Gospel's insistence that Jesus's resurrection and reign confirm that he is, indeed, the (Jewish) messiah?

To begin with, note that this Gospel frequently uses the twin motifs of resurrection and reign to designate God's life-giving power unleashed authoritatively in Jesus the Christ. In John 5, for instance, Jesus explains

---

9. Rudolf Bultmann, *Theology of the New Testament* (Waco, TX: Baylor University Press, 2007), 2.56.

the nature of his relationship to his Father this way: "whatever the Father does, the Son does likewise" (John 5:19). To elaborate, Jesus claims first that, "as the Father raises the dead and gives life, so too does the Son give life to whomever he wishes" (John 5:21). That is, the Son shares in the resurrection power that belongs to God.

Often, John uses the phrase *eternal life* to specify the nature of the life God imparts through Jesus the Christ. Indeed, in John 6, Jesus calls it the "Father's will: that all who see the Son and believe in him will have eternal life" (John 6:40). What is more, "whoever believes has eternal life" (John 6:47; see also 6:50, 54). And as the Gospel's culminating "sign," the resurrection of Lazarus drives home both Jesus's power to give life and its implications for present reality. After Jesus tells Lazarus's grieving sister, "Your brother will rise again," Martha responds, "I know that he will rise in the resurrection on the last day" (John 11:23-24). Though Martha associates resurrection *only* with the "last day," John's Jesus collapses future expectation into the present by claiming, "I am the resurrection and the life. Whoever believes in me will live, even though they die" (John 11:25). God's resurrection power, John says, is available in the present through God's messiah to all who believe. For John, even *before* Jesus has been raised, God is at work to "give life" to believers.

As a result, the special significance of Jesus's own resurrection in John lies in emphatic confirmation of that life-giving power. Like Luke, John emphasizes the bodily nature of Jesus's own resurrection. This Gospel, too, features multiple witnesses to the empty tomb, as well as Peter's discovery of the "linen cloths" (John 20:5; see Luke 24:12), which suggest the absence of the corpse they had enshrouded. John even goes so far as to say that Peter also saw "the face cloth that had been on Jesus' head. It wasn't with the other clothes but was folded up in its own place" (John 20:7). And, in place of a messenger to interpret these details, Jesus himself appears, not just to Mary in the graveyard, but three more times to his rattled disciples.

These encounters only underscore the physical nature of Jesus's resurrection in the Fourth Gospel. Indeed, Thomas confirms through physical touch that Jesus has been raised in the flesh (John 20:27-28). For John,

God's power to bring bodily life out of death confirms Jesus's messiahship. In turn, belief in the messiah yields a corresponding spiritual "life in his name" (John 20:31). Thus in his resurrection, Jesus appears as the anointed one in whom God's resurrection power has grown evident.

Yet if John adjusts the timing of the messianic age to highlight its present dimension, the Gospel has not abandoned the concept's Jewish backdrop entirely. For one thing, such elements as judgment and divine glory that belong to Jewish apocalyptic thought appear in this story as well. For instance, the Fourth Gospel links resurrection power with the reign in judgment it brings, even if that judgment, too, has already occurred. Thus John's Jesus says that "whoever hears my word and believes in the one who sent me has eternal life and won't come under judgment but has passed from death into life" (John 5:24). On the other hand, Jesus pronounces, "Now is the time for judgment of this world. Now this world's ruler will be thrown out" (John 12:31). In John's view, Jesus's arrival on earth means that "this world's ruler stands condemned" (John 16:11); even if this evil figure still seem to hold sway, Jesus affirms, "he has nothing on me" (John 14:30). While believers have gained "life in his name" and thus escaped condemnation, opposing forces of evil have met their match in this messiah, whose divine power has already subdued them. Like Daniel's vision in the heavenly throne room, John's Gospel holds together the view that, while the outcome of judgment has been fixed, the earthly demise of these forces remains on the horizon.

Another dimension of Jesus's reigning power in John has to do with the glory he shares with the Father. From the prologue (John 1:1-18) on, Jesus reflects the "glory like that of a father's only son" (John 1:14), and it is this glory that radiates God's presence through Jesus on the earth. Again, John's Jesus merges temporal and spatial horizons when he says, "Now the [Son of the] Human One has been glorified, and God has been glorified in him. If God has been glorified in him, God will also glorify the [Son of the] Human One in himself and will glorify him immediately" (John 13:31-32). Once again, John combines past (aorist) and future tense verbs to portray Jesus's messianic career as both complete and unfolding at the same time. Like Jesus's defeat of death through resurrection and reign in judgment, his "glorified" nature adds to John's portrait of Jesus as "God striding across the earth."[10] As he bears God's life-giving power and imparts it to the faithful, as he stands in judgment over "this world's ruler," as he shows the world the divine aura that proceeds from the heavenly realm, Jesus appears in John as a messiah who is both authoritative—in that his career reflects these messianic patterns—and inaugural—in that they persist over time. If the Fourth Gospel draws out the present dimensions of Jesus's messianic resurrection and reign, it also incorporates traditions that keep end-time resurrection and reign in view. A few examples will suffice on this point. For instance, having spoken of God's animating power, John's Jesus offers this promise: "The time is coming when all who are in their graves will hear his voice. Those who did good things will come out into the resurrection of life, and those who did wicked things into the resurrection of judgment" (John 5:28-29; see also 5:25).[11] Clearly, Jesus here looks toward a general resurrection of "all who are in their graves." And those who are raised will, in standard messianic fashion, receive "life" on the one hand and "judgment" on the other (see Dan 12:2). Moreover, it is the Son who will preside in judgment "because he is [a Son of] the Human One" (John 5:27).[12]

In the next chapter, Jesus's teachings about the "bread of life" (John 6:35) reiterate hopes for a future, general resurrection when he says, "This is the will of the one who sent me, that I won't lose anything he has given me, but I will raise it up at the last day" (John 6:39-40). As the passage unfolds, he twice repeats the promise to "raise [believers] up at the last day" (John 6:44, 54). Once again, Jesus's life-giving power in the present belongs within a thoroughly eschatological framework. The eternal life

---

10. Ernst Käsemann, "The Structure and Purpose of the Prologue to John's Gospel," in *New Testament Questions of Today*, trans. W. J. Montague (Philadelphia: Fortress, 1969), 159, 161.

11. John 5:25 is a complicated verse, since it includes both the future prediction of a general resurrection and the claim that the hour of such judgment "is here." Because the phrase that introduces the present dimension is absent in Codex Sinaiticus, one of two major early traditions, as well as Tertullian, many think it was added at a later date.

12. In an unusual case, the Greek has no definite article before the phrase "Son of Humanity." Thus some translate the clause to read, "because he is a human being."

Jesus offers now, for John, positions believers as participants in the messianic age that is dawning.

What are we to make of these competing views? Most scholars attribute them to different editorial stages in the Gospel's composition; over time, they say, the traditions included in this Gospel tamed eschatological expectation. But regardless of its origins, the text's final form holds in tension both present and future dimensions of resurrection and reign. As a result, this Gospel both affirms and reworks Jewish messianic expectation to feature a present, spiritual resurrection and reign on the one hand while still looking forward to the "last day."

In this respect, John's portrait of messianic resurrection and reign may not take us as far afield as many would suggest. Recall that Daniel's visions, too, hold in apocalyptic tension present faith in God's sovereign rule on the one hand and its future culmination on the other. While Daniel claims that, in the heavenly realm, the fourth beast was "killed and its body was destroyed, handed over to be burned with fire" (Dan 7:11), Daniel's community faces the reality on earth that this beast is alive and well. Thus Jesus's insistence that "this world's ruler stands condemned" (John 16:11) fits well with such a "two-storied" apocalyptic universe: if on earth evil persists, its defeat has already been secured in heaven. In a similar manner, the Qumran covenanters pronounce condemnation upon the wicked, whose fate is already sealed if not fully manifest (1QS 8:5).

This apocalyptic tension relates closely to connections John forges between Christ and community on the question of resurrection and reign. Already, we have seen the ways in which John's Jesus establishes the resurrection power available through him to those who believe. On the one hand, Jesus appears as the "bread of life" (John 6:48), the "way, the truth, and the life" (John 14:6), and "the resurrection and the life" (John 11:25)—all in an effort to bring life to those who believe in him. On the other hand, Jesus promises to raise believers up "at the last day" to life eternal. In a sense, God's life-giving power at work in Jesus's own resurrection spans the entire Gospel as a message for those who would gain "life in his name" (John 20:31). Resurrection in John is inherently communal, but it is also messianic in the broadest sense, since it characterizes the new creation the messiah has instituted.

Perhaps surprisingly, Jesus's reign in glory extends to the faithful as well. The High Priestly Prayer of John 17 is explicit on this point. First, Jesus affirms his own reciprocal relationship with God, praying, "Glorify your Son, so that the Son can glorify you" (John 17:1; see also Ps 30:1). In a similar way, though, John's Jesus ultimately imparts his own glory to the community, in whom he has "been glorified" (John 17:10): "*I've given them* the glory that you gave me so that they can be one just as we are one" (John 17:22, emphasis added). Thus Jesus the messiah mediates divine glory to the community gathered around his messianic mission.

Several features of this portrait of messianic resurrection and reign seem targeted to the plight of John's own community. For one thing, for Jews who believed that Jesus was the Christ, John's account preserves plenty of traces of a thoroughly messianic framework for Jesus's resurrection and reign. As the one who has been "lifted up"—in crucifixion, resurrection, and reign—Jesus presides over the dawn of a new age in which the forces of evil have met their match.

But John's community faced a reality that could easily challenge that view. Where was messianic resurrection and glory evident, for instance, when they met opposition and exclusion from those closest to them? How could they hold onto hopes for messianic judgment as time passed and a cataclysmic end did not come? If Jesus was indeed the messiah, should not God's palpable power be more clearly in view on the earth? In response to these and other questions, the Gospel of John modifies Jesus's messianic mission without cancelling it out. In a sense, its story of Jesus, with his claims about resurrection and reign *in the present* offer a glimpse into the heavenly realm, where God has surely ensured the defeat of evil on the earth. In this sense, then, John's Jesus is the "way, the truth, and the life": he discloses the reign of God in heaven even as John's audience endures social and religious alienation and dislocation. What is more, by imparting God's glory to them, this messiah Jesus implies that they too will bear witness to God's life-giving power, and its final defeat of death, to the world.

Concluding Thoughts

As the crowning episode in Jesus's messianic career, his resurrection and reign lend emphatic confirmation to his earthly ministry. In all four Gospels, he appears as the one anointed to manifest the life-giving power of God's kingdom. In all four Gospels, his resurrection leads in turn toward his reign at God's right hand. As he assumes a place on the heavenly throne, Jesus the Christ presides over the final establishment of God's dominion on the earth, a dominion characterized by God's righteous, life-affirming ways.

But the Gospel witness to Jesus's resurrection and reign also carries important implications for messianic community. Indeed, each Gospel translates the story of a risen, reigning messiah for his followers, who live between the assurance that the Christ has come and daily reminders, in their sociopolitical reality, that oppression, rejection, and even death persist. Thus the story about Jesus's messianic resurrection and reign offers a hopeful lens through which they might anticipate their own resurrection and reign, as part of an unfolding apocalyptic scheme in which all will indeed be set aright. We conclude, then, with a few observations about messianic resurrection and reign—of both Christ and community—in the Gospels.

First, all four Gospels depict Jesus's resurrection and reign in decidedly messianic terms. Even John's "spiritual Gospel" emphasizes not just the bodily nature of the resurrection but also its reflection of the life-giving power that characterizes the messianic age. The Synoptic Gospels, too, anchor Jesus's resurrection and reign in a wider story about God's unfolding redemption of the world. Their witness, then, grows out of and remains intimately connected with Jewish messianic thought.

Second, within that messianic framework, all four Gospels share underlying assumptions about the communal dimension of resurrection, as well as the broad participation of the faithful in the messianic reign. Not only Jesus the Christ will be raised; not only Jesus the Christ will reign in judgment or in glory. Those who "believe in" him (John 11:25-26), prove themselves righteous (Matt 25:46), endure "until the end" (Mark 13:13), or are "furnished with heavenly power" (Luke 24:49) will take their place as residents of the messianic age that has dawned.

Third, in all four Gospels, Jesus's resurrection and reign mean that their communities reside between the "already" and the "not yet." Like Daniel's vision, they pronounce death's decisive demise, even as their hearers still contend with its power in their daily lives. The promise of Jesus's story, then, becomes a commission as well. To trust God's sovereign power brings not just new life in the present but also life eternal. In the resurrection and reign of the Christ, the Gospels suggest that history moves inexorably toward restoration and wholeness. To lay claim to that resurrection power, and the judgment of evil that it ensures, may be the only way to live "life to the fullest" (see John 10:10) while the ruler of this world still rages.

Study Questions

1. In what ways do resurrection and reign together relate to Jesus's identity as the Christ?

2. How does the "general resurrection" evident in Jewish traditions contribute to the Gospel witness to Jesus?

3. Explain the nature and role of righteousness in the final judgment. (See especially Matt 25:31-46.)

4. Discuss three Gospel passages that highlight the communal implications of messianic resurrection and/or reign.

For Further Reading

Anderson, Kevin L. *"But God Raised Him from the Dead": The Theology of Jesus's Resurrection in Luke–Acts*. Paternoster Biblical Monographs. Milton Keynes, UK: Paternoster, 2006.

Charlesworth, James H., Casey D. Elledge, James L. Crenshaw, Hendrikus Boers, and W. Waite Willis Jr. *Resurrection: The Origin and Future of a Biblical Doctrine*. New York: T&T Clark, 2006.

Koester, Craig R., and Reimund Bieringer, eds. *The Resurrection of Jesus in the Gospel of John*. Tübingen: Mohr Siebeck, 2008.

Madigan, Kevin, and Jon D. Levenson. *Resurrection: The Power of God for Christians and Jews.* New Haven, CT: Yale University Press, 2008.

Vermes, Geza. *The Resurrection: History and Myth.* New York: Doubleday, 2008.

Wright, N. T. *The Resurrection of the Son of God.* Minneapolis: Fortress, 2003.

Part Two
Messianic Identity

So far, we have considered four central dimensions of Jesus's messianic *mission*, as depicted in the NT Gospels. Together, these stories bear witness to his message, his power, his sacrifice, and his resurrection and reign. In each case, the evangelists portray Jesus's career in a messianic light: as God's anointed one, Jesus presides over the dawn of God's coming reign, offering evidence of divine power unleashed on the earth. More than that, each Gospel assumes that the faithful will carry forward Jesus's messianic mission. Paradoxically, his distinctive role as the Christ means that he engages and empowers others to bear witness to God's life-giving power unleashed in the world. Our thematic study has thus detected the Gospels' coherent witness to Jesus, even as it has exposed the ways in which each Gospel adapts that witness for its audience.

In this second section, we turn to the question of Jesus's messianic *identity*. Here we will consider each evangelist's reply to the question, "Who do you say that I am?" (Mark 8:29). In chapter 6, we explore messianic *titles* used to name Jesus in each Gospel. And while all four Gospels use the names "Son of the Human," "God's Son," "Lord," and "Christ" to convey Jesus's messianic identity, our study will examine the epithet that emerges as central for each evangelist's story. In chapter 7, we explore Jesus's messianic *traits*: servanthood, righteousness, prophetic power, and mystical union. As we shall see, both the titles and the traits that the Gospels use to depict Jesus's messianic identity arise out of Jewish hopes for the establishment of God's kingdom on the earth. What is more, the Gospel witness to Jesus's messianic identity shapes in turn the identity of those who call him Lord. It turns out that, for the evangelists, to name and portray Jesus as the Christ carries important implications for the community devoted to him.

Chapter Six

Messianic Titles

Son of the Human, God's Son, Lord, and Christ

All four evangelists call Jesus "Son of the Human," "God's Son," "Lord," and "Christ"—titles that elaborate his messianic identity in significant ways. Yet in each Gospel, one of these titles plays an especially prominent role in casting Jesus's messianic identity in a certain light. In this chapter, we explore these distinctive titles, asking such questions as these: How does each Gospel use terms found in Jewish messianic thought to identify Jesus? In what ways does each title fit both the literary patterns of the Gospel and the historical setting of its original audience? And how does this way of depicting Jesus's messianic identity forge a connection between Christ and community? By first establishing the title's function in Jewish writings, we lay important groundwork for a careful study of the Gospels themselves. As we shall see, each evangelist builds a case for Jesus's messiahship in ways that carry important implications for readers in the first century and beyond.

The Gospel of Mark: Jesus as "the Son of the Human"

Many have noted that, more than any other Gospel, Mark identifies Jesus by calling him "the Son of the Human" ("Human One" in CEB). This term supplies a rather wooden translation of the Greek phrase, *ho huios tou anthrōpou*. Several factors support this admittedly awkward replacement of the more traditional name "Son of Man." First, the word "human" preserves the more inclusive connotation of the Greek noun.[1] Second, our translation retains the definite article (*tou*) that appears throughout Mark (Mark 13:27 is a noteworthy exception, as we shall see). Third, over time, readers have come to read the phrase "Son of Man" in light of their views about Jesus, rather than the other way around. As a result, much of the term's original nuance, which we explore here, has been neglected over time. To translate the title as "the Son of the Human" preserves the title's more enigmatic meaning.

This title is intriguing on many levels. In the first place, Paul never uses it, preferring instead to call Jesus the "Son of God." Since Paul's letters predate all of the Gospels, some think the title originated not in Jesus's ministry but in early Christian tradition. Where the name does appear in the Gospels, "the Son of the Human" refers to a wide range of figures. In some instances, it designates a human being in a generic sense; elsewhere, it indirectly denotes Jesus himself, by way of circumlocution; and sometimes, it seems to correspond to an apocalyptic figure found in Jewish apocalyptic writings such as Daniel and *1 Enoch*. As we shall see, Mark's apocalyptic worldview provides a way of understanding the title that encompasses all of these uses. It turns out that, as in Jewish background texts, Mark uses the "Son of the Human" title to elaborate Jesus's identity as a designated representative for the wider "new humanity" that inhabits the messianic age.

The "Son of a/the Human" in Daniel and 1 Enoch

The title's ambiguous bearings can be seen in Jewish texts that assign a special role to a "Son of a/the Human" in conjunction with the dawn of God's kingdom. The phrase first appears as something of an epithet in the exilic book of Ezekiel, where God repeatedly addresses the prophet as "Son of a Human."[2] On one level, since Ezekiel is clearly a human being, the term underscores his humanity, perhaps in distinction from the di-

---

1. The Greek word *anēr* is used to designate a male human being.

2. The phrase appears some ninety times in the LXX of Ezekiel, almost always in the vocative (voice of direct address).

vine one whose message he bears. Yet already, Ezekiel appears as a human among humans—that is, as one specially designated to convey God's plans to redeem Israel from captivity.

Already, we have considered the importance of Daniel 7 for understanding Jesus's messianic resurrection and reign (see chapter 5). In what follows, we focus on the vision's preeminent figure, the "one like a Son of a Human." As we shall see, this vision provides a helpful interpretive backdrop for our reading of the "Son of the Human" in Mark. First, we should note the figure's relationship to both earthly and heavenly realms. To be sure, this "one like a Son of a Human" takes on a superhuman quality, as he arrives in the heavenly throne room to join in God's reign (Dan 7:13 AT). Yet while some interpreters emphasize this individual's transcendent, heavenly *status*, the text itself highlights his *role* as mediator of divine authority to "the people, the holy ones" (Dan 7:27). To consider the vision in its own literary and historical context draws this representative and incorporative role into view.

As we have noted, Daniel 7–12 addresses those suffering under the oppressive weight of Syrian occupation in the second century BCE by pulling back the veil of heaven to spy on the secure reign of the Ancient One. What is more, as Antiochus IV Epiphanes threatens Jewish practice and identity at every turn, Daniel's vision heralds the coming reign of God within the earthly domain. In Daniel's "two-storied" universe, four successive beasts represent earthly powers in the heavenly realm. Notably, they bear only faint resemblance to human beings (Dan 7:4, 8) and deploy decidedly inhumane tactics: they terrorize and devour (Dan 7:5, 7). Yet from its outset, the vision signals that their end is near, as the Ancient of Days snatches life from "the horn" and authority from the "remaining beasts" (Dan 7:11-12).

After their removal, the seer spies "one like a Son of a Human coming on the clouds of heaven" (Dan 7:13 AT). This enigmatic figure appears in the heavenly throne room just in time to assume the beasts' vacated position of power. In their stead, the "one like a Son of a Human" now receives "dominion and glory and kingship . . . that shall never be destroyed" (Dan 7:14 AT). As their decisive antitype, this latecomer to the heavenly realm surpasses his oppressive predecessors in at least two respects: he bears *full* rather than partial likeness to humanity, and the dominion he receives is *permanent* rather than transitory in nature.

Yet, there is also an important similarity between the beasts and this humanlike figure. For just as his predecessors have represented earthly, human powers, so too does this "one like a Son of a Human" exercise divine authority on behalf of faithful humanity. As a result, the humanlike figure will share his power with the "holy ones of the Most High" who, like him, shall "receive the kingdom [and]...hold the kingship securely forever and always" (Dan 7:18). Even if these "holy ones" are angelic figures, as interpreters often assume, their authority reaches ultimately to the faithful community, as the "kingship, authority, and power / of all kingdoms under heaven / will be given to the *people*, / the holy ones of the Most High" (Dan 7:27, emphasis added). In this vision, then, a sovereign God deputizes first "one like a Son of a Human," then the "holy ones," and finally the "people, the holy ones." For Daniel, God's reign will prevail decisively on earth in and through the faithful "people, the holy ones."

The Similitudes found in *1 Enoch* 37–71 expand and elaborate on this figure, as the "Son of Humanity" appears also as the chosen/righteous one and twice as the "Messiah."[3] While the Similitudes' precise setting proves notoriously elusive, this text clearly addresses an audience under duress. The text itself alludes to the community's plight by noting the persecution faced by the faithful, earthly allies of the Lord of Spirits (probably to the extent of shedding blood; see *1 Enoch* 47:1, 4). Here too, the "kings and the mighty ones" and the "strong ones" (*1 Enoch* 46:4) rule with force over the faithful; these earthly rulers "manifest all their deeds in oppression," and their "power depends upon their wealth" (*1 Enoch* 46:7). Moreover, their misplaced piety means that they co-opt religious life, as "they like to congregate in [the Lord's] houses and [with] the faithful ones" (*1 Enoch* 46:8). In response, the Similitudes offer an apocalyptic glimpse of alternative divine reality, along with the promise that God's justice will ultimately triumph on earth, in and through the "Son of a/the Human."

---

3. Even the term "Son of a/the Human" translates three different Ethiopic phrases, suggesting that the term is more of a descriptor than a title, per se.

Indeed, rather than focusing on the divine status of the "Son of the Human," the Similitudes use the figure to channel the hopes of the "holy, the righteous, and the elect" (*1 Enoch* 38:4). After all, the text itself features parables that address the "congregation of the righteous" (*1 Enoch* 38:1) and "the righteous and the elect" (*1 Enoch* 58:1). Together, these stories promise a time when "those who possess the earth will neither be rulers nor princes, [for] at that moment, kings and rulers shall perish" (*1 Enoch* 38:4-5). Rather than distinguishing between heaven and earth, the Similitudes follow Daniel's impulse to depict the interpenetration of the two realms. For instance, Enoch declares that the "holy ones" come down "from high heaven and ... become one with the children of the people" (*1 Enoch* 39:1). And just as the Lord of Spirits will make "my Chosen One dwell in her [that is, earth]" (*1 Enoch* 45:5), so too will "the chosen ones ... begin to walk with the chosen ones" (*1 Enoch* 61:3). The Similitudes thus envision divine involvement in the created order, through the earthly sojourns of heavenly agents and, we might say, through their incarnation in the midst of the faithful.

Within this dynamic interface between heaven and earth, the chosen/righteous one functions as both mediator and corporate embodiment of the coming age of righteousness. Like Daniel's "one like a human being" (Dan 7:13), he inhabits a throne in the heavenly realm (*1 Enoch* 45:3; 51:3; 55:4; 61:8). Further, when the Enochic Son is revealed, the "congregation of the holy ones shall be planted, and all the elect ones shall stand before him" (*1 Enoch* 62:8); they too shall "wear the garments of glory" (*1 Enoch* 62:16).

Together, both Daniel and *1 Enoch*'s Similitudes assign a pivotal messianic role to a "Son of a Human," who presides over the impending renovation of earth. As he represents the interests of the faithful and mediates God's reign to them, the Son of the Human thus sheds helpful light on Mark's wide-ranging uses of the title. This enigmatic figure is firstborn among the new humanity that will inhabit the messianic age; the Son of the Human thus plays a role that is distinctive and prototypical on the one hand, and representative and inclusive on the other. In Mark, Jesus appears as the Son of the Human whose messianic authority and witness extend ultimately to the faithful community he gathers. In what follows, we explore the title's appearance in several key passages in Mark's Gospel.

"The Son of the Human" in Mark

As an apocalyptic Gospel, Mark uses this enigmatic figure to cast Jesus's identity in a messianic light. As we shall see, to read the title in relation to both Daniel and *1 Enoch* helps make sense of its wide-ranging uses in this Gospel. For Mark, to call Jesus "the Son of the Human" (AT) is to suggest that he imparts God's kingly authority to the new humanity his messianic career establishes.

The title first appears early in Mark, when Jesus heals a paralytic (Mark 2:1-12). Before restoring use of the man's limbs, though, Jesus pronounces divine forgiveness. When the religious leaders nearby respond with (silent) disapproval, Jesus offers this enigmatic reply: "But so you will know that the [Son of the Human] has authority on the earth to forgive sins," he says to the paralytic, "Get up, take your mat, and go home" (Mark 2:10-11). In this instance, Jesus seems to signal, at least obliquely, his own divinely sanctioned authority to pronounce forgiveness.

Later in the chapter, though, a second reference to "the Son of the Human" complicates the notion that Mark applies the title to Jesus in an exclusive sense. When others have challenged his disciples' activity on the Sabbath, Jesus defends them in this way: "The Sabbath was made for humanity, and not humanity for the Sabbath; / So the Son of the Human is lord even of the Sabbath" (Mark 2:27-28 AT). Assuming the title refers to Jesus in an exclusive sense, readers often infer that Jesus here asserts his *own* lordship over the Sabbath. Yet the saying's literary structure and context indicate that the term points both toward Jesus's lordship and beyond Jesus, to suggest his followers' lordship as well. For one thing, the title itself stands in "synonymous parallel" with the claim that the Sabbath serves "humanity" (Greek: *anthrōpon*). That is, the saying about the "Son of the Human" seems to reiterate the previous one by restating it. Thus the term appears here to function somewhat generically, designating humanity as a whole. Moreover, since Jesus responds to the Pharisees' inquiry about the *disciples'* action, not his own, his defense substantiates their authority, not his (see Mark 2:24). In this sense, then, Mark 2:10 and 2:28 together implicitly assign authority to Jesus as "the Son of the Human"—but also through him to those aligned with his messianic mission.

Within the Gospel's central section, three passion prediction sayings call Jesus as "the Son of the Human" whose destiny will bring persecution, death, and resurrection (Mark 8:31; 9:31; 10:33). Clearly, Mark applies the title to Jesus, as the details he foretells anticipate details found throughout Mark's Passion Narrative. And yet, as we have noted in chapter 4, each statement about *Jesus's* destiny leads in turn to an extended teaching his *disciples'* self-sacrifice as well. Like Jesus, his followers will "take up their cross" (Mark 8:34); like Jesus, those who aspire to greatness "must be least of all and the servant of all" (Mark 9:35). As the suffering "Son of the Human," then, Jesus appears as first among those who follow in his way of sacrificial servanthood.

Indeed, after the third passion prediction, Jesus applies this pattern of servanthood to his followers in an explicit way. When James and John inquire about positions of power in "your glory" (Mark 10:37), Jesus depicts the nature of lordship in God's kingdom, which stands in stark contrast to the Gentiles' apparent "rulers" and "great ones," who wield power as "tyrants" (Mark 10:42 NRSV). Like both Daniel and *1 Enoch*, Mark exposes the coercive ways of the prevailing world order. Turning this manner of "lordship" on end, he depicts "greatness" in God's kingdom with these words: "Whoever wants to be great among you will be your servant. Whoever wants to be first among you will be the slave of all, for the [Son of the Human] didn't come to be served but rather to serve and to give his life to liberate many people" (Mark 10:43-45). Here, the title "Son of the Human" establishes the governing nature of Jesus's own messianic authority. The purpose of his coming, Jesus says, lies in the redemptive impact of his vulnerable servanthood. In this lies true "greatness." Yet in context, Mark identifies the Son of the Human both with Jesus and with those who aspire to join in his glory. If only suggestively, even the notion that sacrificial servanthood brings liberation for many may apply to them (see Isa 52:13–53:12).[4]

---

4. See chapter 4 for a discussion of this verse.

Since Mark so consistently refers to Jesus as the "Son of the Human," the title's appearance in the apocalyptic discourse (Mark 13) presents an interpretive challenge. For when Jesus points toward a "Son of a Human coming in clouds" (Mark 13:26 AT), he seems to imply distinction from, rather than connection with, this quasi-divine being. Probably since the verse quotes Daniel's vision, the Greek phrase lacks the definite article ("Son of *a* Human"). In addition, some take this saying to preserve an earlier and more authentic tradition. From this angle, the saying suggests that Jesus awaited the "Son" Daniel envisions. Others infer that Jesus alludes, however obliquely, to his own ascension after the resurrection, suggesting that he will travel on the clouds to the heavenly throne room. What are we to make of Jesus's saying in this case?

To take interpretive cues from both Daniel 7 and the Similitudes of *1 Enoch* leads us to understand this figure as a humanlike intermediary who shuttles between heaven and earth to secure the whole cosmos for God's reign. After all, Daniel's vision heralds the Son's arrival in the heavenly throne room, where he replaces the beastly rulers. It is his humanity—and humane ways—that qualify him to serve as co-regent in God's dominion. Moreover, just as the Ancient of Days imparts the kingdom to this humanlike ruler, so too does that kingdom extend, through him, to the "people, the holy ones." Likewise, the figure in the Similitudes functions as agent of God's power among those who remain faithful.

But what light do these passages cast on the interpretive conundrum of Mark 13? First, they raise the possibility that Mark does indeed identify Jesus with the humanlike figure who assumes authority in God's coming kingdom. Read in this light, Mark's Jesus may anticipate his own reign in the heavenly throne room. In addition, Mark may use the title more suggestively, to signal the broader implications of that reign. As we have seen, the apocalyptic teaching of Mark 13 addresses the plight of Mark's community. In light of their current suffering, Jesus's prediction of a coming "Son of a Human" may extend his heavenly authority to Mark's audience, casting them in the role of the "people, the holy ones of the Most High" (Dan 7:27). Thus, this messianic title extends Jesus's messianic authority to those who endure "until the end" (Mark 13:13).

Mark's portrait of Jesus as "Son of the/a Human" fits well within the apocalyptic framework we have elsewhere discussed. Like the figure in Daniel and *1 Enoch*, and like the "new Adam" in Paul (see Rom 5:12-21; 1 Cor 15:45-59), Jesus appears as the preeminent denizen of the messianic age. In Mark's account, this age is marked by forgiveness, Sabbath rest, servanthood, and the ultimate defeat of any forces that would diminish human wholeness. Yet the Son's authority is not his alone; as he inaugurates that new age, those who inhabit God's kingdom will share in that rule as well.

Mark's message about this "Son of the/a Human," then, carries important implications for our understanding of Christ and community—both for the Gospel's earliest audience and for readers today. For those suffering persecution for their loyalty to God's reign, such a portrait of Jesus the Christ characterizes not only his authoritative earthly mission but also his enduring authority in heaven. Yet his authority extends in turn to those who participate in the "new humanity" he inaugurates. For Mark's community, facing threat of trial and death, this "Son of a/the Human" thus embodies a humane lordship they can both affirm and emulate.

The Gospel of Matthew: Jesus as "God's Son"

While Matthew retains traditions that call Jesus "the Son of the Human," scholars often note that Jesus's identity as "God's Son" lies at the heart of this Gospel message. Not only does Matthew include material from other sources that identify Jesus's divine Sonship (e.g., Matt 2:15; 21:37; 22:2), but also this evangelist sometimes adds the title when editing Mark's account (e.g., Matt 14:33). From the birth narrative (Matt 2:15) to the great commission (Matt 28:19), then, Matthew portrays Jesus as "God's Son."

But what does Matthew mean by the term? Those who stress the term's Hellenistic background tend to agree with Bultmann, that "God's Son" suggests "the divinity of Christ, his divine nature, by virtue of which he is differentiated from the human sphere."[5] More recently, though, scholars have widely challenged this approach. Though the Gospels address a wider Greco-Roman setting, their sources bear the imprint of Jewish thought.

5. Rudolf Bultmann, *Theology of the New Testament* (Waco, TX: Baylor University Press, 2007), 1:129.

Thus, rather than reading Matthew in light of later Hellenistic beliefs, we consider here its origins in Jewish texts that influenced both Jesus and the evangelists. A range of writings use the title "God's Son" to depict figures who *both* enjoy God's special favor *and* mediate God's righteous ways to the faithful in ways that lead to their designation as "sons" as well. The title thus encompasses both Christ and community in Jewish tradition and in Matthew's Gospel.

"God's Son" in Jewish Tradition

While Jewish scripture mentions "sons of God" who belong to the celestial realm (e.g., Gen 6:2-4; Deut 32:8 AT), these references are probably vestiges of ancient Israelite mythology. As biblical traditions evolved, the term came to designate an array of people and groups: King David and his successors; the people of Israel in general; or the righteous community, to name a few. Since Matthew tells the story of a Jewish messiah for a Jewish audience, it will prove helpful to review selected passages that inform this Gospel's portrait of Jesus as "God's Son."

To begin with, the Deuteronomistic History expresses the special relationship between God and the Davidic dynasty in terms of divine Sonship. In a pivotal passage, Yahweh promises, "I will be a father to [King Solomon], and he will be a son to me" (2 Sam 7:14). The psalmist also affirms this father-son relationship, as Israel's king announces, "[God] said to me, 'You are my son, / today I have become your father'" (Ps 2:7). Rather than divine status or nature, the king's sonship simply means he has been divinely appointed; God is the king's "father" in that his earthly authority derives from heaven. Moreover, the psalmist uses the human king's sonship to subordinate his political power to Yahweh's righteous, universal reign.

Both the prophets and wisdom traditions develop the notion of divine Sonship in a more democratic direction, shifting the identity of God's "son(s)" from an individual ruler toward the people of Israel as a whole. For their part, the prophets often use father-son imagery to convey the intimate relationship between God and Israel, a relationship Israel so often violates. For instance, Isaiah delivers this message from God: "Hear, O heavens, and listen, O earth; / for the LORD has spoken: / I reared sons and brought them up, / but they have rebelled against me" (Isa 1:2 AT). Thus the prophet makes a cosmic case for grievances against Israel as an offense against God's parental care. Likewise, Hosea promises that, after a time of repentance, Israel will be called "sons of the living God" (Hos 1:10 AT; see also 11:1). In Jeremiah, God urges "faithless sons" to repent and promises, "I will heal your faithlessness" (Jer 3:22 AT). In each case, God uses the motif of sonship to hold the people to account to a divine Father who has loved and nurtured them. While a special status is implied, God's "son" Israel is neither divine in nature nor consistently faithful. Instead, the term forges the kind of relational intimacy with God that shores up, in turn, God's relational authority.

Other Jewish traditions link "God's Son" to the way of righteousness. In sayings that may lie behind Matthew's Gospel, for instance, the Wisdom of Solomon designates the "man who does the right thing" as "God's son" (Wisdom 2:18; see also 12:21; 16:10, 26). And though righteousness encompasses many attitudes and actions, Ben Sira establishes the social responsibility that characterizes divine Sonship:

> Be like a parent to orphans,
>   and take care of their mothers
>   as you would your own wife or husband.
>   Do this, and you will be like a child
>   of the Most High,
>   and God will love you
>   more than your own mother does. (Sir 4:10)

Being a "son of God" means bearing witness to God's righteous ways within the human community. Expanding the biblical motifs discussed above, then, this later wisdom tradition sees divine Sonship wherever God's righteousness shines forth.

"God's Son" in Matthew

This conceptual backdrop offers important interpretive guidance for our study of Matthew's use of this title. For one thing, it challenges the widespread assumption that Jesus's identity as "God's Son" in Matthew automatically designates his divine nature. Of course, Matthew does use this title to emphasize Jesus's special status and relationship with his Father, along with his righteousness and faithfulness. But rather than forging unique claims about Jesus, Matthew also promotes Jesus's exemplary way of "greater . . . righteousness" (Matt 5:20) as a pattern for others who, like him, will call God "Father." We turn first to Matthew's depiction of Jesus's divine Sonship.

At times, Matthew uses the title "God's Son" to present Jesus as the quintessential representative of God's people. Citing scripture, Matthew sometimes casts Jesus in the role the prophets have assigned Israel. For instance, when Jesus's earthly father Joseph takes his family to Egypt until Herod's death, Matthew explains their return this way: "This fulfilled what the Lord had spoken through the prophet: *I have called my son out of Egypt*" (Matt 2:15; see Hos 11:1). Just as Hosea uses Israel's divine Sonship to convey God's tenderhearted ties with a wayward people, Matthew suggests that even the infant Jesus enjoys such divine intimacy and favor.

Both repeating and revising Mark's account, Matthew uses a wide range of characters to affirm Jesus's status as God's son. At both his baptism and the transfiguration, a voice from heaven speaks these words: "This is my Son whom I dearly love; I find happiness in him" (Matt 3:17; see 17:5; Mark 1:11; 9:7). While in Mark, the voice addresses Jesus directly at the baptism, Matthew makes the pronouncement public, as if to confirm Jesus's identity from the outset of his ministry. In both cases, the words echo Psalm 2:7 and so suggest Jesus's royal—and messianic—status as well. And as in Mark, a voice "from the cloud" reaffirms Jesus's divine Sonship, adding a command to "listen to him" (Matt 17:5; see Mark 9:7). Thus, as we have found in wisdom traditions, this Son appears as one who instructs others about God's righteous ways.

Besides the divine voice, other figures—both friend and foe—recognize Jesus as God's Son in Matthew. This identification often follows Jesus's display of divine power, just as it does in Mark. For instance, when the Gadarene demoniacs hail him as "Son of God" (Matt 8:29; see Mark 5:7), they discern his authority over evil spirits. In Matthew, Peter first names Jesus as "God's Son" just after he has joined Jesus walking upon the sea (Matt 14:33); Jesus's command over chaotic waters thus inspires this unprompted recognition. Ultimately, the centurion and his companions apprehend the cataclysmic events at Jesus's death—including the resurrection of the saints (Matt 27:52)—and see them as his divinely sanctioned defeat of death: "This was certainly God's Son" (Matt 27:54; see Mark 15:39). In all these ways, Jesus is God's Son in part because he manifests divine power at work in creation.

Notably, Matthew makes it clear that Jesus will not invoke his special status as God's Son for his own protection or profit. After his baptism, for instance, the devil tempts Jesus to use his identity as "God's Son" to provide food (Matt 4:3) and show off special powers (Matt 4:6). And at the crucifixion, passersby taunt Jesus, saying, "If you are God's Son, come down from the cross" (Matt 27:40). In both cases, Matthew's Jesus bears the likeness of his Father by refusing to serve his own interests.

Wisdom traditions also seem to lie behind Jesus's identity as "God's Son" when he dispenses the knowledge of God to others. In a Q passage, for instance, Jesus affirms both his own intimacy with his Father and his inclination to disclose God's ways: "My Father has handed all things over to me. No one knows the Son except the Father. And nobody knows the Father except the Son and anyone to whom the Son wants to reveal him" (Matt 11:27; see Luke 10:22). On the one hand, the saying assigns an exclusive quality to this Father-Son relationship, since Jesus personifies God's Wisdom in a unique sense. Yet even this privileged status leads ultimately toward revelation for others. Indeed, in the passage that follows, Jesus invites those who are "struggling hard and carrying heavy loads" to come to him and to learn from him (Matt 11:28-29; see Sir 24:19, 51:23). His divine authority as Son thus equips this messiah to disclose the Father to others.

Within Matthew's Passion Narrative, Jesus speaks allegorically about his impending rejection, casting himself in the role of God's Son in the parables of the wicked tenants (Matt 21:33-46) and the wedding banquet (Matt 22:1-10). In the first, the landowner sends his son to collect the harvest after his servants have been beaten, killed, and stoned; surely, he thinks, "They will respect my son" (Matt 21:37). But it is his status as "son"—and thus heir—that prompts them to kill him as well, a move that leads in turn to their destruction and replacement (Matt 21:41). In a similar vein, when invited guests decline the chance to attend his son's wedding celebration, a king sends servants to the streets, where they "gathered everyone they found, both evil and good. The wedding party was full of guests" (Matt 22:10). Together, these parables cast Jesus in the role of God's Son who has entered the world to preside over messianic restoration and the celebration it elicits. Though these stories draw his impending rejection into view, they also suggest that as God's Son, he plays a vital role in claiming the earth for God's kingdom.

But if Jesus's identity as "God's Son" is distinctive in Matthew, it is not exclusive. Others who join in this "righteous road" (Matt 21:32) become sons of this heavenly Father. For instance, the Sermon on the Mount (Matt 5–7) promotes a way of "greater" righteousness that affirms not just Jesus's divine Sonship but also the divine Sonship of those who, like him, reflect that righteousness. The claim appears explicitly in the Beatitudes, where Jesus promises that those who make peace will be called "sons of God" (Matt 5:9 AT).[6] And throughout the Sermon, Jesus speaks to his audience about "your Father," implying that those who follow his teachings, too, become "sons" of God.[7]

What can we say about divine Sonship in the Sermon? How does the term *God's Son* fit with the view that those whose "righteousness is greater than the righteousness of the legal experts and the Pharisees" (Matt 5:20) call God "Father"? On one level, to be called "God's Son" in the Sermon is to reflect the Father's indiscriminate love. As we have seen, Jesus instructs his hearers, "Love your enemies and pray for those who harass you so that [*hina*] you will be acting as [sons] of your Father who is in heaven" (Matt 5:44-45). For Jesus, the connection is an organic one: The Father's expan-

---

6. In a laudable effort to use gender-inclusive language, many modern translations use the term "God's children" (CEB) or "children of God" (NRSV). For our purposes, it is important to affirm the likeness of the peacemakers' status to Jesus's: like him, they are "sons," regardless of their gender.

7. The word *father* appears sixteen times in the Sermon, and all but one instance modifies the noun with the second-person pronoun (either singular *sou* or plural *hymōn*).

sive, indiscriminate care for creation (see Matt 5:45) manifests the kind of expansive, indiscriminate righteousness Jesus promotes. Jesus's command to "be complete [*teleioi*]," "as your heavenly Father is complete [*teleios*]" (Matt 5:48) only confirms this point. God's likeness can be seen wherever God's "greater...righteousness" (Matt 5:20) comes into view.

If the pattern of divine Sonship is reflected in righteousness throughout the Sermon, it is also evident in Jesus's teaching about utter trust in the Father. After encouraging hearers to look to God for their provision— to ask, search, and knock (Matt 7:7-8)—Jesus likens God to a Father who provides for children. He explains, "Who among you will give your [son] a stone when [he asks] for bread?...If you who are evil know how to give good gifts to your children, how much more will your heavenly Father give good things to those who ask him" (Matt 7:9, 11). Using a rabbinic strategy that argues from the lesser to the greater, Jesus promotes relational dependence on a God whose provision exceeds that of a human parent. Just as Matthew's Jesus has refused to provide his own bread from stones in the wilderness, relying instead on God for sustenance, here he enjoins his hearers to approach the Father with their needs. Thus divine Sonship reflects the trust that arises out of intimate devotion to God as loving parent.

Finally, Matthew underscores the eschatological import of divine Sonship when Jesus interprets the parable of the wheat and weeds (Matt 13:24-30) to his followers. Calling the "good seed" the "sons of the kingdom" (Matt 13:38 AT), he expresses the destiny of the righteous this way: at "the end of the present age...the righteous will shine like the sun in their Father's kingdom" (Matt 13:39, 43). Once again, God's "sons" bear the radiant image of God's righteous in the new age of God's reign.

For Matthew's community, residing in the Father's kingdom meant affirming, with Peter, that Jesus is "God's Son" (Matt 14:33; see 16:16). That is, Jesus's life, death, and resurrection bore for them the likeness of the Father to the world; in so doing, this Son embodied the Father's expansive righteousness and utter trust in God's coming reign. Since this belief about Jesus as crucified and risen Son of God proved to be an increasingly sharp point of religious distinction, Matthew only drew heightened attention to this title.

But according to Matthew, this devotion to Jesus as "God's Son" meant that they, too, were "sons of the kingdom" or "sons of God." In this phrase, Matthew thus merges interest in Jesus's messianic identity with the view that, as the Christ, he promotes a way of greater righteousness. Those who affirmed Jesus's divine Sonship thus found themselves drawn into the "righteous road" (Matt 21:32) he taught and embodied. Already, Paul had written that "whoever is led by the Spirit of God, these are the sons of God" (Rom 8:14 AT). Likewise, Matthew names both Jesus and those who affirm his authoritative witness to God's righteousness as God's "sons." In this Matthew carries forward Jewish tradition. If he also underscores the messianic dimension of Jesus's divine Sonship, so too does he cultivate messianic community among those who, through Jesus's enduring presence, continue to reflect the righteousness of the one who is their Father as well.

The Gospel of Luke: Jesus as "Lord"

As many have noted, the Gospel of Luke uses the term *lord* (Greek: *kyrios*) as a thematic key word in its portrait of Jesus. The noun appears some 104 times in Luke, and almost all instances refer to God or Jesus (occasionally, the distinction is blurred), implicitly or explicitly. In addition, Luke identifies Jesus with the articulated title "the Lord" in a number of verses found only in this Gospel, suggesting the evangelist's deliberate editorial emphasis. In what follows, we explore the term's wide-ranging uses throughout Luke to determine both Jesus's identity with/as "the Lord," as well as the title's implications for the community Luke addresses.

The "Lord" in Jewish Tradition

In terms of background, Luke's Hellenistic setting has led many scholars to explain this Gospel's use of "lord" terminology in terms of Greco-Roman religious and political discourse. We know, for instance, that the god Serapis was called "lord," as were some Roman emperors, especially in the eastern territories. In the latter case, the title provides religious sanction for political power; their divine or semidivine status made these human leaders largely beyond reproach.

Recent scholarship, though, has brought to light the complementary influence of Jewish traditions even on evangelists who wrote for the wider Greco-Roman world. This is clearly the case with Luke, who tells the story of a Jewish messiah for a mostly non-Jewish audience. Indeed, in the Hellenistic world, Jews distinguished themselves in part by their devotion to one and only one "lord"—the God of Israel named in scripture as YHWH (Yahweh). In most cases, they were even exempt from participating in state religion because of this exclusive loyalty. By the first century, the LXX often used the term *lord* (*kyrios*) wherever the divine name appeared.[8] In so doing, Jewish scribes undercut—either subversively or unwittingly—any pretense to human power wielded by the empire. In Hellenistic Judaism, the "lordship" of God subordinated all earthly power to Yahweh's sovereignty.

Though God's identity as "Lord" spans the LXX, we consider here two passages that cast important light on Luke's use of the term. First, we return to the opening line of Isaiah 61 that lies behind Jesus's inaugural proclamation in Luke (Luke 4:18-19). In a post-exilic oracle, the prophet declares that "the LORD God's spirit is upon me, / because the LORD has anointed me" (Isa 61:1) to deliver a message of hope and restoration to Zion. This statement establishes, even reiterates, God's sovereign "lordship"; the prophet speaks not on his own, but at God's instigation. To call God the "lord" is to insist that the message comes only at God's behest. At the same time, the Lord has "anointed" the prophet as human spokesperson to deliver a message of "good news to the poor" (Isa 61:1). In pronouncing God's coming deliverance for those who suffer, the prophet becomes a spirit-empowered agent of reversal. Those who now suffer will soon "be called oaks of righteousness, the planting of the LORD, that he may be glorified" (Isa 61:3 AT). That is, as God's "lordship" restores Zion,

---

8. Philo used *kyrios*, though Josephus seems to have preferred *despotēs*, a word that preserves but recasts the power dynamics we discuss here.

God's people will reflect God's righteous ways. As a result, they will garner for God the world's acclaim.

In addition to Isaiah 61, an enthronement psalm proves vital to Luke's use of the title "lord." In Psalm 110, the LXX calls Yahweh "lord" (*kyrios*). But the psalmist also uses the term to establish close correlation between God's "lordship" and the "lordship" of David, the anointed servant-king. As a result, this psalm offers a biblical window into the nature of the "lordship" that both God and God's anointed reflect. Psalm 110 begins this way: "What the LORD says to my master [Greek: *kyriō*]: / "Sit right beside me / until I make your enemies / a footstool for your feet!' / May the LORD make your mighty scepter / reach far from Zion! / Rule over your enemies!" (Ps 110:1-2; 109:1-2 LXX). By calling both God and the earthly ruler "lord," the psalmist extends divine power to an earthly ruler, an impulse not uncommon in the ancient Near East. And while the LXX calls both Yahweh and David "lord [or "master"]," it is God who holds *absolute* authority. After all, this divine "lord" manages even earthly affairs, while the human king sits (almost idly) by. Affirming God's sovereignty as the one who will "make your enemies a footstool for your feet" and "make your mighty scepter reach far from Zion," this enthronement psalm suggests that the Davidic king's lordship comes from the one who establishes ultimate rule. As king, the human lord wields God's power, in a provisional sense, within the earthly realm.

Both Isaiah 61 and Psalm 110 suggest that God's lordship is both ultimate and shared. That is, the biblical writers use the term to convey God's unsurpassable power in the heavenly realm. At the same time, both passages suggest that God assigns human beings the task of manifesting the values of God's sovereign reign on earth. Thus God's heavenly "lordship" works its way toward earth through prophets and kings who bear its decisive power on God's behalf.

The "Lord" in Luke

In Luke, the title functions in a similar vein, as it designates Jesus the Christ an earthly "lord" who wields God's sovereign authority. Thus the name works less to establish Jesus's divine identity per se than to frame his own "lordship" in messianic terms that reflect the redemptive nature of God's power. Luke's Jesus thus represents "the Lord" as an anointed emissary who manifests God's reign on the earth. As messiah, his "lordship" thus bears distinctive witness to the power that emanates from God's lordship—a power at work to deliver rather than hold captive, to serve rather than to enslave, and to thwart all forces that would compromise human dignity and wholeness.

What role does this title play in Luke? First, in about a third of its uses, the Greek noun *kyrios* refers clearly and distinctively to Israel's God. Most of these instances appear in Luke's birth narrative (Luke 1–2), which plays an important role in tipping the hand of Luke's theological agenda. Here, the repeated references to God as "the Lord" establish that Jesus's power originates with the God of Israel. Early on, devotion to the Lord— expressed by Zechariah, Mary, and Simeon—lays the groundwork for reverence shown toward this child Jesus as well.

Within these opening chapters, Luke also calls Jesus "Lord" unequivocally in two instances and suggestively in a third. First, Elizabeth calls Mary the "mother of my Lord" (Luke 1:43), affirming the infant's authority even *in utero*. Even more emphatically, the messenger greets frightened shepherds by identifying the child born in Bethlehem as "a savior, the messiah, the lord" (Luke 2:11 AT). This triad of titles binds together the deliverance the infant will bring as "savior," his status as the "anointed," and the authority already invested in him as "lord." Together, these roles will coalesce, for Luke, as God's plan unfolds in the person and work of Jesus.

The third use of the title "lord" in Luke's birth narrative connects Jesus's authority with God's in a more nuanced way. In this instance, John's father Zechariah predicts his son's destiny in these terms: "You, child, will be called a prophet of the Most High, / for you will go before the Lord to prepare his way. / You will tell his people how to be saved / through the forgiveness of their sins" (Luke 1:76-77). In one sense, Luke identifies the Most High (God) with "the Lord." As God's authorized messenger, John "will go before the Lord," as does Isaiah's voice (see Isa 40:3). As in Isaiah, this way of "salvation" is God's way, and the people are God's people. Yet in another sense, Luke depicts John as harbinger of Jesus himself; it is his ways, as the anointed one, toward which John will point (see Luke 3:16-17).

This nuanced relationship between God's lordship and Jesus's appears throughout the Gospel, as Luke's Jesus often refers to "the Lord" in ways that hold together both his distinction from God and his intimate involvement in God's redemptive purposes. Several passages anchor Jesus's messianic career in relation to God's Lordship. First, in response to Satan's wilderness testing, Jesus affirms exclusive worship of the one *"Lord"* (Luke 4:8) and cites a prohibition against testing *"the Lord your God"* (Luke 4:12). In both cases, Jesus places himself under God's authority in an exclusive sense. In the passage that follows, Jesus introduces his public ministry by reading the Isaiah scroll in the synagogue at Nazareth. Here, he cites the prophet, affirming that *"the Spirit of the Lord is upon me"* (Luke 4:18) and proclaiming the *"year of the Lord's favor"* (Luke 4:19) has arrived. In these claims, Jesus both affirms that God is Lord and takes the mantle of that authority upon himself.

For Luke, Jesus manifests the spirit God had imparted to him throughout his career. For one thing, his curative powers evince God's healing presence, since Luke says that "the power of the Lord was with Jesus to heal" (Luke 5:17). It is not surprising, then, that many characters in the story call him "lord" (*kyrie*). While this term of direct address may simply convey respect, it appears in Luke on the lips of those who bear witness to Jesus's authoritative word or deed. Most frequently in Luke, it is Peter or other disciples who call Jesus "lord" (Luke 5:8; 9:54; 10:17, 40; 11:1; 12:41; 13:23; 17:37; 19:8; 22:33, 38, 49), reflecting the master-student relationship of authority that he has forged with them. Elsewhere, beneficiaries of Jesus's healing power affirm his authority by addressing him as "lord" (Luke 5:12; 7:6; 18:41). Together, then, Luke uses these encounters to suggest that God's lordship can be seen in Jesus's.

Within the Travel Narrative (Luke 9:51–19:27), Luke often uses the term as a name for Jesus. Once again, the title frequently appears where Jesus displays his power or authority. Sometimes, it is his teaching that leads to his identification as "lord." Thus Jesus is "the Lord" who instructs

Mary and Martha (Luke 10:39, 41), teaches Jewish tradition (Luke 11:39; 13:15), and explains parables (Luke 12:42; 17:5, 6; 18:6). In other instances, Jesus "the Lord" gives life (Luke 7:13) or appoints others to extend his messianic mission (Luke 10:1). And after the passion, his disciples link his lordship to resurrection power, announcing that "the Lord really has risen" (Luke 24:34). In all of these cases, Luke frames Jesus's identity as "the Lord" against the backdrop of his messianic authority, in either word or deed.

Elsewhere in the Travel Narrative, Luke reinterprets earlier traditions about God's coming kingdom (found in both Mark and Q) to portray Jesus's lordship in relation to God's. For instance, Luke uses two parables about a master's delayed return to promote faithfulness in the meantime (Luke 12:35-48; 19:11-27; see Matt 24:42-51; 25:14-30). On the narrative level, the "master" in each case seems to be God, whose kingdom has not yet fully dawned. But Luke's audience still awaited the (second) coming of Jesus as "Lord," so the parables promote their watchful anticipation of his return as well. In any case, the parables reflect Luke's view that links lordship—both God's and Jesus's—with the establishment of God's power on earth.

What then can we infer about Jesus's identity as "the Lord" in a Gospel that clearly applies the title to both Jesus and God, often preserving the distinction between them (see Luke 10:21; 20:37)? An interpretive key may lie in two of the Gospel's three instances where Jesus seems to accept the epithet—all of which derive from either Mark or Q.[9] In the first, Jesus asks, "Why do you call me 'Lord, Lord,' and don't do what I say?" (Luke 6:46; see Matt 7:21-22). Here, Jesus takes for granted his lordship rather than asserting it. As noted above, those who participate in his mission as disciples or benefit from it typically address him as "Lord." Yet Jesus suggests that simply naming him as Lord is of little value. His followers legitimize his identity as Lord only when their actions conform to his teaching about God's kingdom.

---

9. Besides the cases discussed here, Luke includes Jesus's oblique self-reference as the "Son of the Human [who] is lord of the Sabbath" (Luke 6:5 AT; cf. Mark 2:28; Matt 12:8).

In a second passage, Luke uses a tradition from Mark to describe preparations for Jesus's entry into Jerusalem. When he instructs two disciples to retrieve a colt from a nearby village, Jesus tells them to explain to anyone who asks, "The Lord needs it" (Luke 19:31 AT; Mark 11:3; see also Matt 21:3). Yet Luke modifies the underlying tradition in two ways that cast Jesus's lordship in an intriguing light. First, only in Luke do the disciples repeat these words, thus underscoring their narrative significance. Second, Luke calls the colt's owners "lords" (AT; CEB has "owners"; Greek: *kyrioi*). For Luke, of course, their authority over the animal is only provisional; ultimately the colt will serve the need of "the Lord." But who is this "Lord"? On one level, the "Lord" who needs the colt is Jesus, who will ride on its back. From this angle, Jesus asserts his prerogative over that of the so-called lords. But in the triumphal entry passage that follows, onlookers hail Jesus as the "king who comes in the name of the Lord" (Luke 19:38; see Mark 11:9; Matt 21:9), suggesting that Jesus appears not *as the Lord* but *in the Lord's stead*. What are we to make of this tension?

To answer this question, we return to Psalm 110, which Luke cites in the following chapter. Here, Jesus seems to deny the messiah's Davidic lineage when he asks, "How can they say that the Christ is David's son?" (Luke 20:41 AT; Mark 12:35; see also Matt 22:45). He then uses the opening clause of Psalm 110 to maintain that David's son and his "Lord" cannot be the same figure. On the one hand, this tradition may work to tone down any sense in which Jesus's (Davidic) messiahship introduced a political or military threat (see *Psalms of Solomon* 17:21). But the interchange also contributes two insights to our study of Luke's designation of Jesus as "Lord." First, it forges a literary connection between messiahship and lordship, since Jesus equates "the Christ" with the one David would call "my Lord." Second, that messianic lordship derives not from human but from divine power. It is God the Lord who will subdue the "enemies," even as the Christ will "sit right beside" God (Ps 110:1; 109:1 LXX).

Together, the nuanced uses of this title throughout Luke establish Jesus's status as God's designated, and fully authorized, representative of divine lordship over the earth. In this depiction, Jesus remains both separate from and intimately aligned with the "Lord God" as he embodies God's lordship on the earth. For Luke, Jesus is "the Lord" because he shows the world what God's sovereign power looks like. Though Jesus's lordship does not mean he aspires to (provisional) political power, it does mean he exercises (ultimate) divine power, unleashed on the earth as God's anointed one.

How does Luke's view of Jesus's lordship relate to the messianic community? On the one hand, it is important to note that neither the narrator nor Jesus ever calls the disciples "lords." Besides the colt's owners mentioned above, such an ascription among humans is reserved for Jesus himself. On the other hand, as the Gospel story culminates in Jerusalem, Jesus shares a last meal with his disciples, where he instructs his followers about the nature of lordship—both his and theirs as well. First, Jesus tells his followers to divide a cup "among yourselves" (Luke 22:17), suggesting that they will share his destiny (cf. Mark 10:38). Then, Jesus contrasts "lordship" of "kings of the Gentiles" with its practice "among you" (Luke 22:25-26; cf. Mark 10:42). Though their lordship is implicit rather than explicit, Jesus teaches his followers to exercise authority not as "authority over" but by assuming the posture of a servant. That is, their pattern of lordship derives from their Lord Jesus, who in turn reflects the Lordship of their God.

For Luke's community, the message about lordship is both clear and subtly subversive. On the political level, they lived as residents of a first-century Mediterranean world, ruled by the "lordship" of the "kings of the Gentiles." On the religious level, other potential "lords" promised protection and good fortune in exchange for devotion and allegiance. Thus the lordship of Jesus, and the God whose power he manifests, appears in stark contrast to other patterns of political or religious "lordship."

Luke thus uses the title toward at least two ends that address the original audience. First, the close link between Jesus and Yahweh authenticates his story as one rooted in relationship to Israel's God, as part of the unfolding story of Jewish scripture. In this sense, Jesus's messianic lordship promotes exclusive devotion to the one God of Israel, whose coming reign is manifest in and through this anointed agent. Second, Luke uses the language of lordship to redefine prevailing notions of power. For Luke's community, Jesus's divine authority grows apparent neither in political posturing nor personal gain, but through words and deeds that affirm human dignity and wholeness especially among those on the bottom side of earthly power: the poor, the captives, the blind, the oppressed (Luke 4:18). As heirs to his legacy, Luke's audience reflect Jesus's lordship whenever they join in this countercultural enactment of divine power.

The Gospel of John: Jesus as "Christ"

Already we have seen that, of all NT Gospels, John is clearest about its christological intent, since the writer promotes explicit belief "that Jesus is the Christ, God's Son" and thus offer readers "life in his name" (John 20:31). Yet the Fourth Gospel's keen interest in Jesus as "the Christ" is, in some respects, paradoxical, since this account seems farthest from the messianic worldview that heralds God's coming kingdom. Indeed, the word *kingdom* (*basileia*) appears only five times, and in just two passages (John 3:3, 5; John 18:36 [3x]). Where it does occur, the term seems to convey a personal, spiritual experience in the present (e.g., John 3:3, 5; 18:36). And when future resurrection and reign remain faintly in view, the salvation to which they lead has more to do with personal destiny than cosmic renewal. Together, these factors lead us to reconsider the meaning of the "Christ" in John. Has this writer radically interpreted the term, removing it from its Jewish native soil and reinterpreting it in light of Greek thought?

The "Christ" in Jewish Tradition

It turns out that John's view of Jesus as the Christ may not be as far removed from Jewish thought as many assume. In what follows, we review selected Jewish traditions that shed light on the Fourth Gospel's view of Jesus's messianic identity. Rather than setting aside Jewish expectation for God's coming kingdom, John both adopts and adapts it in light of Jesus's mission and the community's own setting.

One messianic motif in Second Temple Judaism that plays an influential role in John is that of the anointed king. After the exile and return to Jerusalem, the prophetic and scribal traditions looked both backward to the golden age of David's rule and forward to a Davidic messiah who would preside over the restored covenant people. These hopes are rooted in earlier prophecy, as the eighth-century BCE prophet Isaiah promises that "a shoot will grow up from the stump of Jesse" (Isa 11:1)—that is, out of the Davidic line. After the exiles' return to the land, Zechariah's apocalypse envisions a "day of the Lord" when the "splendor of David's house" is restored (Zech 12:1–13:1). Though the earlier traditions in Zechariah refer to two "anointed ones" (Zech 4:14)—a priest and a king—the later chapters merge religious and royal leadership as they look forward to Jerusalem's restoration. Closer to John's time, such messianic hope appears in the *Psalms of Solomon*, where the writer implores God to "raise up . . . their king, the son of David" (*Psalms of Solomon* 17:21) to "purge Jerusalem" of foreign rulers. Though John revises such messianic hopes, the motif of anointed kingship plays an important part in the Fourth Gospel's depiction of Jesus as the anointed one.

Jesus's appearance as a prophet like Moses (Deut 18:18) also contributes in important ways to John's account of his messiahship. Though first-century Judaism did not generally assume a connection between messiah and prophet, some writers add a prophetic overlay to the role of the messianic king. For instance, Josephus rewrites the 1 Samuel account of David's accession to the throne by reporting that, under the influence of the "divine spirit," David "began to prophesy."[10] Thus he undergirds David's status as anointed king with a prophetic calling. Though written later, the *Isaiah Targum* probably preserves a first-century strain of messianic Jewish thought in its rendering of Isa 11:1-2: "A *king* shall come forth from the *sons* of Jesse, and *the messiah* shall be exalted from the *sons of* his *sons*. And upon him shall rest *the* spirit of *prophecy*."[11] This targumic flourish both slants the text in a messianic direction and imports the motif of prophecy. Finally, the Dead Sea Scrolls include a cryptic allusion to "Moses His anointed" (4Q377 2 II 5). While elsewhere the Scrolls speak of royal and

---

10. Josephus, *Jewish Antiquities*, 6.8.2, trans. H. St. J. Thackeray and Ralph Marcus (Cambridge, MA: Harvard University Press, 1934).

11. See Bruce D. Chilton, *The Isaiah Targum*, The Aramaic Bible 11 (Wilmington, NC: Glazier, 1987), 28.

priestly messiahs (1QS 9:11), here Moses appears as one anointed by God. Since Moses is the one through whom God gave the Jewish law, hope for renewal grounded in God's righteousness—disclosed in Torah—remains in many instances closely associated with a prophet like Moses (see Mal 3:4-5).

The "Christ" in John

Against the backdrop of messianic hopes for a Davidic king imbued with prophetic powers, John portrays Jesus as "the Christ" in ways that both carry forward and radically revise such expectation. In John's account, Jesus engages—and often corrects—others' views about the messiah that do not fit his own story. The Fourth Gospel thus provides an intriguing window into messianic thought as it continued to develop in generations after Jesus's death.

One question that recurs throughout the Fourth Gospel has to do with Jesus's origins, or where he "comes from." For one thing, John seems unaware of traditions that establish Jesus's ties with Bethlehem (see Matt 2:6-7) and the house of David (see Luke 2:4). As a result, John reinterprets messianic expectation in light of Jesus's well-known Galilean roots. In this Gospel, two different groups object to Jesus's messianic identity on the grounds of his origins. One says that their familiarity with Jesus's native region means he is not the messiah, since "when the Christ comes, no one will know where he is from" (John 7:27; see *1 Enoch* 48:6). Others address his Galilean origins more directly: "Didn't the scripture say that the Christ comes from David's family and from Bethlehem, David's village?" (John 7:42). Rather than directly refuting either tradition, John's Jesus simply rewrites the messianic script. In this Gospel, Jesus's native landscape is heaven itself: he has come "down from heaven" (John 6:38) and is "from God" (John 8:42). Thus Jesus's heavenly origin allows him to sidestep both criteria at once: on the one hand, his detractors do not "know where he is from," and his divine home only confirms that he has been set apart by God.

Besides revising expectations about Jesus's origins, the Fourth Gospel also takes up the question of Jesus's identity as the anointed king. Early in the Gospel, some recognize him as "king" (John 1:49) or even try to "force him to be their king" (John 6:15). But it is in the Passion Narrative that John establishes Jesus's messianic kingship while revising prevailing expectations about his royal office. In what many take to be an authentic tradition, Jesus's entry into Jerusalem in John identifies him as the "messiah" (John 12:12-19 AT; cf. Mark 11:1-10; Matt 21:1-11; Luke 19:28-40). For one thing, only in John do the crowds hail him as "king of Israel" (John 12:13). Further, John explains that Jesus sat on a "young donkey" in fulfillment of Zechariah's prophecy about the coming messiah (John 12:15 AT; Zech 9:9).

If Jesus enters Jerusalem as messianic king, John uses the story of his interrogation by Pilate to reinterpret his identity as the Christ. As in the Synoptic Gospels, the Roman prefect seems reluctant to prosecute Jesus. But only in John does their conversation lead to Jesus's reflection on the nature of his kingdom. When Pilate asks, "Are you king of the Jews?" (John 18:33), Jesus replies, "My kingdom doesn't originate from this world. If it did, my guards would fight so that I wouldn't have been arrested by the Jewish leaders. My kingdom isn't from here" (John 18:36). Not only does Jesus return to the question of origins (his kingdom is not "from here"), but he also distinguishes the nature of his power from other messianic figures of the time. For one thing, he flatly rejects the possibility of violent uprising. Unlike the Zealots whose rebellion led to Jerusalem's destruction decades after his death, Jesus locates his kingly power in the heavenly realm. When Pilate then asks if Jesus is, indeed, a "king," Jesus answers obliquely: "You say that I am a king. I was born and came into the world for this reason: to testify to the truth" (John 18:37). For John, the truth about Jesus's messiahship leads in turn to his exalted death as witness to God's presence and power in the world.

Besides Jesus's identity as anointed king—albeit one whose kingdom is not "from here"—the Fourth Gospel emphasizes Jesus's identity as an anointed prophet whose words and deeds bear witness to his messiahship. While in the Synoptic Gospels, Jesus takes a dim view of "signs" (Mark 8:11-13; Matt 16:1-4; Luke 11:29-32), John finds in Jesus's signs convincing proof that he is God's anointed one. Not only does John expressly link

Jesus's signs to his identity as the "Christ" (John 20:30-31), but the Gospel's first eleven chapters constitute the Book of Signs because they make the case, in one episode after another, for Jesus's messiahship. Together, these signs confirm Jesus's identity as a prophet like Moses, since like Moses, he manifests God's power and presence in the world.

For one thing, the signs confirm his access to divine power. The miracle at Cana makes this point, revealing Jesus's "glory" through his ability to transform water into wine—and "good wine" at that (John 2:1-12). Later, Jesus's healing of a blind man raises the question of his messianic identity. Having witnessed the sign, the man's parents are afraid to speak about it, "because the Jewish authorities had already decided that whoever confessed Jesus to be the Christ would be expelled from the synagogue" (John 9:22). Thus John forges a clear connection between Jesus's healing power and his messianic status. And Jesus's final and most dramatic sign only further confirms that he is the messiah. After he revives Lazarus (John 11:1-17), Martha responds with this affirmation: "I believe that you are the Christ, God's Son, the one who is coming into the world" (John 11:27).

Besides his manifestation of divine power, John's Jesus appears as a prophetic messiah through his access to divine knowledge. For instance, when Jesus calls Nathanael, he says, "Before Philip called you, I saw you under the fig tree" (John 1:48; see Zech 3:10). This knowledge convinces Nathanael that Jesus is "king of Israel" (John 1:49)—that is, a messiah with prophetic insight. Likewise, the Samaritan woman calls Jesus the "Christ" because of his prescience: since the coming one will "teach everything to us" and Jesus accurately recounts her marital history, she considers the possibility that he is the "messiah" (John 4:25-29). Together, then, both Jesus's miraculous power and his divine insight lead believers to ask, "When the Christ comes, will he do more miraculous signs than this man does?" (John 7:31). As a prophet like Moses, Jesus acts as specially designated agent of divine power and knowledge and confirms, for John, that he is indeed the messiah.

Indeed, Jesus's relationship to Moses is an important part of John's portrait of this messiah. Like Matthew, John both validates Moses's witness and thinks that Moses points toward Jesus's messiahship. For one thing, the Gospel's prologue summarizes the messianic era Jesus inaugu-rates this way: "As the Law was given through Moses, / so grace and truth came into being through Jesus Christ" (John 1:17). Thus John suggests that the Law of Moses has prepared for, even led toward, the messianic age. Indeed, Philip calls Jesus the one "Moses wrote about in the Law and the Prophets" (John 1:45). As if to underscore this positive relationship, Jesus says, "If you believed Moses, you would believe me" (John 5:46).

Yet John also forges a sharp distinction between those who believe that Jesus is "the Christ" and those who call themselves "Moses' disciples" (John 9:28). As in Matthew, Jesus takes issue not with Moses or the law but with those who do not keep the law (John 7:19). For the Fourth Gos-pel, Jesus embodies the fullest expression of the "Law and the Prophets" (John 1:45) and so appears as one sent into the world to inaugurate the messianic age. If those devoted to Moses remain unconvinced of his iden-tity as the Christ, John thinks they have misunderstood Moses's witness.

Ultimately, Jesus's identity as the messiah grows clearest, for John, in his sacrificial self-denial. After Jesus's entry into Jerusalem, for instance, Gentiles seek to honor him as the "Christ." John's Jesus responds by quali-fying his messiahship in this way: "I assure you that unless a grain of wheat falls into the earth and dies, it can only be a single seed. But if it dies, it bears much fruit. Those who love their lives will lose them, and those who hate their lives in this world will keep them forever" (John 12:24-25). Not only that, but in John's account, Jesus's teaching about self-denial appears just after his kingly ride into the seat of religious and political power. This move constitutes an emphatic reframing of messianic hopes in light of Jesus's destiny.

Drawing together a range of traditions, then, the Fourth Gospel tells the story of Jesus the messiah. Along the way, John both reaffirms Jew-ish messianic hopes and adjusts them in light of Jesus's life, death, and resurrection. In John, Jesus bears the life-giving power associated with the messianic age. As a prophet like Moses, he is anointed by God to show the "way" to the Father (see John 14:4-6) by teaching his followers to "keep my commandments" (John 14:15; 15:10)—especially the commandment to "love one another as I have loved you" (John 13:34 AT; 15:12). As messianic king, he reigns in a kingdom characterized by eternal life rather than by earthly force. In these respects and others, Jesus appears as the Jewish messiah who embodies and expands hopes for enduring human life.

As much as the Fourth Gospel emphasizes Jesus's *identity* as the messiah, though, the story also works to expose the *implications* of his messiahship for those who believe in him. For one thing, John says that believers come to "know God and Jesus, whom God has sent" (John 17:3 AT). As a result, they secure "eternal life" (see, e.g., John 3:15-16; 3:36; 5:24; and so on). Because they are "born anew" into God's kingdom (John 3:3), they take up residence in the "kingdom [that] doesn't originate from this world" (John 18:36), a kingdom that both transcends and eclipses all notions of earthly power. In the end, the eternal life his followers gain by believing in Jesus the messiah means that they "hate their lives in this world" (John 12:25) and thus follow his self-emptying way of sacrifice.

The Fourth Gospel thus makes a robust case for Jesus's identity as "the Christ" that both engages traditional Jewish hopes for God's kingdom and recasts them in light of Jesus's career as well as the community's own setting. On the one hand, this "messiah" is an anointed prophet-king endowed with divine power and knowledge. On the other hand, his kingdom is not of this world, and his ultimate self-offering manifests the very life-giving power of God. For John's community, such a portrait of Jesus's messiahship helped make sense both of his destiny and of their own circumstance.

After all, for John's community, the belief that Jesus was indeed the Jewish messiah set them apart from the wider stream of rabbinic Judaism from which they had emerged. For the rabbis, God's way of life was disclosed in Moses and the interpretation of Torah. To the degree that they held out messianic hopes, those hopes mostly meant that God's rule would supplant Rome's, in an earthly sense. For many, the claim that the messiah had come stood at odds with both Jesus's death on a Roman cross and the enduring harsh reality of military occupation. What is more, Jesus's messianic call to self-sacrifice may have seemed downright foolish in light of such oppressive force.

For John's audience, then, this Gospel both reiterates that Jesus *was* the messiah and, perhaps more importantly, establishes *what kind* of messiah he was. From their vantage point decades after Jesus's death, expectations for the end of the present age were fading from view. As a result, John recalibrated the core belief in Jesus's messiahship in ways that addressed the community's setting. First, John points to Jesus's "signs" evidence of God's life-giving power wielded by this anointed one. Second, John transposes the coming kingdom into a present, spiritual dimension called "eternal life," secured through trust in Jesus as messiah-king. And third, John portrays the Christ's death and resurrection as the exemplary reflection God's sacrificial love for the world, unleashed in the messianic age. In all these ways, the Fourth Gospel traces out the contours of Jesus's messiahship so that it leads, for those who believe in him, to "life to the fullest" (John 10:10).

Concluding Thoughts

In this chapter, we have explored titles that each Gospel uses to depict Jesus's messianic identity. By calling Jesus "Son of the Human," "God's Son," "Lord," and "Christ," the evangelists connect Jesus's story with traditions that have come before and further expose the messianic contours of his mission. Both the titles' background in Jewish thought and their use in each Gospel lead to three synthetic observations about the evangelists' view of Jesus's messianic identity.

First, though modern studies in Gospel Christology tend to focus on Jesus's ontological status—that is, Jesus's (divine) nature—our findings here suggest a different direction for our inquiry. For rather than emphasizing Jesus's identity in an exclusive or isolated sense, the Gospels employ names taken from Jesus's Jewish landscape to interpret his messianic function. In each case, the favored title captures Jesus's role as one who establishes a foothold for God's reign on the earth, among the faithful.

Second, the messianic title that dominates each Gospel fits the wider narrative tendencies of the evangelist's story. Mark's apocalyptic story thus features the enigmatic but iconic "Son of the Human," who presides over God's coming kingdom and the new world order it establishes. Matthew's Torah-centered portrait of Jesus associates his identity as "God's Son" with the righteousness that lies at the heart of Jewish practice. Luke's depiction of Jesus's relationship to "the Lord" reconstitutes the nature of power in an imperial setting. And John's insistence that Jesus is, indeed, the "messiah" seems to appropriate and retool messianic expectation in conversation with mainstream Judaism.

Third, in each case, the Gospels use messianic titles to forge connection, rather than distinction, between Christ and community. To be sure, the Gospels ascribe privileged status to Jesus as the messiah in terms of his authority and relationship to God. While both "Son of the Human" and "Son of God" are titles that carry implicitly inclusive connotations, neither "Lord" nor "Messiah" applies, as a name, to the community. Yet in each case, Jesus's messianic identity sets the terms for the new world order he establishes. Thus those who locate themselves within God's unfolding story of redemption find in the Gospels not just evidence of Jesus's messiahship but a reminder of its bearings on their life together as well.

Study Questions

1. Explain the significance of each messianic title in Jewish thought.

2. What distinctive elements of Jesus's messianic identity seem most important to each Gospel?

3. In what ways do the Gospel writers connect Jesus's messianic identity to the identity of his followers? Give an example from each Gospel.

4. What remains distinctive about Jesus in each Gospel? How do the evangelists set him apart from his followers?

For Further Reading

Rowe, C. Kavin. *Early Narrative Christology: The Lord in the Gospel of Luke.* Grand Rapids: Baker Academic, 2009.

Casey, Maurice. *The Solution to the "Son of Man" Problem.* New York: T&T Clark, 2007.

Gathercole, Simon J. *The Pre-Existent Son: Recovering the Christologies of Matthew, Mark, and Luke.* Grand Rapids: Eerdmans, 2006.

Longnecker, Richard N., ed. *Contours of Christology in the New Testament.* Grand Rapids: Eerdmans, 2005.

Malina, Bruce J., and Jerome H. Neyrey. *Calling Jesus Names: The Social Value of Labels in Matthew.* Sonoma, CA: Polebridge, 1988.

Meeks, Wayne. *The Prophet-King: Moses Traditions and the Johannine Christology.* Leiden: Brill, 1967.

Smith, D. Moody. *The Theology of the Gospel of John.* Cambridge: Cambridge University Press, 1995.

Wink, Walter. *The Human Being: Jesus and the Enigma of the Son of Man.* Minneapolis: Fortress, 2002.

Chapter Seven
Messianic Traits

Servanthood, Righteousness, Prophetic Power, and Mystical Union

Besides using titles to identify Jesus as the Christ, the evangelists also highlight attributes that further elaborate the nature of his messiahship. The Gospel witness to Jesus thus moves beyond names to expose character traits that identify him with God's sovereign power and presence unleashed in the world. In Mark, Jesus appears as servant, while Matthew emphasizes his righteousness. Luke points to his prophetic power, while John draws into sharp focus his mystical union with God. In each case, Jesus's messianic identity grows clearer in light of these traits.

Once again, the messianic features discussed here appear in all four Gospel accounts. Yet each evangelist exhibits keen interest in certain attributes. In this sense, they fit the genre of ancient biography, which gives "particular attention to the marks and indications of the souls of men," according to the Roman writer Plutarch.[1] For the Gospels, these "marks and indications" point to Jesus's messianic identity even as they embody Jewish hopes for a world redeemed by God's kingly power. In the end, Jesus's attributes help forge important ties between Christ and community, since those who come after Jesus will continue to bear witness to the messianic age he has established.

---

1. Plutarch, *Life of Alexander*, in *Lives, VII: Demosthenes and Cicero. Alexander and Caesar*, trans. Bernadotte Perrin, Loeb Classical Library 99 (Cambridge, MA: Harvard University Press, 1919).

The Gospel of Mark: "Rather to Serve" (Mark 10:45)

As we have seen, Mark's portrait of Jesus as "servant" lies at the heart of the Gospel's central section (Mark 8:27–10:45), which features three predictions of Jesus's destiny in Jerusalem. Indeed, many take the "suffering servant" motif to be this Gospel's defining christological trait, since the story moves inexorably toward the passion. Yet the theme of servanthood works throughout Mark's story, where Jesus's service to others constitutes a defining trait of his messianic identity. More than in any other Gospel, Jesus appears in Mark as God's faithful servant *both* within his earthly ministry *and* as he turns toward the cross. In the end, Jesus's servant posture establishes an authoritative pattern for his followers to emulate.

Servanthood in Jewish Tradition

Already, we have considered in some detail the fourth Servant Song (Isa 52:13–53:12) as interpretive backdrop for Jesus's messianic sacrifice (see chapter 4). To complement our earlier discussion, we consider here the first three Servant Songs found in Second Isaiah (Isa 42:1-9; 49:1-7; 50:4-11). Together, these passages expand our view of the servant's role in Isaiah—a role that includes sacrificial suffering but goes beyond it as well. As we shall see, for Isaiah and for Mark, the servant's devotion to God as Lord subtly asserts God's life-giving sovereignty upon the earth, even where human rulers seem to rule and oppress.

Several observations about the servant in Isaiah will anchor our study of this trait in Mark's Gospel. To begin with, Isaiah uses the image of Israel as God's "servant" to cast the people's submission to their Babylonian overlords as a temporary condition.[2] Notice, for instance, Isaiah's promise of the coming new world order:

> The LORD, redeemer of Israel and its holy one,
> says to one despised,
> rejected by nations,

---

2. See chapter 3 for a discussion of the servant's collective identity.

> to the slave of rulers:
> Kings will see and stand up;
> commanders will bow down
> on account of the Lord, who is faithful,
> the holy one of Israel,
> who has chosen you. (Isa 49:7)

If the people of Israel are the "slave of rulers" for the moment, soon God's sovereign lordship will bring their vindication (see Isa 50:8). In due time, they will appear as God's "servant, / Israel, in whom I show my glory" (Isa 49:3), because the Lord is the "Redeemer of Israel" (Isa 49:7).

Besides this ultimate loyalty to God as Lord, these oracles also consistently celebrate the servant's favored status before God. In the first Servant Song, for instance, God says, "I've put my spirit upon him" (Isa 42:1). Indeed, just as the Lord "gave breath to [the earth's] people and life to those who walk on it" (Isa 42:5), so too this God has "called" and taken the servant's hand and guarded him (Isa 42:6). In the second song, the servant claims that "the Lord called me before my birth" (Isa 49:1) and that he is "honored in the Lord's eyes" (Isa 49:5). Indeed, God upholds this special status on a daily basis, as "morning by morning [God] wakens— / wakens my ear / to listen as those who are taught" (Isa 50:4 NRSV). Together, these passages establish the servant's privileged relationship to God.

This prized calling, though, carries with it a vital part in God's unfolding redemption of the whole earth. On one level, the servant will gather a dispersed and wayward people; the servant has been chosen "to restore Jacob to God, / so that Israel might return to him" (Isa 49:5). Yet since this mission seems "not enough," God expands it exponentially: "I will also appoint you as light to the nations / so that my salvation may reach to the end of the earth" (Isa 49:6; see 42:6). As God's "chosen one," then, the servant radiates the glory of God's reign throughout the whole earth.

Indeed, the servant discloses God's reign in a number of ways. First, the servant will teach others about God's kingdom. Not only do the "coastlands await his teaching" (Isa 42:4), but the servant also claims that "The Lord God gave me an educated tongue / to know how to respond to the weary / with a word" (Isa 50:4). Ultimately Isaiah equates the fear of the Lord with obeying "the voice of his servant" (Isa 50:10). This one whose mouth is "like a sharp sword" (Isa 49:2) bears God's message to those who would listen and obey.

But the servant's revelation of divine authority entails more than verbal instruction. As one who "bring[s] justice to the nations" (Isa 42:1; see 42:3), this servant manifests God's power in part by deploying it on behalf of those held captive, either physically or spiritually. This servant, then, is called "to open blind eyes, to lead the prisoners from prison, / and those who sit in darkness from the dungeon" (Isa 42:7). As we have seen in chapter 3, these deeds of power thus constitute the early signs of the restored human condition associated with God's coming reign.

Of course, to manifest God's liberating ways is also to threaten earthly powers that depend on others' oppression. Thus, the servant will be "despised" and "rejected by nations" (Isa 49:7). Yet, even in the face of abuse and scorn, God's servant does not engage in the adversaries' tactics: "I gave my body to attackers, / and my cheeks to beard pluckers. / I didn't hide my face / from insults and spitting" (Isa 50:6). Perhaps surprisingly, such vulnerability to the rulers' fierce derision only brings God's power into clearer view; indeed, it lies close at hand (Isa 50:7-8).

To be sure, none of these Servant Songs is messianic in a technical sense, since none explicitly equates the servant with the anointed one (but see Isa 61:1). Yet together they assign the faithful people a central role in God's coming redemption. As "servant" of God rather than Babylon, those who affirm God's lordship become vessels in whom divine power makes its way to earth, restoring human dignity and wholeness not through coercive violence but through vulnerable loyalty to God's just reign. In and through this chosen servant, God promises deliverance to a captive people in exile and through them, salvation to the "end of the earth."

Servanthood in Mark

The portrait of God's servant found in Second Isaiah sheds important light on Mark's witness to Jesus, who comes not "to be served but rather to serve" (Mark 10:45). For one thing, this role as servant relates, in both Isaiah and Mark, directly to God's coming kingdom, which we have found to be a central theme for this Gospel. What is more, the pattern established in Isaiah's oracles helps explain Mark's bifocal interest in Jesus's messianic power and his messianic sacrifice. Finally, the corporate notion of Isaiah's servant makes sense of the correlation Mark consistently forges between Christ and community.

Throughout much of this Gospel, connections with Isaiah's servant are more implicit than explicit. Still, the features we have detected in Second Isaiah also characterize Mark's Jesus. For instance, like Isaiah's servant, Jesus stands specially favored by God in Mark. Already in its opening chapter, the heavenly voice at baptism confirms that Jesus is God's "Son, whom I dearly love" (Mark 1:11). Later, a voice out of the cloud at the transfiguration reaffirms his identity as beloved son while adding the injunction to "listen to him" (Mark 9:7; see Isa 49:1). Near the Gospel's end, a Roman centurion at the foot of the cross confirms Jesus's privileged status: "This man was certainly God's son" (Mark 15:39).

Like the servant's mission, too, Jesus's mission in Mark begins with the restoration of Israel and reaches outward to the nations. To be sure, Jesus first appears in the Galilee, where he gathers disciples who will play a role in restoring Israel (Mark 1:16-20; see Jer 16:16). Indeed his own ministry is based in the Galilee (Mark 1:30), where he proclaims the good news, heals the sick, and casts out demons. And when he appoints the twelve apostles, he establishes the foundation of a New Israel who will inhabit God's coming (Mark 3:13-19).

Yet Jesus's itinerary in Mark takes him into Gentile territory as well, where he becomes a "light to the nations" (Isa 42:6). Jesus and his disciples cross the Sea of Galilee three times, landing in explicitly Gentile territory twice (Mark 5:1; 6:53). Jesus also travels to the "region of Tyre" (Mark 7:24), where he encounters a woman Mark identifies as "Greek, Syrophoenician by birth" (Mark 7:26). Later, he traverses "the region of the Ten Cities" (Mark 7:31), where he feeds a large Gentile crowd (Mark 8:1-10). While Jesus's journeys in Mark make little geographic sense, these details suggest that, for Mark, Jesus crosses social and religious borders to inaugurate God's coming reign both within Israel and among the nations.

Jesus also fulfills the servant's role of disclosing God's sovereign authority in both word and deed. Early on, the crowds marvel at his authoritative instruction (Mark 1:22, 27). Later, just as the servant sustains "the weary with a word" (Isa 50:4), Jesus addresses the needs of a "great crowd" by beginning to "teach them many things" (Mark 6:34). Finally, Mark underscores Jesus's role as teacher when the story's brisk narrative pace pauses for instruction about God's coming reign in Mark 4 and 13. Along the way, Jesus's instruction not only enlightens and comforts but also challenges and offends, often carrying the force of a "mouth like a sharp sword" (Isa 49:2).

Even more than this instruction, Mark uses Jesus's miraculous deeds to portray him as God's servant who opens "blind eyes" and delivers "the prisoners from prison, / and those who sit in darkness from the dungeon" (Isa 42:7). For instance, just after Jesus asks the disciples, "Don't you have eyes? Why can't you see?" (Mark 8:18), he performs a two-staged healing of a man from Bethsaida (Mark 8:22-26). As many have noted, this story signifies the progressive revelation of Jesus's messiahship: while his earthly ministry suggests its sketchy contours, his "way of the cross" will disclose its sacrificial nature.

Indeed, after three predictions of Jesus's suffering destiny, Mark's central section concludes with the healing of blind Bartimaeus (Mark 10:46-52), a story that follows Jesus's pronouncement that the Son of the Human has come not "to be served but rather to serve" (Mark 10:45). In this second story of restored sight, then, Mark presents Jesus's servanthood in a decidedly messianic light, since Bartimaeus calls him by the title "Son of David" (Mark 10:47). And this time, after Jesus opens "blind eyes" (Isa 42:7), Bartimaeus follows him "on the way" (Mark 10:52).

Finally, Mark implies that, like the servant's, Jesus's power brings freedom from darkness and imprisonment. In the story of the Gerasene demoniac (Mark 5:1-20), Mark reports that the possessed man "lived among the tombs" and had "been secured many times with leg irons and chains" (Mark 5:3-4; see 5:2, 5). The evil forces holding him captive, though, mean that "no one was ever strong enough to restrain him" (Mark 5:3; see 3:27) and "no one was tough enough to control him" (Mark 5:4).

Thus he is prisoner to a spiritual power that surpasses human strength. In response to such palpable captivity, Jesus introduces astonishing liberty. After the demons depart, Mark reports that the man was "sitting there fully dressed and completely sane" (Mark 5:15). In this story, God's power works through the servant Jesus to set the man free.

Of course, Mark's portrait of Jesus as servant culminates in Jesus's passion. Like Isaiah's suffering servant, he faces rejection and scorn (Isa 53:3), he dies through an "unjust ruling" (Isa 53:8), and he ultimately rises again (Isa 52:13). In this way, Mark portrays Jesus's life, death, and resurrection in redemptive terms, highlighting his role as God's faithful servant. Like the servant, Jesus becomes vulnerable to earthly powers, and it is that vulnerability that unleashes the true nature of God's power. After all, their violent ways will not prevail. By absorbing the full measure of earthly force, God's servant, Jesus the Christ, ultimately brings salvation and life.

If Mark depicts Jesus in servantlike terms, so too does this Gospel promote this pattern of sacrificial servanthood among those who call him Lord. Throughout this study, we have seen evidence of this pattern. Thus Jesus the servant engages others in his gathering of Israel and in his shining the light of God's glory to the nations, as he calls his disciples to "fish for people" (Mark 1:17; see Jer 16:16-18). He equips others to spread the word about God's kingdom, and he imparts divine power to those who would bring God's wholeness to the world (Mark 3:14-15; 6:12-13). Ultimately, Mark's Jesus assigns his servant posture—and the suffering destiny it brings—to his disciples: "Whoever wants to be great among you will be your servant. Whoever wants to be first among you will be the slave of all" (Mark 10:43-44). If Jesus the messiah embodies the trait of servanthood in Mark, he also models servanthood for those who, like him, would cast their loyalty with God's coming reign.

For Mark's community, Jesus's role as God's servant helps make sense not just of his messianic identity but also of their own circumstance. Like Isaiah's servant and Jesus himself, they too faced dire, even life-threatening, challenges from those whose power derived from the religious or political establishment (Mark 13:9). But Jesus's status as God's servant raises questions of ultimate allegiance. Whose servant will they be? Will they seek "greatness" based on self-protective domination like the "apparent rulers of the Gentiles" (Mark 10:42 AT)? Or will they bear the image of God's life-affirming power to the world—a power unleashed, for Isaiah's servant, for Jesus, and for Mark's own community, in vulnerable service to others? Rather than the humiliated "slave of rulers" (Isa 49:7), Mark suggests, they will find salvation and life when they become "slave of all." As God's servant, they thus participate in the reign of God as it draws near.

The Gospel of Matthew: "To Fulfill All Righteousness" (Matt 3:15)

If Mark points suggestively to Jesus's servant-like identity, Matthew makes his righteousness explicitly clear throughout this Gospel. Even a simple word count points to Matthew's editorial interest in this theme, since the word family related to the Greek word for "righteousness," *dikaiosynē*, appears some twenty-six times in Matthew. Moreover, Matthew speaks of righteousness at pivotal points in the story: Jesus declares that his baptism will "fulfill all righteousness" (Matt 3:15); the Sermon on the Mount contains frequent references to "righteousness" (Matt 5:6, 10, 20, 45; 6:1 [in the Greek], 33); and, in the Passion Narrative, Pilate's wife pronounces Jesus "righteous" (Matt 27:19 AT). Clearly, Matthew's Jesus embodies righteousness to a degree that is unparalleled in the other Gospels.

Righteousness in Jewish Tradition

Of all messianic traits discussed in this chapter, righteousness may be the one most widely associated with both individual figures and the faithful community in Jewish tradition. For texts reflecting prophetic, wisdom, and apocalyptic streams of thought together promote faithfulness to God in terms of human righteousness. What is more, they see in that righteousness evidence of God's own righteous ways prevailing on earth.

Within the book of Isaiah, for instance, righteousness appears as a defining trait for an ideal ruler as well as for the restored community that will inhabit the messianic age. On the one hand, the prophet heralds a Davidic king who will reign in peace and "with justice and righteousness" (Isa 9:7). Isaiah describes the ideal leader's rule this way: "He will judge the needy with righteousness, / and decide with equity for those who suffer in the land. / . . . Righteousness will be the belt around his hips, / and faithfulness the belt around his waist" (Isa 11:4-5; see also 16:5; 32:1). From the exile on, the oracles found in Isaiah democratize this quality of righteousness, extending it to the faithful community. In Isaiah 60, for instance, the "shoot that [God has] planted" is not an individual ruler but "the people [who] will all be righteous" (Isa 60:21). In the restored community, the people will both "seek" and "know" righteousness through God's instruction (Isa 51:1, 7). Indeed, their righteous ways (Isa 58:2) show forth God's glory and, ultimately, "make many righteous" (Isa 53:11).

The Wisdom of Solomon establishes a similar correlation between righteous rulers, especially Solomon himself, and the community, including the "day laborer who does what's right" (Wisdom 2:10). Probably written sometime in the first century CE, the pseudepigraphical writer appeals, in Solomon's name, to those "who judge the earth" to "love what is right" (Wisdom 1:1). Indeed, the plan of creation requires that human beings will "govern the world by holiness and by doing what is right" (Wisdom 9:3). Notably, this vision of righteousness applies not just to the powerful. Just as the righteous will find vindication, those oppressed and rejected by the ungodly will find their reward at the coming judgment (Wisdom 5:1, 15). What is more, both God and Wisdom herself instruct the people in righteous ways (Wisdom 8:7; 12:19).

Finally, the Similitudes of Enoch (*1 Enoch* 37–71) depict both a messianic figure and the faithful community in terms of righteousness. Like the Wisdom of Solomon, the Similitudes presuppose a gaping existential chasm between the righteous people's experience of oppression by the "strong ones" (*1 Enoch* 46:4; see also 46:7; 47:1-2) and the justice that the Lord of the Spirits will soon deliver. Their present experience notwithstanding, the writer boldly pronounces: "Blessed are you, righteous and elect ones, for glorious is your portion" (*1 Enoch* 58:2). Rather than promising the immortality of the righteous, though, the Similitudes depict their deliverance in apocalyptic terms.

Within this scheme, the messianic righteous one serves as both the heavenly embodiment of God's righteous ways and the one who imparts righteousness to his earthly counterparts, the "holy, the righteous, and the elect" (*1 Enoch* 38:4). On the one hand, the righteous one "shall reveal light to the righteous and the elect who dwell upon the earth" (*1 Enoch* 38:2). As a result, "the holy, the righteous, and the elect" will bear the "light of the Lord [that] has shined upon [their] face" (*1 Enoch* 38:4). The righteous one thus bridges the divide between heaven and earth, affirming the righteous community and endowing them with the light of God's reign.

Elsewhere in the Similitudes, the righteous community participates actively in the dawn of that reign. For instance, the "prayers of the righteous ascended into heaven" until "judgment is executed for them" (*1 Enoch* 47:1-2). Moreover, the writer promises that God will deliver kings and mighty landowners "into the hands of my elect ones" (*1 Enoch* 48:8). In other words, both the righteous one and his earthly counterparts will mete out God's impending justice and righteousness. The righteous one thus plays a mediating and paradigmatic role, as his heavenly righteousness takes root among the faithful.

In all these cases, then, righteousness characterizes both ideal figures and the communities identified with them. Ultimately, the righteousness in question reflects God's righteousness. It is God's righteous ways that confirm God's holiness (Isa 5:16), and the Wisdom of Solomon likens knowing God to "complete righteousness" (Wisdom 15:3 NRSV). This divine righteousness exists not in theory or in isolation from just human society; indeed, wherever the poor and meek find equitable judgment, God's righteousness shines most brightly.

Righteousness in Matthew

The depiction of Jesus's righteousness thus fits within Matthew's decidedly Jewish setting. And though scholars often distinguish ethical from eschatological righteousness on the one hand, or human from divine righteousness on the other, close reading of the Gospel itself yields a portrait in which such distinctions fade from view. For Matthew, righteousness is both ethical *and* eschatological, both human *and* divine. In this Gospel, righteousness becomes a defining quality of Jesus's messianic identity, as through him the kingdom of heaven takes root on earth.

But for Matthew, God's righteousness can be seen not just in Jesus but also among those who heed his call to messianic community. Like the Similitudes' righteous one, Matthew's Jesus both discloses and engenders God's righteousness among the faithful. Indeed, Matthew casts Jesus's mission within a broader stream of righteousness, running from his forebears—including both Joseph (Matt 1:19) and John the Baptist (Matt 3:15)—to those deemed righteous at the final judgment (Matt 25:37, 46). As preeminent exemplar of God's righteousness, Jesus inculcates this trait among those who seek "first and foremost God's kingdom" (Matt 6:33).

From the outset of Jesus's public career, Matthew shows keen interest in his righteousness. For one thing, Jesus appears at the baptism in response to John's call to repentance, likely taken from the Q account (see Luke 3:7-9). As we have seen in chapter 5, Matthew thus accentuates the judging task that Jesus will perform: "The shovel he uses to sift the wheat from the husks is in his hands. He will clean out his threshing area and bring the wheat into his barn. But he will burn the husks with a fire that can't be put out" (Matt 3:12). Though John does not mention righteousness explicitly, the imagery is clear: his successor will preside over God's righteous judgment at the end time (see Matt 7:24-27; 13:47-50; 25:31-46).

Yet Jesus approaches John not alone but alongside the "people from Jerusalem, throughout Judea" (Matt 3:5) who come to prepare for that judgment by way of ritual cleansing. When he sees Jesus, John protests, saying, "I need to be baptized by you" (Matt 3:14). But Jesus insists that it is "necessary to fulfill all righteousness" (Matt 3:15). In a striking move, Jesus locates himself on *John's* "righteous road" (see Matt 21:32), which will characterize, for Matthew, God's eschatological reign.

If at the baptism, Matthew's Jesus joins John's "righteous road," his most significant teaching—the Sermon on the Mount—also sketches the contours of that road for his followers. Here, Matthew's Jesus promotes righteous human behavior that will secure eschatological reward. Thus the Beatitudes promise those who are "hungry and thirsty for righteousness" will be satisfied within God's coming kingdom (Matt 5:6). And Jesus says that kingdom belongs to those persecuted "because of righteousness" (Matt 5:10 AT). And though readers sometimes assume Matthew refers to a heavenly reward in the afterlife, the Gospel itself presses toward the earthly disclosure of God's reign (see Matt 6:10).

As the Sermon continues, Jesus sets forth the way of "greater" righteousness that befits God's kingdom (see Matt 5:16-20). A series of "antitheses" combine Jesus's appeal to tradition ("you have heard that it was said") with his authoritative interpretation ("but I say to you"). Along the way, he recasts Torah's commandments on such ethical concerns as murder, adultery, divorce, oaths, and treatment of the evildoer. But again, Jesus instructs his hearers in light of the coming judgment. Those who are angry, Jesus says, "will be in danger of judgment [*krisei*]" (Matt 5:22); when body parts compromise righteousness, he warns, "It's better that you lose a part of your body than that your whole body go into hell" (Matt 5:30). In other words, the antitheses are both ethical, in that they concern human relationships, and eschatological, in that they carry ultimate implications. What is more, these teachings forge a likeness between human righteousness and the righteousness of "your heavenly Father [who] is complete in showing love to everyone" (Matt 5:48).

Besides ethical concerns, Matthew's Jesus also includes traditional religious practices in this discourse on "righteousness" (Matt 6:1-24). Notably, this chapter opens with a call to be alert against doing righteousness (AT; Greek: *dikaiosynēn*) "in front of people to draw their attention" (Matt 6:1).[3] While other Jewish writers call these acts of religious devotion "pieties," Matthew forges an explicit connection between God's righteousness and the habits that engender such righteousness among the faithful. Jesus discourages their public display, since "your Father who sees what you do in secret will reward you" (Matt 6:4, 6; see 6:18). Finally, Jesus's com-

---

3. Most English translations do not preserve the thematic bridge between Matt 5 and 6, preferring to translate the Greek word for "righteousness" as "religion" (CEB) or "piety" (NRSV).

mand to "desire first and foremost God's kingdom and God's righteousness" (Matt 6:33) weaves together ethical and eschatological dimensions of righteousness in a way that pursues God's will "on earth as it's done in heaven" (Matt 6:10). Ultimately, the Sermon concludes with warnings against evildoers (Matt 7:21-23) who face cataclysmic destruction (Matt 7:24-27). For Matthew, God's righteousness, disclosed through Jesus, also carries weighty implications for believers' eschatological destiny.

Outside the Sermon, Matthew frequently returns to the motif of righteousness. Perhaps surprisingly, the word never applies uniquely to Jesus. Two passages considered earlier in our study shed important light on this trend. First, having explained the parable of the weeds (found only in Matthew) in terms of coming judgment, Jesus promises that the "righteous will shine like the sun in their Father's kingdom" (Matt 13:43; see Dan 12:3; Phil 2:15); moreover, "at the end of the present age," "the angels will go out and separate the evil people from the righteous people" (Matt 13:49). Like Daniel and *1 Enoch*, Matthew connects righteousness with an eschatological destiny marked by glory.

The judgment of the nations "when the Son of the Human comes in his glory" (Matt 25:31 AT) also combines ethical and eschatological righteousness. Here, not only is the judging figure implicitly righteous, but he also adjudicates between righteous and unrighteous people on clearly ethical terms: their treatment of the "least of these" (Matt 25:40). At the same time, Jesus promises that the righteous will "inherit the kingdom" (Matt 25:34). Matthew's view of righteousness, then, can be seen in care for society's most vulnerable members.

Finally, an ironic editorial twist in Matthew's Passion Narrative reiterates the significance of Jesus's righteousness in this Gospel. Only in Matthew does Pilate's wife identify Jesus as "this righteous one," urging her husband to "have nothing to do with [him], for I have suffered much because of him in a dream" (Matt 27:19 AT). To translate the adjective *dikaios* as "innocent" (NRSV) is to miss Matthew's use of a Gentile woman as mouthpiece for this vital christological claim.[4] Like "righteous" Joseph

---

4. Such a move is consistent, for instance, with Matthew's genealogy, which features four women within Jesus's lineage, which is otherwise dominated by Israelite men (Matt 1:3, 5, 6, 16).

(Matt 1:19), she has gained divine knowledge through a dream, and here she approaches Pilate while he is on the "judgment seat" (Matt 27:19 NRSV). The irony of course lies in Matthew's view of true righteousness: while Jesus will be condemned by earthly powers, he stands before God's judgment seat as the "righteous man" Pilate's wife has identified.

Given the pervasive concern with righteousness in Jewish tradition, Matthew's redactional interest in the motif fits well within the Gospel's socioreligious setting. As a story that portrays Jesus as a "new Moses," Matthew makes it clear that Jesus is to be counted as one who both fulfills all righteousness—as related in the law and prophets—and cultivates righteousness among the messianic community he establishes. For Matthew, as for the Jewish traditions that shape this Gospel message, that righteousness is both ethical and eschatological. As the anointed one who heralds the dawn of God's reign upon the earth, Jesus walks a "righteous road" marked by expansive care for the vulnerable more than by religious distinction, even when such righteousness leads to suffering. For Matthew's community, still awaiting the judgment associated with God's coming kingdom, Jesus's own righteousness provides a paradigm that entails sacrifice that leads inexorably to vindication (Wisdom 5:1, 15).

The Gospel of Luke: "A Prophet Powerful in Deed and Word" (Luke 24:19 AT)

In Luke's first post-resurrection encounter, Jesus meets two men on the road to Emmaus who at first do not recognize him. They explain "the things about Jesus of Nazareth" this way: "Because of his powerful deeds and words, he was recognized by God and all the people as a prophet. But our chief priests and our leaders handed him over to be sentenced to death, and they crucified him. We had hoped he was the one who would redeem Israel" (Luke 24:19-21). Rather ironically, this report conveys their dashed hopes to the risen Lord who fulfills them, even as it offers a summary account of Luke's story of Jesus. In what follows, we consider Jesus's prophetic power in relation both to his messianic identity and to the messianic community Luke addresses.

Though some interpreters deemphasize this element of Luke's Christology as either too human or not unique enough, two observations suggest this evangelist assigns central importance to Jesus's prophetic power. First, Luke often introduces or elaborates the prophetic motif in ways that highlight Jesus's anointed—and thus messianic—identity (see, e.g., Luke 4:16-30). Second, Jesus's identity as a prophet provides a coherent framework for features that scholars widely take to be distinctive emphases in Luke's messianic story: the role of the Spirit, the motif of social reversal and inclusion, the rejection by religious leaders, and—more suggestively—even his resurrection.

Prophetic Power in Jewish Tradition

Before we turn to Luke's account, it will be helpful to situate the prophetic role in relation to God's coming reign in Jewish thought. In what sense might a prophet's career relate to the dawn of God's kingdom and especially to the "messiah" who would herald it? For our purposes, several aspects of the prophetic tradition contribute to the backdrop of Luke's christological portrait of Jesus.

Already we have seen that the Fourth Gospel depicts Jesus as a messianic prophet like Moses (see Deut 18:18; see also Mark 9:2-8 and parallels; Acts 3:22-23; 7:37). And though Second Temple writings barely mention this verse,[5] it does offer a conceptual bridge between Torah and God's coming reign. On this point, Malachi is helpful, since this prophet looks for a "messenger of the covenant" (Mal 3:1), often associated with Elijah, who will "turn the hearts of fathers to their children and the hearts of children to their fathers" (Mal 4:6 AT; see also Sir 48:1, 7-10). Here, the prophet as God's spokesperson sounds a sharp warning—a call to repentance according to covenantal values—designed to evoke a faithful response that leads to redemption.

As we have seen throughout this study, the oracles of Isaiah associate the prophetic calling with God's coming kingdom of God. We have

---

5. One passage that does allude to Deut 18:18 is 4QTest (4Q175), which weaves together several verses from the Pentateuch to herald the "prophet" whose unheeded messsage will bring a "reckoning" (vv. 1-7).

already noted that Isaiah 61, so important for Luke's portrait of Jesus, says the prophet "anointed" by the spirit declares the "year of the LORD's favor" and the reversal of fortune it brings (Isa 61:1-2; see 58:6; Luke 4:18-19). Likewise, several passages from the Dead Sea Scrolls seem to characterize Israel's prophets as "anointed," sometimes explicitly by the "spirit" (e.g., CD 2:12; see also CD 6:1; 1QM 11:7). Moreover, 11QMelchizedek identifies the one who announces the good news of God's reign (see Isa 52:7) with "[the one an]ointed of the spir[it]" (2:15-20). Finally, 4Q521 combines mention of God's messiah with a description of God's "eternal kingdom" that features many of the elements of social justice reflected in Isaiah 61: good news for the poor, release to the captives, and recovery of sight for the blind, among others (2 II 1-14).

Taken together, these representative examples provide a starting point for our study of Luke's portrait of Jesus as messianic prophet. On one level, they establish Jesus's prophetic role in relation to what has come before. Together, the biblical prophets summon the people to follow faithfully the Sinai covenant. More specifically, the prophetic message often calls for renewal of social and religious commitment to the justice that covenant stipulates. Yet the prophets also herald what lies ahead—the coming reign of God—by delivering a message of both promise and warning. For those who would heed the call to renewal, to reflect the values of God's coming kingdom, the prophet casts a vision of social order recalibrated to God's scales of justice. On the other hand, the prophet warns those working to subvert God's kingdom values of their impending judgment.

Prophetic Power in Luke

How then does Luke portray Jesus as prophet, and what implications does this messianic attribute have for Jesus's followers? To begin with, Luke includes several passages in which Jesus emphasizes his own prophetic role. For instance, in the programmatic scene at Nazareth (Luke 4:16-30), Jesus not only assumes the voice of one anointed by God's spirit by reading from the Isaiah scroll, but he adds by way of explanation that the good news heralded by the prophet has been "fulfilled" in his presence (Luke 4:21). Moreover, Luke's Jesus accounts for his coming rejection as prophet—expressed in a traditional saying (Luke 4:24; see Mark 6:4; Matt 13:57)—by likening his mission to the careers of Elijah and Elisha (Luke 4:25-27). Both in his mission to the Gentiles and in the resistance he will face, Luke's Jesus finds a biblical precedent for this role as anointed prophet.

In a story that seems crafted to forge this connection, Luke reports Jesus's raising of a widow's son (Luke 7:11-17; see 1 Kings 17:17-24; 2 Kings 4:8-37). Just as Elijah and Elisha have wielded God's life-giving power, Jesus performs this miracle of new life for a grieving widow. Besides the literary parallels, though, Luke reports the "awestruck" response from the crowd: "A great prophet has appeared among us.... God has come to help his people" (Luke 7:16). Here, Luke combines an emphasis on Jesus's prophetic identity with the notion that this "prophet" bears the very presence of God on earth.

Luke elsewhere reworks traditional sources to emphasize Jesus's prophetic calling. For instance, Luke adapts the story of the woman who anoints Jesus in ways that draw narrative attention to this role (Luke 7:36-50; see Mark 14:3-9; Matt 26:6-13). In Luke's account, Jesus dines at a Pharisee's home and there allows a woman identified as a "sinner" (Luke 7:37, 39) to anoint him. Jesus's host reflects on the event by both acknowledging and questioning Jesus's prophetic reputation: "If this man were a prophet, he would know what kind of woman is touching him...that she is a sinner" (Luke 7:39). For Luke, though, the Pharisee's musings are deeply ironic. While they assume Jesus does not know the woman's status and so cannot be a prophet, Luke thinks Jesus's association with sinners only confirms his prophetic role (see Luke 5:32). And since Luke places this story early in Jesus's earthly ministry, the sinful woman's "anointing" signals divine confirmation of Jesus's entire prophetic career, not just his death (cf. Mark 14:8; Matt 26:12).

After Jesus sets his face toward Jerusalem (Luke 9:51), Luke introduces the lament over Jerusalem, likely taken from Q (see Matt 23:37-39), with a conversation that highlights Jesus's rejection as prophet. After a warning from some Pharisees that Herod "wants to kill you" (Luke 13:31), Jesus explains his movement away from Herod's domain—Galilee and Perea—

not in terms of self-preservation or escape but in terms of his prophetic destiny: "Look, I'm throwing out demons and healing people today and tomorrow, and on the third day I will complete my work. However, it's necessary for me to travel today, tomorrow, and the next day because it's impossible for a prophet to be killed outside of Jerusalem" (Luke 13:32-33). Like the prophets of old—especially Elijah and Elisha—Jesus wields divine power to defeat the forces of evil. Here, Luke combines this prophetic power with his impending prophetic rejection, forging an explicit identification with the prophets Jerusalem has historically killed.

Finally, Luke's post-resurrection story of two men on the Emmaus road points to Jesus's role as a "prophet mighty in deed and word before God and all the people" (Luke 24:19 NRSV). What the men fail to grasp is not Jesus's messianic identity—he is, in Luke, a prophet mighty in deed and word—but the fact that this prophet has accomplished the redemption of Israel (Luke 24:21). As prophet, Luke's Jesus has played a typical role as mediator between God and "all the people"—a phrase that nicely captures Luke's inclusive vision of the messianic kingdom.

Besides portraying Jesus's identity as anointed prophet in an explicit way, Luke elsewhere depicts his prophetic legacy more subtly, often positioning his career in continuity with "ancient prophets" (Luke 9:8, 19) who have come before him. For one thing, Jesus affirms his predecessors' place in God's coming reign, where those excluded from it will see "Abraham, Isaac, Jacob, and all the prophets in God's kingdom" (Luke 13:28). Luke's Jesus also positions both his mission and John the Baptist's in continuity with prophetic tradition. Noting that, "Until John, there was only the Law and the Prophets," he adds, "Since then, the good news of God's kingdom is preached" (Luke 16:16; see Isa 52:7). Though the saying leaves open the question of who proclaims the "good news"—Jesus and John, or just Jesus—both figures build on the message conveyed in the Jewish prophetic tradition. Finally, in Luke's distinctive story of the rich man and Lazarus (Luke 16:19-31), Abraham twice refuses to provide additional warning to the condemned man's brothers, explaining that "they have Moses and the Prophets" (Luke 16:29; see 16:31). Like these "ancient prophets," Luke's Jesus points out the covenant's ethical mandate while noting the dire consequences that await those who fail to follow it.

For Luke, Jesus's identity as messianic prophet sets the terms for his followers' prophetic calling as well. Already, we have seen that Luke highlights the miraculous powers wielded by those sent in Jesus's name (Luke 10:1-20). Like Elijah and Elisha, and like Jesus himself, they perform deeds of power associated with God's defeat of evil, resistant forces (Luke 10:18). Indeed, their witness to Jesus's prophetic ministry affords them unprecedented insight: "I assure you that many prophets and kings wanted to see what you see and hear what you heard, but they didn't" (Luke 10:24). In Luke's view, Jesus's followers have become privileged witnesses to the disclosure of "all things" (Luke 10:22) in this prophet-messiah.

For Luke, though, Jesus's prophetic office extends to the disciples mostly after his resurrection. When the risen Lord explains the fulfillment of scripture, he includes not only his own messianic destiny (Luke 24:46) but also its aftermath: "a change of heart and life for the forgiveness of sins must be preached in his name to all nations, beginning from Jerusalem" (Luke 24:47). That is, the "witnesses of these things" will carry forward Jesus's prophetic task (Luke 24:48) once they have been "furnished with heavenly power" (Luke 24:49; see Acts 1:8). Jesus thus confirms an earlier promise to "send prophets and apostles to them and they will harass and kill some of them" (Luke 11:49; see 13:34-35). If Luke's Jesus bears the prophetic power wielded by Israel's prophets before him, so too does he insist that "prophets and apostles" will continue to disclose God's kingdom.

Of course, the faithful community's prophetic calling grows clearer in the book of Acts. Like Jesus who was "anointed" by the "Spirit of the Lord" (Luke 4:18), the disciples too are "filled with the Holy Spirit" (Acts 2:4) on Pentecost and, as a result, testify to Jesus's prophetic, messianic mission. What is more, Peter's opening address in Acts begins by citing Joel's promise of God's spirit pouring out "on all people" (Acts 2:17; see Joel 2:28 LXX). Like Jesus, too, the spirit-filled messengers face rejection and persecution, even to the point of death (Acts 7:54-60). Yet

Jesus's relentlessly inclusive vision of God's just reign extends, through the post-resurrection community, from Jerusalem to the "end of the earth" (Acts 1:8; see 28:28).

Luke's broadly imperial setting makes good sense of this prophetic emphasis. Written in part to legitimize Jesus's messianic career and the movement that carried it forward after his death, this Gospel makes it clear that Jesus belongs to an established socioreligious landscape as anointed Jewish prophet. That is, he points authoritatively to God's renewal of the whole world. Thus Luke accounts for the "foolishness" of Jesus's fate (see 1 Cor 1:23) by noting that Israel's prophets have shared his destiny (Luke 13:33). For Luke, such a prophetic portrait diminishes neither Jesus's messianic significance nor his distinctive role in God's plan of salvation. He is the channel through whom the prophetic tradition must run, in Luke's view. Among prophets, Luke's Jesus emerges as preeminent, authoritative, and even the decisive turning point in God's story. Yet the channel does not stop with him. Luke's portrait of Jesus's own spirit-filled mission leads rather seamlessly to the community's spirit-filled mission. As they continue to proclaim God's coming kingdom in deed and word, they bear witness to the messiah in whose life, death, and resurrection it has dawned. Through them, "a change of heart and life for the forgiveness of sins must be preached in his name to all nations, beginning from Jerusalem" (Luke 24:47).

The Gospel of John: "I and the Father Are One" (John 10:30)

While all the NT Gospels maintain that Jesus shares an intimate relationship with God, the Fourth Evangelist makes Jesus's oneness with God a defining messianic trait. Not only does the Prologue (John 1:1-18) present Jesus as the human being ("flesh") in whom God has taken up residence (*eskēnōsen*; John 1:14), but throughout the Gospel, Jesus also frequently alludes to his unity (e.g., John 10:30) and mutual indwelling with the Father (e.g., John 10:38; 14:10, 20; 17:11, 21-23). Moreover, John's Jesus claims to disclose the Father in a definitive sense: "I am the way, the truth, and the life. No one comes to the Father except through me. If you have really known me, you will also know my Father. From now on you know him and have seen him" (John 14:6-7). In all these ways, then, scholars widely agree that Jesus's intimacy with the Father emerges a prominent christological attribute in John's portrait of Jesus.

Scholars differ, though, on the question of the Gospel's inconsistent claims about Jesus's divine nature. After all, statements that point to his union with God stand in some tension with other sayings that maintain distinction between Jesus and "the Father." Some explain this tension by attributing it to different sources that the evangelist has combined, if clumsily. Others suggest the Gospel itself grew over time, adding sayings that reflect developing ideas about the person of Jesus and his relationship to God. Our study takes a different tack. Without setting aside either hypothesis, the discussion that follows explores the notion that, in its final form, John's portrait of Jesus's mystical union with God encompasses *both* his identity as God's "only son" (*monogenous*; John 1:14) *and* his separateness from, even subordination to, the "only God" (John 5:44). Read in this light, even Jesus's "way" of intimate indwelling with God becomes an inclusive rather than exclusive trait.

Union with God in Jewish Tradition

We explore the question of conceptual background in a rather focused way: Where, in Jewish tradition, does God make a "home" on earth? Where else do we find union with God that yields authoritative exposition (*exēgēsis*, John 1:18) of God's ways for the world? As we shall see, John depicts Jesus's intimacy with God in ways that both adopt and adapt Hellenistic Judaism in light of the conviction that Jesus was, indeed, God's anointed one.

In the wilderness narrative, God instructs Moses to build a portable sanctuary "so I can be present among" the people (Exod 25:8). Not only will this tabernacle provide the sacred space for the sacrifices commanded in Exodus, but it will also house the ark of the covenant, where God promises to "meet with you" and "deliver to you all that I command you concerning the Israelites" (Exod 25:22). Already, then, Israel's sacred lore insists that this God seeks a presence in the midst of the people for the express purpose of interactive instruction.

As the story progresses, God defers David's proposed temple to the reign of Solomon. God's reticence about inhabiting a permanent building may stem from the editors' exilic or post-exilic perspective; God's "traveling around in a tent and in a dwelling" (2 Sam 7:6) implies a divine portability that would have been vital to those who left Jerusalem with the destruction of Solomon's temple in 586 BCE. Still, the Deuteronomistic History recounts in splendid detail the specifications for that temple.

The exilic prophet Ezekiel addresses the question of God's dwelling place explicitly, first reporting that God's presence (Ezek 10:6, 18; Hebrew: *kavod*) leaves the temple before its destruction. Later, the vision of the valley of dry bones anticipates a kingdom restored under "my servant David" in the "land that I gave to my servant Jacob" (Ezek 37:25). With a reestablished covenant and rebuilt sanctuary, God promises: "My dwelling will be with them, and I will be their God, and they will be my people" (Ezek 37:27). In a similar vein, the post-exilic prophet Zechariah heralds the ingathering of the lost tribes to Zion, which serves in turn as hub of universal worship: "Many nations will be joined to the LORD on that day. / They will become my people / and I will dwell among you / so you will know that the LORD of heavenly forces sent me to you" (Zech 2:11). Both the law and the prophets, then, make a case for God's dwelling among the people. Notably, passages from a wide array of literary and historical settings share at least two convictions about God's dwelling on earth: first, Israel's God is an immanent God whose relationship with the people depends at least in part on maintaining a presence in their midst; second, God's dwelling among them consistently engenders covenant loyalty—either in association with the ark, or in the temple that houses it, or even in the hearts of the people (see Jer 31:31-34).

Finally, Jewish wisdom traditions that emerged in conversation with the wider Hellenistic world sometimes personify God's immanent presence in terms of Wisdom herself. As we have seen, Sirach 24 depicts an intimate relationship between God and Wisdom, who "came forth from the mouth / of the Most High" (Sir 24:3) and surveyed "every land" and "every people and nation" (Sir 24:6) in search of an earthly habitation. At the Creator's command, she finds herself established in Zion where "I ministered before [the Creator]" (Sir 24:10).[6] Again, this depiction of Wisdom provides a glimpse of a widespread linkage in Jewish thought between Wisdom and the divine *logos* as an aspect of the monotheistic deity, as well as the implicit ties to the covenant itself. Together, these concepts suggest that God is present wherever faithfulness to the covenant discloses God's ways to the world.

Union with God in John

John's Prologue provides a helpful starting point for understanding Jesus's union with God as a signature trait in this Gospel. Already, we have seen that Hellenistic Jewish traditions often acknowledged that God's *logos* played an active part in creation (see chapter 2). What is distinctive about John's Christology, then, is not the idea that this word was "with God in the beginning" (John 1:2) nor even that "everything came into being through the Word" (John 1:3). Rather, John's interpretive twist comes with the claim that "the Word became flesh / and made his home among us. / We have seen his glory, / glory like that of a father's only son, / full of grace and truth" (John 1:14). The shift is pronounced: rather than taking up residence in Zion, in the (now destroyed) temple, or even in Torah and its interpretation, God's *logos* has made a home in a human being named Jesus.

That the person of Jesus bears God's "word" or "message" to the world only grows clearer as the Prologue ends. There, the writer explains, "As the Law was given through Moses, / so grace and truth came into being through Jesus Christ. / No one has ever seen God. / God the only Son, / who is at the Father's side, / has made God known [*exēgēsato*]" (John 1:17-18). From this opening passage, then, already we gain a sense of the twofold significance of Jesus's relationship to the Father. First, rather than in the law, God has chosen to dwell in Jesus the messiah. Moreover, this indwelling serves a messianic function, since this Christ "draws out" or

---

6. Cf. *1 Enoch* 42, where Wisdom fails to find a suitable dwelling place on earth and retires to heaven.

"exegetes" the knowledge of God. That is, more than just privileged status, Jesus's closeness to the "Father's side" signals his messianic purpose, which is to make God known on the earth.

Throughout the Gospel, John returns to the question of Jesus's intimate union with God in ways that emphasize this purpose: to convey God's word of life on earth. To begin with, in a discourse that many interpreters ascribe to an earlier stage in the Gospel's development, Jesus counters charges that he "called God his own Father, thereby making himself equal with God" (John 5:18). On the one hand, he insists that "the Son can't do anything by himself except what he sees the Father doing" (John 5:19). On the other hand, he insists that "these works I do testify about me that the Father sent me" (John 5:36). That is, Jesus is the one who comes in the "Father's name" to make known the "praise that comes from the only God" (John 5:43-44).

Later in the Gospel, Jesus responds to a similar accusation that "you are human, yet you make yourself out to be God" (John 10:33; see also 10:30). Again, in his reply, Jesus reiterates both his *distinction from* God and his *union with* God. Notably, he calls himself both "the one whom the Father has made holy and sent into the world" and "God's Son" (John 10:36). He operates in the world as a designated agent who does the "works of my Father" (John 10:37)—works that confirm in turn that "the Father is in me and I am in the Father" (John 10:38).

Both passages, then, hold claims about Jesus's intimacy with God together with the view that they remain separate, since he is one "sent" to do God's "works" in a way that brings God's life to the world. As one writer notes, the "Gospel of John, which testifies most vigorously to the unity of Father and Son, nevertheless also unequivocally differentiates between them."[7] Already we see that Jesus's union *with* God does not mean, in John, that he *is* God.

Within the Farewell Discourse (John 13–17), Jesus draws his followers together for an extended "exegesis" of his own mission. Again, John's Jesus works deliberately to convey to the community their calling in the

---

7. Marianne Meye Thompson, *The God of the Gospel of John* (Grand Rapids: Eerdmans, 2001), 233.

post-resurrection age to which he points. When Jesus tells his followers about his imminent departure, Philip asks Jesus to "show us the Father" (John 14:8). Jesus's reply underscores his mystical union with God. After saying that "whoever has seen me has seen the Father" (John 14:9), Jesus reaffirm his mutual indwelling with God: "I am in the Father and the Father is in me" (John 14:11; see 10:38).

Even here, though, Jesus's union with God is not unique. As he anticipates the time "soon" when "the world will no longer see me" (John 14:19), he says that others will share in his life with the Father. Indeed, those who keep his commandments (John 14:15) will receive the advocate/comforter (*paraklētos*, John 14:16). As a result, "On that day you will know that I am in my Father, and you in me, and I in you.... The one who loves me will keep my word, and my Father will love that one, and we will come to that one and make our residence [literally, *abiding*; Greek: *monēn*] with him or her" (John 14:20, 23 AT).[8] In the post-passion age, then, God will continue to dwell on earth among the faithful community, where both Father and Son will find a home.

What will that "abiding" look like? Jesus uses the extended metaphor of the vine and the branches to depict his relationship with his followers after he has departed. Just as God's word has taken up residence in Jesus during his earthly career, so too will those who "remain in me and I in [them]... produce much fruit. Without me you can't do anything" (John 15:5). Like Jesus, the faithful are both authorized as agents of God's works on earth and utterly dependent on Jesus and his love (John 15:9).

Indeed, this extension of Jesus's own intimacy with God to the faithful community plays a momentous role in his prayer that concludes this section of the Gospel. Not only does he ask that his own disciples be made "holy in the truth" (John 17:17, 19; see 1:18), but he also prays for those "who believe in me because of their word" (John 17:20). That is, as authorized agents of Jesus's messianic mission, his followers will in turn bear the *logos* of God, made known through Jesus, to the world.

---

8. To preserve an inclusive sense, the CEB translates John 14:23 with plural pronouns. I have chosen a more awkward rendering to convey the singular sense of the Greek, while maintaining gender neutrality.

Strikingly, Jesus applies the pattern of his own intimacy with God to this inclusive, and expanding, group of believers. When he prays that "they will be one," he adds this petition for their mystical union with both Father and Son: "Father, just as you are *in me* and I am *in you*," may they also "be *in us*, so that the world will believe that you sent me" (John 17:21, emphasis added). Though some textual traditions (e.g., ℵ, A, C³) tone down this notion of mystical union with the divine by stating, "may they be one in us," John's Jesus asks, of his followers, that they "be one just as we are one. I'm in them and you are in me so that they will be made perfectly one" (John 21:22-23). In other words, since the Father dwells in Jesus, and Jesus dwells in the faithful, then the divine word makes its home not just in Jesus but, through him (and ultimately the paraclete), in the faithful community that bears witness to his messiahship.

Though interpreters often maintain that, in the Fourth Gospel, Jesus has become God, John's story offers a portrait of Jesus's messianic intimacy with God that is not quite so simple. If on the one hand God is fully evident in Jesus, and if God's word has indeed become flesh, John's Jesus often maintains his distinction from the "only God" (John 5:44). It turns out that John emphasizes Jesus's union with God as a way of authorizing his disclosure of God for all who would believe in him. In turn, those who "remain" in his words—that is, in his message about God's self-giving love—participate through him in a similar union with God, and thus with one another. As one interpreter puts it, in the incarnation, "Jesus is brought down, but on his way back up believers latch on and become elevated as well."[9]

Clearly, the contours of this messianic attribute reflect the social and religious landscape of John's own setting. To begin with, we have seen that the Fourth Gospel stakes claims about God's dwelling in the person of Jesus that would have been both consistent with and a radical departure from first-century Judaism, especially the rabbinic traditions gaining ground in the late first century. For John, Jesus does not deny Torah's

9. Jaime Clark-Soles, "'I Will Raise [Whom?] Up on the Last Day': Anthropology as a Feature of Johannine Eschatology," in *New Currents Through John: A Global Perspective*, ed. Francisco Lozada and Tom Thatcher (Atlanta: Society of Biblical Literature, 2006), 29–54 (34).

validity but interprets it (see John 5:46); he does, though, undermine and challenge its contemporary interpreters, subordinating its authority along the way to traditions that "testify about me" (John 5:39). As the word-become-flesh, Jesus embodies the Father in human form—a radical notion indeed for John's own place and time.

It is this notion, for John, that lies at the heart of Jesus's messiahship. As a result, those in John's community who trust that Jesus reveals the "way, the truth, and the life" (John 14:6) assume in turn the task of bearing witness to the messianic age. Not surprisingly, their unity emerges as indispensable to that witness; it is through their oneness that the world will come to see the Father, made known through Jesus. Thus John's sectarian concerns function to promote social cohesion within the fledgling—and marginalized—community. Yet, perhaps paradoxically, the Fourth Gospel also promotes their own "exegesis" of God's word-become-flesh in the world. Just as Jesus's union with God both authorizes and empowers his own "works," so too will their union with Christ, and thus with God, authorize and empower them to do greater works (John 14:12) as testimony to the messianic age.

Concluding Thoughts

Taken together, the qualities discussed in this chapter deepen our understanding of the Gospel witness to Jesus as the Christ. In his servant posture, in his embodiment of righteousness, in his prophetic office, and in his union with God, Jesus appears in the Gospels as the one anointed to preside over the dawn of God's coming kingdom, as well as the disclosure of God's "way, truth, and life." Yet while each Gospel identifies messianic traits that are distinctive to Jesus, these attributes are not exclusive to him. Thus we return to the persistent paradox of this study: in their witness to Jesus as the Christ, the Gospels depict his messiahship in continuity with both Jewish tradition that has come before and the faithful community that bears the contours of his messiahship—and God's reign that it heralds—in the post-resurrection age.

Despite their differences, then, the Gospels understand Jesus's messianic identity in relation to the new world order anticipated among a range of Jewish writings. Each trait or role situates Jesus as a pivotal part of the regime change at hand, as he presides over the dawn of God's kingdom on earth. As agent of God's life-giving power, this anointed one seeks not his own advantage but the well-being of others (see Phil 2:1-11). As the Christ, he thus reflects God's righteousness—a righteousness that cares for the vulnerable, includes the excluded, and that culminates in self-giving love.

But for the Gospel writers, this christological story has little to do with Jesus's divine nature per se. Instead, it is a story of God's redemption that is rooted in Jesus's earthly ministry but reaches beyond it into the life of the community. In our final chapter, we draw together our findings to sketch the contours of messianic community each Gospel promotes. How might the faithful community—then and now—carry forward the vision of God's dawning kingdom for a new place and time? How might the interpreting community today reclaim the Gospels' first-century vision of christological community for our own place and time?

Study Questions

1. Explain each Gospel's dominant trait in light of the Jewish traditions discussed.

2. Which features of each Gospel seem most vital to its portrait of Jesus's messianic identity?

3. Which texts discussed here forge the most surprising connection between Christ and community?

For Further Reading

Morna D. Hooker. *Jesus and the Servant: The Influence of the Servant Concept in Deutero–Isaiah in the New Testament.* London: SPCK, 1959.

Powell, Mark Allen, and David R. Bauer, eds. *Who Do You Say That I Am? Essays on Christology.* Louisville: John Knox, 1999.

Hagner, Donald A. "Holiness and Ecclesiology: The Church in Matthew."

In *Holiness and Ecclesiology in the New Testament*, edited by Kent E. Brower and Andy Johnson, 40–56. Grand Rapids: Eerdmans, 2007.

Howell, David B. *Matthew's Inclusive Story: A Study in the Narrative Rhetoric of the First Gospel.* Journal for the Study of the New Testament: Supplement Series 42. Sheffield: Sheffield Academic Press, 1990.

McWhirter, Jocelyn. *Rejected Prophets: Jesus and His Witnesses in Luke–Acts.* Minneapolis: Fortress, 2014.

Przybylski, Benno. *Righteousness in Matthew and His World of Thought.* Society for New Testament Studies Monograph Series 41. Cambridge: Cambridge University Press, 2004.

Thompson, Marianne Meye. *The God of the Gospel of John.* Grand Rapids: Eerdmans, 2001.

Conclusion
Christ and Community

The Gospel Witness to Jesus

By all accounts, the movement that grew out of Jesus's earthly career should have failed. After all, its founding figure died a criminal's death on a Roman cross, hardly the fitting outcome for a messianic ruler. Word about the empty tomb met mostly disbelief and scorn. And if Jesus promised that God's kingdom would arrive "in power" within a generation (see Mark 9:1), it did not—at least not in the cataclysmic way that most expected. Indeed, decades after Jesus's death, Rome's heavy-handed response to a Jewish insurgency in Palestine only confirmed, for many, that messianic hopes were at best a fairy tale and at worst the cause of Jerusalem's destruction.

But somehow, that movement did not die. Something happened to convince believers that in Jesus the Christ, God's kingdom was taking root on earth in a palpable way. Perhaps that "something" was a series of post-resurrection encounters, as Paul suggests (1 Cor 15:5-8). Perhaps it was the compelling testimony or spirit-filled deeds of Jesus's followers, as Luke's story in Acts would have it (Acts 2:41, 43). In any case, despite evidence to the contrary, a small but growing group embraced the view that in Jesus Christ, God had staked a decisive claim for the power of life, redemption, and wholeness in a world gone awry.

In a sense, the four Gospels considered here offer a window into early Christian efforts to honor Jesus's messianic mission in light of present reality. In each story, we find a portrait of Jesus the Christ that preserves and

213

extends Jewish hopes for God's renewal of the earth. Yet each story also refracts both Jewish hopes and Jesus's own messianic career through the experience of those devoted to him. As we have seen, the Gospel witness to Jesus traces contours of his mission and identity that extend, in turn, to the shared life of those who call him Lord.

On the one hand, then, the Gospel witness to Jesus is emphatically christological. That is, these four accounts have much to say about who Jesus was and what he stood for as the "Christ." Though not written as dogmatic treatises, they do cast Jesus in a certain messianic light. For all four Gospels, Jesus is the authoritative Son of God who channels God's life-affirming power, even as social, religious, and political forces rise up against him. For all four Gospels, both his earthly ministry and his passion manifest God's redemptive purposes at work in the world. And for all four Gospels, Jesus lives on after the resurrection, reigning in heaven until that day when God's justice prevails throughout the whole earth.

But this Gospel witness to Jesus is also deeply communal in at least two respects. On one level, the Gospels are "community literature" by their very nature. That is, they tell the story of Jesus's messiahship for those devoted to him. Indeed, as Papias puts it, the evangelists even adjust the gospel story to meet the "needs of [the] hearers."[1] On another level, the Gospels bear witness to Jesus as one who summons others to reflect his messianic vision for the world. Rather than a solitary figure who sets himself above the masses, this Jesus eats with sinners, washes his followers' feet, and ultimately involves others in his redemptive work—both during his ministry and in the post-resurrection age. In this way, the Gospel witness to Jesus is indeed a witness to Christ and community.

This connection between Christ and community grows out of Jewish hopes for God's redemption of the world. Though over time, Christians increasingly turned to Jewish scripture to confirm doctrinal views about Jesus's divine nature, the Gospels themselves make no such move. Instead, they preserve and adapt Jewish tradition to frame Jesus's messiahship against the wider horizon of God's coming kingdom. For the Gospels, as for a wide range of Jewish traditions, the messiah presides over God's

---

1. Eusebius, *Ecclesiastical History*, 3.39.

214

renewal of the world, imparting divine wisdom, authority, and judgment to those who trust in God's sovereign power.

Our study of Christ and community concludes with a synthetic summary of the Gospel witness to Jesus. Taking each story on its own terms, we draw together findings from the preceding chapters to capture the Gospel message for those devoted to Jesus the Christ. In its call, its challenge, and its promise, each story engages readers in the redemptive work of God, begun in Jesus of Nazareth and extending to his followers in the first century and beyond. To read the Gospels as community literature allows us to reclaim their vital word of life, hope, and renewal in a world still awaiting redemption.

The Gospel of Mark: Servant Power

Mark writes for a community facing persecution—even to the point of death—because of their loyalties to a messianic movement (Mark 13:9-13). The repercussions of the Jewish War probably meant that they lived under the suspicious watch of political and religious leaders alike. After all, the Jewish Zealots who rose up against Rome did so in the name of God's kingly power. As a result, those devoted to Jesus the messiah probably drew the attention of rulers invested in the Roman peace as well as religious leaders who wanted to safeguard the Jewish people from further retaliation.

But rather than promoting coercive force or defensive self-protection, Mark's Gospel responds with a message about vulnerable servant power. Mark interprets the story of a crucified Christ for those who, like him, would "take up their cross" (Mark 8:34). In this Gospel, Jesus urges his followers to look beyond present oppression and trust that God's power would soon reclaim the world. For Mark, the trials faced by both Jesus and those who joined his messianic movement were "sufferings associated with the end" (Mark 13:8)—that is, the end of the present evil age. Indeed for Mark, the community's suffering only confirms that the messianic age established in the life, death, and resurrection of Jesus continues to unfold.

As dominant as this "way of the cross" motif is in Mark, it goes hand in hand with another, complementary dimension Jesus's messiahship: his

215

demonstration of God's kingly power in word and deed. Taken together, *both* Jesus's authoritative ministry *and* his embattled destiny expose the nature of servant power that characterizes his messianic story. As he travels through the Galilee and beyond, proclaiming the good news and subduing evil forces, Mark's Jesus deploys God's power in service to human dignity and wholeness. When he hangs on a Roman cross, this anointed one forfeits his very life for others and reveals, in the end, that God's life-giving power is stronger than death. For Mark, Jesus's christological servant power is still at work among those who trust that, in and through his enduring presence, God's kingdom continues to draw near. In what follows, we consider the call, the challenge, and the promise of Mark's message about Christ and community.

The Call: "To Be with Him, to Be Sent Out" (Mark 3:14)

From the story's outset, Jesus calls followers to remain in his presence and to participate in his messianic mission. As his first public act, Jesus summons four fishers with these words: "come after me, and I will make you fish for people" (Mark 1:17 AT). In the first command, to "come after" him, Jesus recruits followers who place themselves under his authoritative guidance. This is no company of equals. Rather, to "come after" Jesus is to submit to his commanding witness to God's coming kingdom. Yet Jesus's call already implies that "coming after" him will lead, in turn, to their involvement in his gospel movement. These fishers, he says, will become fishers of people in their own right, as they gather others to populate God's kingdom (see Jer 16:16-21).

Jesus reiterates this call to discipleship when he commissions the Twelve on a mountaintop (Mark 3:13-19). Those whom he gathers are "to be *with him* and to be *sent out* to proclaim the word and to have authority to cast out demons" (Mark 3:14-15 AT, emphasis added). Like Jesus, the apostles will "proclaim the word" about God's coming kingdom (see Mark 1:14-15). Like him, they will exercise the divine authority to defeat demonic forces (see Mark 3:27). In this way, they too manifest the servant power that characterizes his mission.

The nature of their servant power comes to light as the story progresses. For one thing, Jesus instructs those who remain with him about their role in spreading the "word" about God's coming kingdom (Mark 4:1-34). Indeed, Mark offers this account of their own missionary journey: "They went out and proclaimed that people should change their hearts and lives. They cast out many demons, and they anointed many sick people with olive oil and healed them" (Mark 6:12-13). Even in the feeding of the five thousand (Mark 6:30-44), Jesus's followers participate in his display of servant power, as they provide the loaves and fish and then work alongside Jesus to enact God's economy of abundance in a wilderness feast.

Ultimately, of course, this call to be present with Jesus and to participate in his messianic mission leads to the cost of discipleship. "If anyone wants to follow after me," Jesus says, "let that one deny the self and take up [a] cross and follow me" (Mark 8:34 AT). Again, Mark uses the language of "following" to promote devoted discipleship. Again, Mark suggests that this call to discipleship means participating in the servant power—even the loss of life (see Mark 8:35)—that leads to salvation and life.

The Challenge: "Whoever Stands Firm until the End" (Mark 13:13)

This call to manifest Jesus's servant power carries with it implicit challenges for Mark's readers. Early in the Gospel, Mark hints at the resistance that Jesus will eventually meet head-on. After a Sabbath-day healing, Mark says, "The Pharisees got together with the supporters of Herod to plan how to destroy Jesus" (Mark 3:6). Already, religious and political leaders forge an alliance that will conspire against Jesus. Jesus's three predictions of his own destiny (Mark 8:31-33; 9:30-32; 10:32-34) only confirm its inevitability.

But for Mark, the challenge Jesus faces as he wields God's servant power is not his alone. In this Gospel, whenever Jesus predicts his own destiny, he explains its implications for those who follow him. Like him, they will "take up their cross" (Mark 8:34). To be "first" in God's kingdom is to "be least of all and the servant of all" (Mark 9:35). Indeed, the Son of the Human One, as a pattern for the faithful, "didn't come to be served but rather to serve and to give his life to liberate many people" (Mark 10:45). In all these ways, the challenge associated with the call to servant power intensifies as the story unfolds.

Mark 13 speaks to this challenge in a deliberate way. While Jesus's words seem to predict his followers' destiny, Mark probably adapts Jesus's teachings to address the harsh realities faced by the Gospel's first audience. Thus, Jesus says, "Watch out for yourselves. People will hand you over...because of me" (Mark 13:9). In the face of inevitable resistance, betrayal, and hatred, Jesus challenges them to endure "until the end," when they will "be saved" (Mark 13:13). In this endurance, their servant power comes to light.

As Jesus approaches the passion itself, the disciples increasingly fail to meet this challenge. In Gethsemane, Jesus begs Peter and James and John to "stay here and keep alert" as he grapples with his destiny, but they keep falling asleep (Mark 14:32-42). At his arrest, his closest companions all "left him and ran away" (Mark 14:50). Even a mysterious man in a linen cloth left it behind when he too "ran away naked" (Mark 14:52). Finally, Peter follows him only "from a distance" (Mark 14:54) and denies his loyalty to Jesus three times (Mark 14:66-72). Understood on human terms, both the robust call to servant power and the daunting challenge it brings prove too much for even the most willing disciples.

The Promise: "I Will Go before You" (Mark 14:28)

Despite the disciples' lapses, Mark's story of Christ and community ends on a more hopeful note. Knowing that his followers will both desert and deny him, Jesus promises, "But after I am raised up, I will go before you to Galilee" (Mark 14:28). Even when the women at the empty tomb greet news of the resurrection with silence and fear (Mark 16:8), their somber reaction is not the final word. For one thing, the angel sends them back to "tell his disciples, especially Peter, that he is going ahead...into Galilee" (Mark 16:7). Though Mark's earliest ending probably leaves their report out of account, the Gospel story itself suggests that they did declare this "good news" that God's servant power leads to new life.

This promise of Jesus's enduring presence—to the disciples, to Mark's community, and to faithful readers in any age—means that Mark's story of servant power hinges not on human will or cognition but on God. For Mark, it is God's act of renewal in the messianic mission of Jesus that unleashes life-giving power on earth. After the resurrection, that mission lives on, for Mark, only through Jesus's abiding presence. As he continues to "go before" his disciples, he empowers them to become "servants of all," wielding God's power to repair and restore the world. For Mark, this servant power operates not through military, economic, or social strength but through vulnerable sacrifice that works, albeit mysteriously, to undercut the power of the present evil age.

For Mark's audience, then and now, this call to messianic community promotes a dynamic Gospel witness, activated through enduring dependence on, and trust in, their risen Lord. After all, those persecuted for their practice of God's servant power tend either to cut and run or to draw inward toward personal piety or sectarian isolation. But for those who trust that God's kingdom has indeed drawn near (Mark 1:14-15), Mark's story of Christ and community sounds a more daring, costly, and rewarding appeal: to show forth God's servant power in word and deed, to endure when opposition arises, and to live lives animated by the abiding presence of the risen Lord.

Matthew: Expansive Righteousness

If Mark's community faced external pressure from religious and political authorities, the crisis of Matthew's community has more to do with internal matters, as this nascent group forges its social and religious identity against the backdrop of its own Jewish heritage. As messianic Jews, its members both followed Jewish law and thought that in Jesus, the kingdom of heaven had dawned. As a result, their relationship to rabbinic Judaism was, for the moment, an open question. On the one hand, like the rabbis (the Pharisees), they found in God's covenant a mandate for faithful community. But on the other hand, the "way of righteousness" they found in Jesus differed in important ways from the rabbis' emerging view. Rather than a way of life that safeguards the distinctive identity of

God's people, Matthew's Jesus espouses a "greater... righteousness" (Matt 5:20) that draws "all the nations" into its scope.

In Matthew, Jesus is the one who fully embodies God's righteousness. At his baptism by John, he submits himself in order to "fulfill all righteousness" (Matt 3:15). In his Sermon on the Mount, Jesus offers authoritative instruction that fulfills "the Law and the Prophets" (Matt 5:17). He is, in Matthew, the "one teacher" (Matt 23:8) who discloses the expansive righteousness that reflects God's coming reign. It is, he says, a righteousness that appears wherever human deeds reflect God's sweeping provision for creation, extending beyond self-interest to care for the "least of these" (Matt 25:40).

But rather than bringing religious status or acclaim, this expansive righteousness brings rejection, persecution, and calumny (Matt 5:10-11). Indeed, like other righteous figures from Israel's past, Jesus dies at least in part because his views of God's coming reign challenge those invested in the political and religious status quo (Matt 26:64). Yet Matthew also confirms Jesus's way of righteousness as the way of life: only in Matthew does his death mean that the holy ones rise from the dead to participate in the dawning reign of God (Matt 27:53). Thus Jesus's messianic mission continues to spread after the resurrection, as Matthew's Gospel sounds a call to righteous community that looks forward to God's kingdom come "on earth as it's done in heaven" (Matt 6:10).

The Call: "Be Perfect, Therefore, as Your Heavenly Father Is Perfect" (Matt 5:48 NRSV)

At the heart of Jesus's teachings about "greater... righteousness" (Matt 5:20; see also 6:33), the jarring command to "be perfect" (Matt 5:48 NRSV) captures Jesus's call to discipleship in Matthew.[2] Interpreters have long bristled at this saying's rigor, since it signals just the kind of Western perfectionism that can be dangerous at both the personal and the social

---

2. The CEB offers an important departure from standard translations on this verse: "Therefore, just as your heavenly Father is complete in showing love to everyone, so also you must be complete." The discussion here supports such an understanding of this verse.

levels. As a result, some think these words prompt readers to recognize the profound need for grace.

Yet the call to "be perfect" does not necessarily denote the flawlessness that readers usually assume. Both the saying's context and its language suggest a different reading: "Be expansive [in your love], as your Father in heaven is expansive [in caring for creation]" (Matt 5:48 AT). After all, the verse follows the command to love enemies—a practice that grows out of God's indiscriminate care for the "good and evil...the just and the unjust" (Matt 5:45 AT). The sweeping nature of God's righteousness leads in turn to Jesus's command to be "complete" or "all-encompassing" (*teleios*; Matt 5:48) by extending love even to "your enemies and...those who harass you" (Matt 5:44). For Matthew's Jesus, to reflect God's righteousness is to be "sons of your father in heaven" (Matt 5:45 AT).

Elsewhere in Matthew, we find that the "way of righteousness" consistently involves concern for others—often those who suffer the burden of religious practice. Using a familiar image of Torah-observance as a "yoke," Jesus calls those who are "struggling hard and carrying heavy loads" to "put on my yoke, and learn from me" (Matt 11:28-29). Elsewhere, he lambasts those who "put [heavy packs] on the shoulders of others" (Matt 23:4). Rather than practicing righteousness in a way that avoids public acclaim (Matt 6:1), they broadcast religious practice: "Everything they do, they do to be noticed by others. They make extra-wide prayer bands for their arms and long tassels for their clothes" (Matt 23:5). What is more, they "give to God a tenth of mint, dill, and cumin, but...forget about the more important matters of the Law: justice, peace, and faith" (Matt 23:23). In these negative examples, Jesus warns against a so-called righteousness that promotes self-interest, often at others' expense.

Indeed, Matthew's call to expansive righteousness comes into clear view when the Son of the Human sits on a throne of eschatological judgment (Matt 25:31-46). For one thing, God's righteousness can be seen not just among God's chosen people but among "all the nations," even when they claim ignorance of it. Moreover, the deeds of "righteousness" that secure life in God's kingdom have nothing to do with religious belief or practice. Rather, those deemed righteous show simple care for the "least of these"—that is, society's most vulnerable members. In this way, they heed the call to "be perfect" because they have provided food and drink, clothing and companionship. Setting aside personal gain to meet the needs of the weak, they have displayed God's "way of righteousness" and secured a place in God's eternal reign.

The Challenge: "Until the Harvest" (Matt 13:30)

This call to expansive righteousness brings with it, for Matthew, several challenges. Already we have seen in Mark that those aligned with God's coming kingdom face harsh scrutiny, even rejection. In Matthew, such resistance only escalates. For instance, Matthew highlights family divisions that arise in response to the disciples' messianic mission (Matt 10:34-37; see also Luke 12:51-53). To follow in a "way of righteousness" that defies social and religious distinction often elicits the vigorous opposition of those whose identity depends on such distinction.

In the face of such division, though, this "way of righteousness" brings a complementary challenge. Though the Twelve will sit in judgment "when everything is made new" (Matt 19:28), Jesus cautions against judgment in the meantime. For one thing, he warns his followers: "Don't judge, so that you won't be judged. You'll receive the same judgment you give" (Matt 7:1-2). Only upon examining one's own foibles can others' offenses, which pale in comparison, be seen clearly (Matt 7:3-5). What is more, Jesus tips the scales of justice toward mercy, telling Peter to forgive repeat offenders "not just seven times, but rather as many as seventy-seven times" (Matt 18:22).

Finally, the parable of the weeds among the wheat (Matt 13:24-30, 36-43) also challenges the human impulse to separate the righteous from the unrighteous, at least in the short term. There, the householder warns against gathering the weeds prematurely, "because if you gather the weeds, you'll put up the wheat along with them" (Matt 13:29). By allowing them to "grow side by side until the harvest" (Matt 13:30), Jesus suggests, the coming judgment arrives through divine, not human, initiative. The call to expansive righteousness thus brings profound challenges for those who, growing among the weeds, are persecuted because of it. Yet perhaps the deeper challenge lies in trusting even the weeds to God.

The Promise: "I Myself Will Be with You Every Day" (Matt 28:20)

In a similar way, this call to expansive righteousness ultimately depends not on human effort or initiative but on Christ's perpetual presence among the community. For if Mark's Jesus promises to "go before" his disciples (Mark 14:28), in Matthew the risen Lord is more explicit: "I myself will be with you every day until the end of this present age" (Matt 28:20). In their life together, in their expansive efforts to "make disciples," and even in their end-time judging task, the disciples continue to operate as students of their "one teacher" (Matt 23:8) who alone discloses that "way of righteousness."

This promise of Jesus's presence works its way back into the Gospel as well, as Matthew sometimes signals a post-resurrection perspective even within Jesus's earthly teachings. For one thing, when Jesus addresses the question of wrongdoing within the community, he offers the reminder that "where two or three are gathered in my name, I'm there with them" (Matt 18:20). Though Jesus speaks these words while physically present, the promise for the post-resurrection community is clear. It is the risen Lord, Matthew implies, who will be with believers when they come together in his name. And since this passage concerns the church's response to an offending member, any judgment they pronounce comes only "in his name"—that is, on his behalf, not of their own accord. Their authority remains anchored in his Lordship even after the resurrection.

The Gospel's Great Commission only confirms this promise of Jesus's enduring and authorizing presence. After saying that "I've received all authority in heaven and on earth" (Matt 28:18), the risen Lord extends this sweeping authority to his followers: "*Therefore*, go and make disciples of all nations, baptizing them in the name of the Father and of the Son and of the Holy Spirit, teaching them to obey everything that I've commanded you" (Matt 28:19-20, emphasis added). Here, Jesus charges the messianic community with promoting his "way of righteousness" among all nations. In so doing, their teaching conforms to his, and their authority derives from his. His perpetual presence, which continues until the "end of this present age" (Matt 28:20), ensures that they are not alone.

In Matthew, those who follow a messianic rabbi named Jesus find their identity in his call to reflect God's expansive righteousness throughout the earth. This is not a law-free righteousness, as if God's covenant with Israel were null and void. Instead, it is an indiscriminate righteousness that works its way outward, toward all the nations. Along the way, it can be seen among those who care for the "least of these," regardless of religious or ethnic status. For Matthew, the stakes are high, since the final judgment will render God's justice according to such deeds of mercy. Yet those who follow along this "way of righteousness" are not alone. The risen Lord remains present. The one who lived and died as God's "righteous one" lives on, showing the way of God's righteousness that leads to eternal life.

Luke: Subversive Citizenship

Luke writes for a community that seems farther removed from Jesus's Jewish roots. For one thing, this mostly Gentile audience may have been only vaguely familiar with Jewish scripture and its story of God's covenant relationship with Israel. For another thing, they probably lived in a more cosmopolitan and urbane setting than that of Jesus and his first followers. As a result, Luke crafts a sophisticated Gospel narrative that both anchors Jesus's messianic mission in Israel's story and suggests its relevance for the wider Greco-Roman world.

Scholars differ about Luke's attitude toward the empire to which its audience belongs. Some find in Luke an apologetic defense of Christianity, while others read it as a narrative charter for a more subversive movement. But Luke seems to work both angles. In one sense, Luke's message reassures Roman officials—perhaps even the addressee "Theophilus" (Luke 1:3)—that this Jewish "messiah" had no interest in hard political power secured through conventional means. For Luke's audience, then, the Gospel may have offered a useful defense against those who would assume their group's treasonous intent. But in a more subtle way, Luke highlights the radical implications of God's lordship. For one thing, this "good news" concerns a savior far removed from imperial power structures. What is more, Luke's Jesus uses women disciples, a poor man named Lazarus, a hated Samaritan, and a wonton younger son as narrative signposts to God's kingdom values that turn on end prevailing notions of gender, social status, and religious distinction.

In this way, Luke translates the very Jewish story of Jesus's messianic mission and identity for a wider Greco-Roman audience. Luke's portrait of Jesus as "lord," for instance, not only identifies him with Israel's God but also implies that his (and God's) sovereignty ultimately trumps Caesar's. In addition, Luke explains the crucifixion not as a tragedy Jesus laments but as a divine necessity he willingly accepts. Finally, Luke adds stories that work to persuade those who might be suspicious of claims about Jesus's bodily resurrection. In all these ways, Luke reframes this "good news" about Jesus the Jewish Christ for those in the wider imperial world.

But Luke's story of Jesus the Christ also lays a foundation for a community marked by subversive citizenship. Though Luke works deftly to tone down any political threat Jesus might pose, this messiah engenders human dignity and wholeness in ways that undermine imperial values and systems. When Luke's Jesus says that "God's kingdom is already among you" (Luke 17:21), he calls followers to reflect God's reign and the sweeping deliverance and forgiveness it brings. To be sure, this Gospel issues no rallying cry to take up arms against the powers that be. It does, however, suggest that God's power is taking root in the world in ways that turn social and religious systems radically on end. To bear witness to such soft power, in Luke's view, is to affirm that God has worked decisively in Jesus the Christ to extend God's life-giving reign to the "end of the earth" (Acts 1:8).

The Call: "Go and Do Likewise" (Luke 10:37)

In many ways, Luke's call to messianic community grows organically out of Jesus's inaugural preaching. In his first appearance in Nazareth, Jesus signals the terms of his own messianic career (Luke 4:41-30; see Mark 6:1-6; Matt 13:53-58). Reading from Isaiah, Jesus lays this foundation for his own witness to God's coming kingdom: "*[God] has anointed me. / He has sent me to preach good news to the poor, / to proclaim release to the prisoners / and recovery of sight to the blind, / to liberate the oppressed, / to proclaim the year of the Lord's favor*" (Luke 4:18-19). As the story unfolds, he enacts these redemptive ways in word and deed, asserting authority over oppressive powers that threaten human dignity and wholeness.

But Luke's Jesus does not act alone. Rather, he engages others in this mission, both implicitly and explicitly. Only Luke includes both the missionary journey of his twelve disciples (Luke 9:1-6) and the sending of seventy(-two) "others" to spread word of God's coming kingdom (Luke 10:1-12). When the larger group returns, Jesus says he "saw Satan fall from heaven like lightning" (Luke 10:18). Working "in [his] name" (Luke 10:17), they have played an active part in the defeat of God's resistance. Thus Luke draws the community's role into sharper focus.

Besides this explicit call to proclaim the dawn of God's kingdom, Luke offers a narrative glimpse of subversive citizenship in a range of stories that illustrate the values of that reign. For instance, Luke includes special traditions that destabilize conventional notions about status, wealth, and power. Only in Luke does Jesus tell a story about a merciful Samaritan to explain the command to "love your neighbor as yourself" (Luke 10:27; see Lev 19:18). In this account, Jesus defines a "neighbor" as one who shows mercy, rather than as one belonging to a religious or ethnic group. What is more, the Samaritan's deed of mercy points the way to eternal life, and Jesus tells the lawyer to "go and do likewise" (Luke 10:37).

The subversive nature of God's kingdom also comes to light in the story of Mary and Martha (Luke 10:38-42). Here, Martha faithfully performs domestic duties generally assigned women in the ancient world, while Mary assumes the (male) posture of discipleship, sitting "at the Lord's feet" (Luke 10:39). When Martha challenges her sister's violation of social order, Jesus replies that Mary has "chosen the better part" (Luke 10:42). In a world that saw women as biologically and socially inferior, Luke's Gospel assigns them a prominent role as disciples, even patrons (see Luke 8:1-3), within the community devoted to Jesus's lordship.

For Luke, the story extends into the book of Acts, where the risen Lord commissions his followers to "be my witnesses in Jerusalem, in all Judea and Samaria, and to the end of the earth" (Acts 1:8). After the gift of the spirit at Pentecost, the believing community only expands the impact of its witness to Jesus the Christ—and to the kingdom he has inaugurated. Part of that witness, of course, means convincing others that Jesus was indeed the Jewish messiah. But it also includes wielding God's power in the "many wonders and signs [done] through the apostles" (Acts 2:43). And Luke twice points out that the early Christians "shared everything" (Acts 2:44; see also 4:32). Thus this fledgling community subverts a social order in which the wealth of a few entails the poverty of many (see 1 Cor 11:17-34).

For Luke, the Gospel message is subtly subversive rather than overtly combative. Writing for those who span the social and economic spectrum, Luke tells the story of Jesus's messiahship in a way that promotes their realignment with the values of God's kingdom. While Luke is not working to overthrow Roman forces in a military or political sense, this Gospel promotes a life together under Jesus's lordship that challenges imperial values at their core. Its vision of God's kingdom on display in Christian community destabilizes the empire from the bottom up, through lives that promote human well-being without respect to ethnic and religious identity, gender, or economic status.

The Challenge: "The One Who Would Redeem Israel" (Luke 24:21)

Before they recognize their risen Lord, two travelers on the road to Emmaus explain why they find Jesus's death so troubling. After all, this prophet with "powerful deeds and words" (Luke 24:19) has been crucified. His fateful end leaves them disillusioned, since they had "hoped that he was the one who would redeem Israel" (Luke 24:21). For Luke, the challenge of the Gospel story lies, at least in part, in such dashed hopes. After all, both Jews and Gentiles found it hard to fathom that the "one who would redeem Israel" would die on a Roman cross. Jesus's destiny fit neither Jewish hopes for Rome's defeat nor the imperial view of crucifixion, which was shameful, not honorable. For both Jews and Gentiles, Jesus's death only undermined the notion that the reign of Israel's God had dawned.

Luke lays important groundwork for meeting this challenge. For one thing, such a "shameful" destiny fits within the scheme of prophetic reversal found throughout the Gospel. After all, in this "world upside down," salvation arrives at the home of a loathed tax collector named Zacchaeus when he repents and sets scales of justice to the right (Luke 19:1-8). A father disgraced by his profligate son runs to meet him on the road, kicking up his heels for joy even before the son repents (Luke 15:11-32). A Roman centurion's beloved slave (Luke 7:1-10; see Matt 8:5-13) and the only son of a destitute widow (Luke 7:11-17) live again, when all hope is lost. In Luke's story, reversals of both status and fortune are the order of the day. In a sense, both Jesus's death and his resurrection belong to this Gospel pattern and thus confirm the Gospel's challenge to see God's work in the world through new lenses.

Luke also supplies a scriptural explanation for the challenge of Jesus's suffering destiny. As if to underscore God's command of this story, the risen Lord declares that it was "necessary for the Christ to suffer these things and then enter into his glory" (Luke 24:26). To make the point, Jesus "interpreted for them the things written about himself in all the scriptures" (Luke 24:27). For Luke, the challenge of Jesus's messianic destiny only exposes the true nature of God's redemption. Paradoxically, this Jewish messiah who died on a Roman cross has thereby secured the release, the salvation, the redemption of Israel, and indeed the whole world. For Luke's community, this challenge becomes their own whenever they subvert the present world order to bear witness to God's kingdom—and in so doing, face shame and even death (see Acts 7:54-60).

The Promise: "Heavenly Power" (Luke 24:49)

As vital as the crucifixion is for Luke's way of subversive citizenship, it is not the end of the story. Instead, it is a necessary step as Jesus prepares to "enter into his glory" (Luke 24:26). And it is from that position of glory, Luke says, that Jesus will empower the community established in his wake. Already the earthly Jesus has sent them out as agents of his messianic mission. But after his death and resurrection, the risen Lord continues to endow the faithful with divine power.

As is fitting for Luke's story, the gift of the spirit occurs not in Galilee (see Mark 16:7; Matt 28:16) but in Jerusalem. After all, Luke emphasizes the central role that Jerusalem and its temple play in Jesus's story. Though his message of repentance and "forgiveness of sins must be preached in his name to all nations," it will begin "from Jerusalem" (Luke 24:47). Indeed, the risen Jesus urges them, "stay in the city until you have been furnished with heavenly power" (Luke 24:49). In Luke, Jesus's promise comes not as the disciples flee the religious and political authorities but in the city where their power converges. Meanwhile, they live not as outlaws but as observers of religious tradition; they were, Luke says, "continuously in the temple praising God" (Luke 24:53). In this Gospel conclusion, the disciples stand in between the resurrection and Pentecost, faithful to Jewish practice while they await the power of God's kingdom (see Acts 1:6).

Ultimately, for Luke, that power arrives weeks later, though not in the way many expected. Rather than a cataclysmic end or a day of cosmic judgment, Luke describes the "heavenly power" this way: "They were all filled with the Holy Spirit and began to speak in other languages as the Spirit enabled them to speak" (Acts 2:4). That is, the power of the spirit breaks down even boundaries of language that would separate one group from another. Jesus's message about God's kingdom thus translates across time and place, through followers filled with God's power from on high.

On many levels, Luke's story of subversive citizenship is a matter of unfinished business. As in Mark, the ending of this Gospel itself leaves readers hanging, as the disciples await Jesus's promised return. Yet even Luke's sequel, which tells of that return and more, suggests that the outcome of Jesus's messiahship depends in part on those who carry it forward. For Luke, of course, Jesus's roots in Jewish hopes for God's salvation are vital to the story. But Luke understands that salvation in sweeping terms. As it moves outward, from Jerusalem toward the "end of the earth" (Acts 1:8), it draws in all who respond to this message of "a change of heart and life for the forgiveness of sins" (Luke 24:47) and reorient their lives according to God's subversive reign.

John: Divine Love

Scholars widely agree that John's audience experienced increasing tension with mainstream Jewish leaders who took a dim view of belief in Jesus the Christ. Indeed, in its final form, the Fourth Gospel shows that socioreligious tension stretched to the breaking point. In three cases, John mentions those who have been, or will be, "expelled from the synagogue [*aposynagōgos*]" (John 9:22; see 12:42; 16:2). The term is anachronistic, since Jesus's followers were not excluded from the Jewish community in his lifetime. But the issue was apparently a pressing one for John's community, at least some of whom were probably deemed "heretics" for their devotion to a crucified Jewish messiah.

The mounting conflict, even division, between John's audience and the wider Jewish community plays an influential role in the shaping of John's witness to Jesus. For one thing, John explicitly names the Gospel's purpose in these terms: it is "written so that you will believe that Jesus is the Christ, God's Son, and that believing, you will have life in his name" (John 20:31). Though belief in Jesus plays at best a minor role in the Synoptic Gospels, here it comes to separate those who believe that he is the messiah from those who do not. Such distinction also moves to the present: "Now is the time for judgment of this world" (John 12:31). For John, that judgment rests squarely on the question of Jesus's christological identity.

Perhaps to confirm Jesus's unique status in the face of such dispute, this Gospel makes much of his intimate ties with God. Sometimes, John's Jesus says outright that "I and the Father are one" (John 10:30), or that "the Father is in me and I am in the Father" (John 10:38). Elsewhere, Jesus speaks of himself as both dependent on and utterly faithful to God's own initiative (e.g., John 5:19; 8:28). And at times, John insists that God has "sent" Jesus (e.g., John 6:57; 8:16) and "given" him "everything" (John 13:3; see also 5:22). Jesus's messianic credentials, as one who bears God's image and will to the world, are beyond question.

Yet John's lofty view of Jesus's union with God does not diminish this Gospel's interest in cultivating a community whose life together is marked by union with both Jesus and God, and in turn with one another. Indeed, of all the Gospels, John may cast the boldest vision for what it means to live as those who believe in Jesus the Christ. Like the other evangelists, John sounds a call that finds in Jesus's own life, death, and resurrection a pattern for his followers. Like them, this Gospel takes stock of the (increasingly) adversarial response they seem to receive. But in an unprecedented way, John insists that even Jesus's way of divine love is inclusive rather than exclusive. Through the "Companion" (*paraklētos*, John 14:16) he promises, his followers will participate in the life he shares with God. As a result, they will bear God's glory to the world (John 17:22; see also 1:14).

The Call: "Love Each Other" (John 13:34)

In the Gospel's first major section, the disciples play a diminished role in Jesus's ministry. Again and again, they serve as passive bystanders whose misunderstanding sometimes means they serve as foils to Jesus's display of divine authority. More than the Synoptic Gospels, John casts the limelight on Jesus's messianic power, prescience, and privilege; at least through the first twelve chapters, his followers propel the story along mostly through their ignorance.

As Jesus turns toward his destiny, though, John devotes five chapters to the Farewell Discourse (John 13–17), an extended set of teachings that culminate with the High Priestly Prayer of John 17. Here, Jesus gathers his own as part of a messianic community that extends, through them, to those who will "believe...because of their word" (John 17:20). Saying that he is only here "a little while longer," Jesus announces: "I give you a new commandment: Love each other. Just as I have loved you, so you also must love each other" (John 13:34; see also 15:12). Moving beyond belief in him, John's Jesus inculcates among this gathered community the pattern of God's self-giving love found in his own life and death (see John 3:16).

As we have seen, while love of neighbor lies at the heart of Jewish law (see Lev 19:18), Jesus promotes a "new commandment" that underscores the sacrificial dimension of that love. After Jesus displays this kind of self-giving love by washing his disciples' feet, he offers it as an example for those devoted to him: "You call me 'Teacher' and 'Lord,' and you speak correctly, because I am. If I, your Lord and teacher, have washed your feet, you too must wash each other's feet" (John 13:13-14). Thus Jesus invokes his status as "Lord and teacher" to engender his own divine love—evident in sacrificial service to others—among his disciples.

Throughout this section, Jesus further explains his call to divine love. Indeed, to love Jesus is to keep "my commandments" (John 14:15; see also 14:21). He goes on to encourage his own to "remain in my love" (John 15:10). Yet the sacrificial love of one another is never far from view: "No one has greater love than to give up one's life for one's friends" (John 15:13). In this claim, Christ and community converge, as Jesus's impending death establishes the pattern by which the world will recognize his disciples (John 13:35).

The Challenge: "If the World Hates You…" (John 15:18)

Given John's setting, it is not surprising that opposition to Jesus, and thus to his followers, only intensifies in this Gospel. Along with Jesus's commanding call to self-giving love, the Fourth Gospel includes dire predictions of the hatred his disciples will face. The challenge that accompanies this call to messianic community, then, probably reflects the hostility John's audience encountered from those who saw their belief in Jesus's messiahship as a dangerous sectarian perversion of sacred tradition.

John's dualistic worldview leads to a sharp contrast between the wider "world" and the small group of believers the Gospel addresses. For the Fourth Gospel, the world's antagonistic stance toward Jesus's messiahship makes it an inhospitable environment for his followers. Indeed, they do not "belong to the world" but have come "out of the world" (John 15:19; see also 17:6) to align themselves with God's life-giving ways. Like the synoptic writers, John warns of the challenge the community already faces. In John, though, the resistance they encounter comes not just from religious or political leaders. It seems to permeate the "world" at large (John 16:33) as part of a cosmic showdown between good and evil. For John, God's glory has entered human flesh and, as a result, evoked a powerful response from the legions of evil—a response that brings hatred, exclusion, and even rejection.

For John's audience, this formidable challenge of social and religious dislocation brings another challenge as well. As an increasingly marginalized, sectarian community, this group could well have turned inward in a spirit of defensive self-protection. Yet the risen Jesus passes through doors that were closed "because [the disciples] were afraid of the Jewish authorities" (John 20:19) to deliver a word of peace to followers who have hunkered down after his death. Indeed, he challenges them to leave their seclusion: "As the Father sent me, so I am sending you" (John 20:21; see 17:18). Just as God's love has entered the world in the mission of Jesus to bring salvation (John 3:16) so too does John's Jesus send forth this band of disciples into a world still awaiting redemption.

John's message includes one more challenge: "remain in me" (John 15:1-10). Using the imagery of a vine and its branches, Jesus urges his companions to find their life in union with him, just as he finds life in union with the Father. For just as Jesus's words and deeds come from God alone, he says to believers, "Without me, you can't do anything" (John 15:5). To remain in him is to bear the fruit of embodied divine love, which Jesus himself has disclosed. Remaining in this love, they meet the challenge to enter the world and overcome its hostility.

The Promise: "I'm in Them and You Are in Me" (John 17:23)

Indeed, John's Jesus equips the faithful to meet the Gospel's challenge when he reassures them with these words: "But be encouraged! I have conquered the world" (John 16:33). From the Gospel's outset, Jesus's entry into the world has brought judgment (John 3:19). And while John preserves hopes for a decisive final judgment, this Gospel repeatedly reminds its audience that the decision has already been rendered, since "now is the time for judgment of this world. Now this world's ruler will be thrown out" (John 12:31). On one level, then, John's Jesus offers a word of promise grounded in an accomplished feat. Because God's victory over the "world's ruler" is clearly in view, the faithful are fortified to meet the resistance they face in the meantime.

But the Farewell Discourse includes other promises as well—promises that will sustain the faithful community left to carry forward Jesus's message. For one thing, Jesus repeatedly promises to send his disciples "another Companion [literally, "one called beside"; Greek: *paraklētos*], who will be with you forever" (John 14:16). Just as he has been called to their side in his earthly career, Jesus promises not to leave them "as orphans" (John 14:18) after his death. Elsewhere, Jesus identifies this advocate with the Holy Spirit, who will "teach you everything" (John 14:26). Like Jesus, then, this spiritual companion mediates God's ways to the messianic community.

Besides this Companion, Jesus offers an even more stunning word of hope. Even his mystical union with God will expand to include the faithful. To those who love him and "keep [his] word," Jesus promises, "My Father will love them, and we will come to them and make our home with them" (John 14:23). Just as God has taken on human flesh in Jesus of Nazareth, Jesus says, his followers will be the earthly "home" for the Father and Son. For John's community, the message is clear; when they heed the call to self-giving love ("my word"), they make room for God's residence on earth.

To drive the point home, John's Jesus strains the limits of language to convey the community's union with one another and with God. On behalf of his disciples as well as those who believe through them, he asks that "they will be one, Father, just as you are in me and I am in you. I pray that they also will be in us, so that the world will believe that you sent me. . . . I'm in them and you are in me so that they will be made perfectly one. Then the world will know that you sent me and that you have loved them just as you loved me" (John 17:21, 23). The likeness John forges between Christ and community thus brings the Gospel story full circle. Just as God has sent the Son into the world, so now Jesus asks God to include believers in the divine union they share. As a result, John seems to say, the "world might [yet] be saved" (John 3:16-17) through Christ and, by extension, through those he draws into union with God. It is within this mystical union, forged in divine love, that they find "life in his name" (John 20:31).

It is understandable that the Fourth Gospel is rife with evidence of sectarian thought. Pushed to the margins and beyond by their own religious communities, John's audience likely found in this Gospel a story that resonated with their own: a messiah rejected by his people, convincing evidence of God's palpable power at work in their midst, and a compelling vision of sacrificial divine love that somehow brings new life. Besides lending credence to their beliefs about Jesus's messiahship, John's Gospel casts a vision of messianic community in which his own divine love lives on. By remaining in him, through the presence of the Comforter, John's community extends the reach of Jesus's messiahship not just among their own but also into a world that will inevitably spew hatred and violence. Indeed, in the Gospel's epilogue, Jesus tells Peter that to love him means feeding his flock, a flock that includes "sheep that don't belong to this sheep pen" (John 10:16). In this way, the divine love that has taken human form in Jesus the Christ pushes inexorably outward to bring salvation and life to the world.

The Gospel Witness to Jesus: Reclaiming the Vision of Messianic Community

In this study, we have focused mostly on the Gospel texts and their first-century contexts. But like the Christian movement itself, the Gospels have endured for almost two millennia. Across time, believing communities have found in these four stories compelling claims about God's power at work through Jesus the Christ. Even today, the Christian church looks to these complementary accounts to understand who Jesus was, what he stood for, and what his messiahship means for his followers in any generation.

Along the way, though, readers have sometimes lost sight of the fact that the Gospels are, first and foremost, community literature. After all, when we mine these ancient stories only for what they say *about Jesus*, we bracket out a fundamental aspect of their message. Indeed, the Gospels tell the story of Jesus the Christ for those who would align their lives with his messianic mission by trusting that God's kingdom—with its life-giving power—has indeed drawn near. The Gospels thus bear witness to Jesus the Christ in part by laying the groundwork for those who carry his messianic movement forward.

And yet, the Gospels are not quite succession plans, as if their readers perpetuate Jesus's dream for the world without him. Rather, each evangelist promises Jesus's abiding presence as an active agent in the post-resurrection age; each Gospel somehow confirms Jesus's assurance not to "leave you as orphans" (John 14:18). As the living Lord, Jesus continues to authorize, empower, and sustain those who would embody his messianic agenda as communities that disclose the contours of God's kingdom.

Though this mysterious, even mystical, sense of Jesus's enduring presence is elusive to many, it persists among believing communities to this day. Some meet the risen Lord in prayer or meditation, while others experience it in the Eucharist or when the body of Christ manifests divine love for one another or for the world at large. Many encounter Jesus's presence in the eyes of the poor and oppressed. As Paul puts it, "There are different spiritual gifts [*charismatōn*] but the same Spirit;... and there are different activities but the same God who produces all of them in everyone" (1 Cor 12:4, 6). To live as a community activated by the risen Lord is to lay claim to the gifts of God's palpable presence, in all its variegated forms.

The time is ripe for Western Christianity to reclaim the vision of messianic community that lies at the heart of the Gospel witness to Jesus. Already, such an impulse is gaining ground. When a pope washes the feet of a young Muslim woman prisoner, when a church in Los Angeles translates the Gospel into clean laundry for the homeless, when a denomination refuses to profit from instruments of oppressive military occupation, there we find glimpses of messianic community taking root. Perhaps sociologists of religion are right. Perhaps we stand on the threshold of the "age of the spirit," a time when doctrinal concerns give way to vital, embodied witness to Jesus's lordship. If so, we may find ourselves more closely attuned to the Gospels, and especially Jesus's life-giving reminder: "I myself will be with you every day until the end of this present age" (Matt 28:20).

Study Questions

1. Identify the central elements of each Gospel's vision of messianic community.

2. How do the Gospel challenges discussed in this chapter make sense in light of each community's setting?

3. Which Gospel passages stress Jesus's enduring presence?

4. What connections do you see between the Gospels' first-century audience and the social location of Christianity today?

For Further Reading

Bass, Diana Butler. *Christianity after Religion: The End of Church and the Birth of a New Spiritual Awakening.* New York: HarperOne, 2012.

Burridge, Richard A. *Imitating Jesus: An Inclusive Approach to New Testament Ethics.* Grand Rapids: Eerdmans, 2007.

Henderson, Suzanne Watts. *Christology and Discipleship in the Gospel of Mark.* Society for New Testament Studies Monograph Series 135. Cambridge: Cambridge University Press, 2006.

Johnson, Luke Timothy. *Prophetic Jesus, Prophetic Church: The Challenge of Luke–Acts to Contemporary Christians.* Grand Rapids: Eerdmans, 2011.

Kee, Howard Clark. *Community of the New Age: Studies in Mark's Gospel.* Philadelphia: Westminster, 1977.

Longenecker, Richard N., ed. *Patterns of Discipleship in the New Testament.* Grand Rapids: Eerdmans, 1996.

Segovia, Fernando F. *The Farewell of the Word: The Johannine Call to Abide.* Minneapolis: Fortress, 1991.

Stanton, Graham D. *A Gospel for a New People: Studies in Matthew.* Edinburgh: T&T Clark, 1992.

Stassen, Glen H. *Living the Sermon on the Mount: A Practical Hope for Grace and Deliverance.* San Francisco: Jossey-Bass, 2006.

CPSIA information can be obtained
at www.ICGtesting.com
Printed in the USA
LVOW12s0434291117
557981LV00006B/503/P